MENDING A SHATTERED HEART

HEART

A Guide for Partners
of Sex Addicts

MENDING A SHATTERED HEART

A Guide for Partners of Sex Addicts

Edited by: Stefanie Carnes, Ph.D.

Gentle Path

P R E S S

GENTLE PATH PRESS
P.O. BOX 3172
Carefree, AZ 85377
www.gentlepath.com
800-708-1796

First Printing, January 2008

Editors: Stefanie Carnes, Amy Campbell, Rebecca Post
Assistant Editors: Suzanne O'Connor, Jan Shook
Graphic Design: Adam Wheat
Cover Design: Adam Wheat

GENTLE PATH PRESS
P.O. BOX 3172
Carefree, AZ 85377
www.gentlepath.com
800-708-1796

Contents

Part Two:
For Special Populations 117

INTRODUCTION

If you're reading this book, chances are your heart has been shattered. Your world has been turned upside down in a whirlwind of betrayal, anger and confusion. The authors of this book want you to know that you are not alone. Hundreds of unsuspecting people wake up every day to discover their loved one, the one person that they are supposed to trust completely, has been living a life of lies and deceit because they suffer from a disease – sex addiction.

The most conservative current estimated prevalence rates for sexual addiction are between 1 and 3 percent of the general population. Even those conservative numbers translate into more than 9 million people in the United States alone.[1] Furthermore, sex addiction is not just an epidemic in the Unites States; it reaches all cultures and ethnicities spanning the globe. However, this is a disease shrouded in secrecy and shame.

Even in our progressive society, we seldom speak of sex addiction. Those afflicted tend to cautiously guard their identities, so they are not labeled and stigmatized. The general population remains uneducated. Misinformed, they often equate sex addiction with sex offending or pedophilia, even though the majority of individuals with problematic sexual acting out cannot be classified into either of those categories.

Support groups, treatment centers, and literature for sex addiction have proliferated in the past 20 years. Addicts can now turn to many confidential resources for support. Despite this support for individuals, sex addiction is a family disease because it impacts the entire family system. The wreckage of pain and suffering rips through the family. Spouses or partners are devastated and angry. Children are frightened and confused. Parents of the sex addict wonder, *What did I do wrong?*

As the spouse or partner of a sex addict, you feel the responsibility to sort through this wreckage and to help your family do the same. Yet the resources for spouses and partners are few and far between. You may feel like you cannot reach out for help because you want to preserve the confidentiality of the addict. Or you may feel shame, embarrassment, and worry what others might think of you. The stress generated from this experience is akin to a major medical trauma; however, people going through a major medical trauma often have a community of people providing support. You, on the other hand, are left to suffer silently.

This book is designed for the spouse or partner in the initial phases of learning about the sex addiction in their lives. During this time, you'll be flooded with questions and feel confused. Each chapter is based on frequently asked questions by partners. These questions include: "Should I stay or should I go?" "Is my partner a pedophile?" and "What should I tell the kids?" At the back of the book, you

will find a list of resources, such as 12-step meetings, inpatient treatment and recommended books.

This book would not have been possible without the expertise of the people who contributed to it: Jennifer Schneider, Cara Tripodi, Patrick Carnes, Omar Minwalla, Mavis Humes, Sonja Rudie, Barbara Levinson, Robert Weiss and Joe Kort. Their willingness and diligence was amazing and driven by genuine compassion for the partner's struggle. The authors of this book have collectively worked with thousands of sex addicts and their families. Families like yours have taught us about their suffering. Many of the authors have experienced sex addiction in their own lives and have been touched deeply. Here, they share some of their own personal wisdom.

The communities that support compassionate treatment for sex addicts and their families have also been instrumental in the development of this book. These organizations include the Society for the Advancement of Sexual Health, the International Institute for Trauma and Addiction Professionals, and the network of Certified Sex Addiction Therapists. My employer, Pine Grove Behavioral Health and Addiction Services, also made this book possible. My Pine Grove colleagues' commitment to treating people with love and acceptance has been a constant inspiration; their open-mindedness, patience and support of my work has been immeasurable. I would also like to express appreciation to Gentle Path Press, especially to Amy Campbell, Rebecca Post and Suzanne O'Connor for their assistance with this book. Finally, I would like to thank Patrick Carnes, for his loving support, encouragement and advice.

It is my sincere hope that this book will provide information and comfort to individuals and families struggling with sexual addiction. Many people have walked this path before you. Allow their wisdom to guide you and provide you with the answers to your questions Know that you are not alone and you do not have to suffer silently.

- Stefanie Carnes, Ph.D., CSAT

PART ONE:
For All Partners
of
Sex Addicts

Chapter 1
What is Co-Sex Addiction?

Stefanie Carnes, Ph.D., CSAT

Tiffany could not believe what she just heard. After all of the sexual impropri-
eties her husband Jason had engaged in, he was blaming her for his acting out.
According to Jason, Tiffany was critical, blaming, non-supportive, and wasn't
meeting his sexual needs. He had attempted this bait-and-switch before, shortly
after she discovered his first affair, and she had fallen for it - hook, line and
sinker. She thought, *Maybe I have been pushing him away. I have been emotionally and physically distant in recent months.* The birth of their daughter Amy had
placed a strain on their marriage. The love and intense connection they had in the
beginning of their relationship just wasn't there anymore. Life had taken over,
and it had gotten busy.

Jason rationalized to Tiffany that his affair was just a meaningless sexual
fling. Jason told Tiffany that his affair partner had come on to him, but he tried
to resist her advances. He eventually succumbed to a one-night stand. He promised Tiffany he would immediately cut the ties with the woman, but Tiffany suspected he still had contact with her. She confronted him a few times, but he
always had an explanation. Tiffany began to wonder if she was being paranoid.
She ignored her gut instinct and chose instead to keep the peace and move on
with life.

Two years after Amy was born, Jason lost his job. He was underperforming
at work and it cost the family dearly. He was distracted in all areas of his life,
including his duties as a parent and helping out around the house. He even
became financially irresponsible. He seemed to be living in a fantasy world that
Tiffany couldn't penetrate. She found herself in the role of primary breadwinner,
primary parent, housekeeper and accountant. With all these extra burdens,
Tiffany became resentful of Jason, and she didn't have much time to invest in her
marriage. Admittedly, she became more critical and unsupportive of Jason. As
her anger and distance increased, his neediness increased. Occasionally, their
love would spark and they would reconnect. *He's such a good guy,* she would tell
herself. *He's going to snap out of this funk he's been in soon.*

Tiffany's nightmare escalated when she came home from work unexpected-
ly to get some files. As she pulled into the driveway, a partially clad woman
scrambled out the door. It was one of the most traumatic moments of her life.
She was so shocked that she barely spoke to Jason, who was apologizing profuse-
ly and making excuses. She turned around and went back to work. There, alone,
she tried to take in what she saw. Then she cried. She stayed late at work that

evening, not wanting to face the circumstances. When she got home, Jason told her he believed he was a sex addict and needed help. "A sex addict? Come on, get real!" she responded sarcastically.

Tiffany gave Jason the cold shoulder for weeks. Her anger and resentment colored every interaction with him. She had become a nagging, angry "mommy" figure to Jason and she detested every minute of it. She harassed him about being unemployed and not following through on his responsibilities. She was embarrassed to tell anyone about Jason's acting out, so she confided only in her sister, who advised her to divorce Jason. She thought about the impact divorce would have on Amy. She considered taking Amy and moving in with her parents, or asking Jason to move out.

Jason finally snapped under all the pressure. He told Tiffany he felt like he could never live up to her expectations, and that he would never be good enough for her. He said her nagging and criticism drove him to seek solace from women who believed he was worthwhile and attractive. He told her that she was stingy with sex and even when she did agree to it, it was routine and boring.

Tiffany was astonished that he was blaming all of the dysfunction in their relationship on her. He was a master at deflecting blame and accountability and the best defense was a good offense. When Tiffany thought through the situation logically, she wondered why she tolerated all of this abuse from Jason. But on the emotional level, she questioned herself, *Maybe I have been condescending. I have been pretty horrible to be around. I know I haven't put much energy into our sexual relationship recently.*

As in the case of Tiffany, the betrayal experienced by most partners of sex addicts is enormous. Discovering your partner is a sex addict is a trauma that for many partners causes an acute stress reaction and possibly symptoms of post traumatic stress disorder, such as hypervigilance and intrusive thinking about the trauma. The deception and violation of the covenant of the partnership shatters the trust in the relationship. Feelings of loss, pain and shame can be overwhelming. Many partners find themselves overwhelmed with questions: *What is sex addiction? How did I not know this was going on? Is there any hope for this relationship? How can I protect myself in the future? How do I look at my part so I don't replicate past mistakes?* This book addresses many of these important questions.

How do I know if my partner is a sex addict?

Sex addiction can be defined as an unhealthy relationship to any sexual experience (thoughts, fantasies, activities, etc) that an individual continues to engage in despite adverse consequences. As with other addictions, many sex addicts report feelings of withdrawal, such as irritability or restlessness when unable to act out sexually. Furthermore, some report a tolerance to sexual behaviors, where their sexual behaviors escalate over time, increasing in intensity. For example, someone with an addiction to pornography may find themselves needing more and more stimulation to achieve the original effect. There are 10 key criteria for sex addiction. If an individual meets three or more of these criteria he or she would be considered a sex addict:

1. Recurrent failure to resist sexual impulses in order to engage in specific sexual behaviors.
2. Frequently engaging in those behaviors to a greater extent, or over a longer period of time than intended.
3. Persistent desire or unsuccessful efforts to stop, reduce, or control those behaviors.
4. Inordinate amounts of time spent in obtaining sex, being sexual or recovering from sexual experiences.
5. Preoccupation with sexual behavior or preparatory activities.
6. Frequent engaging in the behavior when expected to fulfill occupational, academic, domestic or social obligations.
7. Continuation of the behavior despite knowledge of having a persistent or recurrent social, financial, psychological or physical problem that is caused or exacerbated by the behavior.
8. The need to increase the intensity, frequency, number or risk level of behaviors in order to achieve the desired effect; or diminished effect with continued behaviors at the same level of intensity, frequency, number or risk.
9. Giving up or limiting social, occupational or recreational activities because of the behavior.
10. Distress, anxiety, restlessness or irritability if unable to engage in the behavior.

How did I not know this was going on?

Sex addiction thrives in secrecy. Addicts will often go to any length to protect their double life. The addict's thinking process becomes impaired and they minimize the severity of their behaviors and take risks that can cause tremendous consequences. The majority of partners are kept completely in the dark about the sexual acting out. Others might know about some of the sexual activities, but not the extent of the behaviors. When the addict starts to "hit bottom," it usually involves heart-wrenching discoveries for the partner.

There are many ways you may find out about the behavior, such as stumbling across pictures or websites on a computer, arrests, contracting a sexually transmitted disease, finding incriminating phone records, receipts, etc. The addict may demonstrate other signs as well such as unaccounted time and money, late hours, decreased interest in sexual activity, or anger and irritability. You may have experienced suspicions about the addict's behavior that you dismissed until more evidence came to the surface and it became impossible to ignore. You'll read more about the discovery process in Chapter Two.

How do I look at my part so I don't replicate past mistakes?

Most partners find that they spend a great deal of time focusing on the addict. The addict is often the focus of treatment and the partner's pain is often overlooked or seen as secondary. Sometimes the partner is included as part of couples therapy during the course of treatment. But many spouses find themselves in a great deal of pain and confusion and also need support. When the addict's treatment is primary, the partner's issues are frequently neglected. It is important for you to have an opportunity to get the support you need, as well as the opportunity to look at the issues that you bring to the table so you can learn from this painful experience.

Many partners of sex addicts exhibit an array of common characteristics, and it can be extremely helpful to examine these to prevent future pain and loss. Some examples of these characteristics for partners of sex addicts are:

- tolerating behaviors in the relationship that others would never tolerate
- sacrificing with the unexpressed expectation that it would create loyalty and appreciation
- doing things for others that you should be doing for yourself while mired in self-neglect
- becoming someone you don't like – such as a nag, a "parent" to the addicted spouse, blamer or rager
- setting rules, agreements, contracts or boundaries but not abiding by them
- rescuing others compulsively
- believing tall tales – giving the addict the benefit of the doubt when it's not warranted
- being disabled by the addict's crazy-making behavior
- being overly concerned with the opinions of others – trying to keep up the appearance that all is well
- holding a firm belief that if the addict could be convinced to do "X" ever thing would be better
- attempting to keep the peace in the relationship at all costs
- living with a high degree of intensity, drama and chaos

If you are in a relationship with an addict and you identify with any of the characteristics listed above, you're likely struggling with *co-addiction* or *codependence*. In the field of sex addiction, the term *co-sex-addiction* is often used. This concept of co-addiction originally came out of the field of chemical dependency. Practitioners conducting family therapy with addicts began to perceive common characteristics in their spouses and family members.

They began to notice that family members struggled with issues such as rescuing behaviors, boundary problems, efforts to control, and sacrificing at the expense of self. They recognized that these behaviors were often taught in the families that bred addiction and traveled from one generation to the next. Even though the addict was the "patient," the family members desperately needed help too and were at times even more distressed than the patient. They often struggle with anxiety and depression, and report feeling unstable. Clinicians began calling this syndrome *codependency.*

The book that brought this phenomenon to everyone's attention was *Codependent No More.* In this classic book, Melody Beattie writes,

A codependent person is one who has let another person's behavior affect him or her, and who is obsessed with controlling that person's behavior.[1]

She outlines core characteristics of codependency including: caretaking, low self-worth, repression, obsession, controlling, denial, dependency, poor communication, weak boundaries, lack of trust, anger and sexual problems.

Timmen Cermak describes codependency as a disorder that involves relationship enmeshment with a person who suffers from a personality disorder, drug or alcohol dependency, or impulse-control problems. According to Cermak these relationships usually contain boundary distortions and anxiety relating to intimacy, self-sacrificing behaviors, and attempts to influence and control the other party in the relationship.[2]

Another author, Pia Mellody says codependency is caused by dysfunctional, less than nurturing family systems which can result in difficulties experiencing appropriate self- esteem, setting functional boundaries, and taking care of adult needs and wants.[3]

As sex addiction has become more acknowledged, this concept of codependency has been applied to family members of sex addicts as well. Some of the first authors to publish in the area of co-sex addiction include Jennifer Schneider, Deborah Corley, Dr. Patrick Carnes, Robert Weiss, Doug Weiss and Judith Metheny. For a list of published works on co-sex addiction please see the Resource Guide.

While there are many parallels between codependency and co-sex addiction, there are also differences. Sex addiction carries a stigma and a sense of shame and betrayal that is very profound. Many partners can understand addiction to a chemical, but when the addiction involves being sexual outside of the relationship, it's much harder for partners to find understanding and compassion. Sexual addiction results in a broken covenant that is extremely painful and difficult to comprehend. What you thought was true, is not. The deception and the secret life of the sex addict bring unprecedented turmoil, fear and pain to the partner.

What Is Co-Sex Addiction?

A co-sex addict is someone who is married to, or in a significant relationship with a sex addict and demonstrates a common set of behavioral characteristics. These characteristics include: denial, preoccupation, enabling, rescuing, taking excessive responsibility, emotional turmoil, efforts to control, compromise of self, anger and sexual issues. Like sex addiction, co-sex addiction can range in severity, and some individuals will find they experience few of these characteristics.

For others, they may demonstrate the vast majority of them, and may also find they cause severe disruption in their life. Here they are described in greater detail:

Denial

Denial is a hallmark of co-sex addiction. It is through the mechanism of denial that the addicts get away with their behavior for as long as they do. Co-addicts commonly find themselves believing tall tales or far-fetched explanations. Sex addiction is an illness of secrecy and deception, and addicts can be very convincing and persuasive.

Many co-addicts come from dysfunctional family backgrounds, so they often want to hold on to that image of the perfect family or the happy couple. There may have been times you didn't want to believe the problems were really as bad as they were. For example, maybe you knew about the pornography, but didn't see it as out of control. Other co-addicts use self-distraction or overwork, which are other common mechanisms of denial.

Preoccupation

Many co-addicts struggle with being preoccupied with the addict or the addict's behavior. You may have experienced anxiety or worry about the addict, and may have found yourself constantly wondering what the addict is up to. Much of your energy may be focused on trying to fix the addict – at the expense of your own self-care. When you're preoccupied with another person in the throes of a destructive addiction, it's hard to nurture and care for yourself.

Enabling or Rescuing

"Enabling" is a word that many perceive as stigmatizing. Really, enabling behavior is a normal response to an abnormal situation. As addicts start to hit bottom, they become desperate. Their life starts to crash around them. They lose their jobs, face financial ruin, or experience other consequences of their addictive behaviors. It's a normal response for family members to try and rescue the addict as he or she spirals out of control.

Unfortunately, for many addicts, it's important they experience the full impact of the consequences of their behaviors. The desperation they experience is the gift that propels many into recovery. Once they feel like their world is crashing around them, many become internally motivated to recover.

When a partner or relative rescues the addict, they're taking a little of this gift of desperation away. They make the bottom softer, so the addicts don't have to face their consequences and feel as desperate.

This is why it's called "enabling," because the family member is unwittingly helping the disease to progress to a worse stage. Examples of enabling behaviors for co-sex addiction include (the following was list developed by S. Carnes and C. Tripodi):

- supporting the addict's decision to work overtime when he often acted out at work
- handling the majority of childcare responsibilities
- handling the majority of household responsibilities
- engaging in sexual behaviors with the addict which make the spouse or partner uncomfortable
- changing one's appearance to be more sexually appealing to the addict
- normalizing and overlooking sexual acting-out behaviors
- expecting little or no financial accountability when money is being spent on his or her sexual acting out behaviors
- rescuing the addict from consequences of the addiction
- making excuses to cover up the addict's behavior

Many of these behaviors are not conscious on the part of the co-addict. However, they do unwittingly support the addictive process and allow the addiction to progress.

Excessive Responsibility

Many partners are caretakers and feel responsible for others, often at the expense of taking care of themselves. The 12-step fellowships for family members of addicts have a slogan: *You didn't cause it, you can't cure it, and you can't control it.* In the past, you may have felt that your actions or behaviors could influence the addictive process. For example, "If I were just sexier, he wouldn't need pornography." This type of thought distortion promotes excessive responsibility for the addict's behaviors. It is these faulty beliefs that keep the co-addict stuck in an unhealthy and exploitive relationship. You may have been taught at a young age to be a caretaker for others and to feel and be responsible for their well-being. Recovery will include learning to take care of yourself, and to let go of caretaking and excessive responsibility for others, especially the addict.

Emotional Turmoil

Living with an active addict is chaotic and overwhelming. Whether you knew or didn't know about the addictive behavior, you were likely being impacted by the addict's out-of-control behavior. The consequences of the addiction, such as financial problems or job loss, have far-reaching implications that impact the entire family. You may have experienced confusion, anger, sadness, loneliness and outrage. Many co-sex addicts report that life is a rollercoaster.

Efforts to Control

Many co-addicts find themselves thinking, *If the addict would just do _____, everything would fall into place.* You may have lived through painful events with people who have been out of control, so it is especially painful when this type of behavior resurfaces in your adult life. You might have found yourself using strategies such as helplessness, guilt, coercion, threats, advice-giving or manipulation to get the addict to change. As a matter of fact, you may have even turned into someone you don't like, such as a parent figure to the addict, a blamer or a nag.

Unfortunately, most of these tactics don't work and only leave you feeling more frustrated. In most *coupleships* where addiction is present there is plenty of blaming, controlling, and playing the victim, and these behaviors are typically exhibited by both parties. The problem for co-addicts is that after these behaviors are manifested, the co-addict typically feels guilty and horrible about themselves. So, recovery for co-addiction focuses on examining these behaviors to ensure that the co-addict can respond with integrity and feel good about his or her responses.

Compromise or Loss of Self

Many partners find themselves making compromises in the relationship that lead to the loss of their sense of self. Examples include acting against your own morals, values or beliefs, as well as giving up life goals, hobbies and interests. Other examples include changing your dress or appearance to accommodate the addict, or accepting the addict's sexual norms as your own. Along with this loss of self often comes erosion of self-esteem. You may have struggled with feelings of unworthiness or perfectionism. As a result, you may have settled for feeling needed in the relationship and compromised yourself to keep the peace or feel valued.

Anger

Understandably, most partners of sex addicts are devastated by the betrayal of the relationship and are justifiably very angry. Anger can manifest in the relationship in a multitude of ways. It can be expressed directly and appropriately. It can also be expressed in the form of rage, blame or punishment. Or conversely, it can also be expressed covertly, such as in passive-aggressive behavior, withdrawal or subtle indirect forms of communication. Depending on the rules you were taught in your family growing up, you may have learned that it was either acceptable or unacceptable to express anger, and this is likely influencing the current way you're coping with this emotion. Recovery for you will require you to learn to express you anger directly and appropriately, as well as let go of resentments – whether you remain in the relationship or not.

Sexual Issues

Similar to addicts, partners of sex addicts also have high rates of past sexual abuse. Since these relationships often contain more than one sexual abuse victim, naturally, there are higher rates of sexual issues with these coupleships. Furthermore, for many partners the addict's sexual acting out is a form of sexual trauma. We go into this topic in more detail in Chapter Six. For example, you may have given in to the sexual demands of the addict believing this would deepen your love, when for the addict it was another fix, which makes the betrayal even more painful. Because of the often complex issues that couples struggling with sex addiction experience around sexuality, they often experience difficulty with sexual intimacy. This can manifest in many ways, such as unmet sexual needs and wants, sexual avoidance, and even sexual dysfunction. Given this trauma history, the addict's sexual acting out can trigger many feelings for the co-addict. It's no coincidence that addicts and co-addicts find each other. For many couples their sexual issues complement one another.

Characteristics of Co-Addiction (Adapted from P. Carnes[4])

Denial
- 83% of co-addicts denied their personal intuitions.
- 43% denied the problem existed.
- 72% of co-addicts kept overly busy and over extended.

Preoccupation
- 62% of partners reported constantly thinking about the addict's behavior and motives.
- 67% of partners found they focused totally on the addict to avoid feelings.
- 58% found themselves participating in detective behaviors, such as checking the addict's e-mail, briefcase, purse, etc.

Enabling and Rescuing
- 71% of co-sex addicts joined the addict to present a united front to others.
- 66% kept secrets to protect the addict.
- 53% lied to cover up for the addict.
- 37% became "hyper" sexual in an effort to connect with the addict.

Excessive Responsibility
- 75% of co-addicts blamed themselves for the problems in the relationship.
- 62% agreed with the statement, "If I changed, the addict would stop."
- 62% of co-addicts took responsibility for the addict's behavior.
- 59% were in a dependency situation where the co-addict was indispensable.

Emotional Turmoil
- 74% of co-addicts reported experiencing free-floating shame and anxiety.
- 63% felt they always had a crisis or a problem.
- 79% felt that their emotions were out of control.

Efforts to Control
- 61% of partners indicated they failed at efforts to control the sexual acting out of the addict.
- 92% identified with playing the martyr, hero or victim role.

Loss of Self
- 59% of co-addicts reported they acted against their own morals, values or beliefs.
- 61% gave up life goals, hobbies and interests.
- 53% changed their dress or appearance to accommodate the addict.
- 43% accepted the addict's sexual norms as their own.

Anger
- 64% of co-addicts perceived themselves as self-righteous and punitive.
- 36% acknowledged homicidal thoughts or feelings.

Sexual Reactivity
- 43% made excuses not to be sexual.
- 68% reported they numbed their own sexual wants and needs.
- 66% rarely felt intimate during sex.
- 34% changed clothes out of sight of the addict.

For many co-addicts, these behaviors were learned in dysfunctional households during childhood. Here are some startling statistics: 98 percent of co-addicts have other family members with an addiction. Ninety-one percent were emotionally abused as children. Seventy-one percent were physically abused.[5] Research has shown that between 43 percent[6] to 81 percent of co-addicts have been sexually abused. Sixty-three percent came from households that were both "rigid" and "disengaged".[7] Rigid, disengaged families are unable to teach healthy intimacy and connection, and these families pass along many negative, shame-based messages about sexuality. Raised in these dysfunctional households, most co-addicts learned how to relate and behave when in a relationship with an addict.

I didn't even know this addiction was going on. Why am I considered a "co-sex addict?"
Addiction presents a series of predictable problems to the partner of the addict, and there are commonalities in the ways that partners respond to these problems. For many partners these responses were learned in childhood in families that also contained addiction.

When addicts are in the throes of their addictive processes, they lie, manipulate, and act hopeless and helpless. These behaviors elicit responses in their loved ones that are also predictable to a certain degree. Many of these problems may have manifested in your relationship before you knew the addiction was even happening.

For example, Tiffany at the beginning of this chapter experienced a lot of chaotic behavior prior to her discovery of the addiction. Her life with Jason was unmanageable. He was under-functioning in many areas of his life, including at work, home and financially. She found herself overcompensating for him and tolerated behavior that was unacceptable on many levels.

Isolating those areas of the relationship where you compromised your values or gave too much of yourself will help you understand how co-sex addiction applies to you. By learning about addiction and co-sex addiction, you will gain insight into the common dynamics in addictive relationships and discover tools to prevent yourself from being manipulated again in the future.

I am so embarrassed about this situation! I don't feel like I can talk to anyone about this. How common is this problem?
According to current estimated prevalence rates about 3 to 6 percent of the general population struggles with sex addiction.[8] That translates into an incredible number of spouses and partners who are also affected. The problem is that even in circles of recovering people, sex addiction is rarely discussed or addressed. Families are left to suffer in silence due to societal stigma and shame. Many co-addicts feel they can't even tell their family or close support networks. Fortunately, there are small groups of recovering co-addicts emerging across the country, supporting one another through anonymous, confidential programs like COSA and S-Anon. (For a list of support groups and contact information see the Resource Guide at the back of this book.)
Consider these situations which are based on real case scenarios:

Deborah had always been concerned about her husband Joe's pornography use. Imagine her distress when her adult daughter called and said she had walked in on her father having sex with a 19-year-old woman. Deborah was worried about rocking the boat, so instead of confronting Joe, she swallowed her anger and pain.

Ken was upset when he discovered his wife Leslie had repeated sexual encounters with different men from her office. He learned that she engaged in sexual acts that he found distasteful and had never engaged in with him. He struggled with ruminating on her sexual behaviors and could not forgive her. Ken eventually decided to divorce Leslie in order to move on with his life.

Lauren was upset when she found women's underwear in her bedroom that didn't belong to her, but she became outraged when she found out they belonged to her niece. Her husband later admitted he had been molested when young and forced to wear girl's underpants. Over time he developed a panty fetish. Lauren came to understand the nature of her husband's sexual trauma and the couple reconciled.

Penny discovered her husband Andy was a sex addict when she found thousands of images of downloaded pornography on her computer. She was so hurt, she immediately threatened divorce. Andy decided he was going to commit suicide and called his father to tell him where to find his body.

He jumped off a 100-foot cliff but survived. The paramedics found him with suicide notes in his pocket. He was released from the hospital and sent to treatment.

James found out his wife Jennifer was having another affair – her third. This time it was with her priest with whom she engaged in ongoing phone sex. Jennifer tried to commit suicide through carbon monoxide poisoning while sitting in her running car.

Rita's 9-year-old son came to her after he found her husband Scott pornography stash. Rita was unaware that Scott was using pornography. She was shocked and struggled with how to explain it to her son. She was infuriated with Scott and decided to seek divorce.

Pat discovered his wife Ellen was meeting up with men at adult bookstores and having sex with them in the parking lot. Although he was very distressed about the dangerous situation she was putting herself in and concerned about sexually transmitted diseases, he began to join her in her acting out and they began acting out sexually with strangers and couples together.

While each family's situation is unique, all of them contain the commonalities of unmanageability, drama, intensity and crisis. These are core elements of relationships that contain active sex addiction. These attributes are features of the addictive cycle that can be seen in many relationships between the sex addict and the co-addict.

Co-Sex Addiction and Sexual Addiction Compared

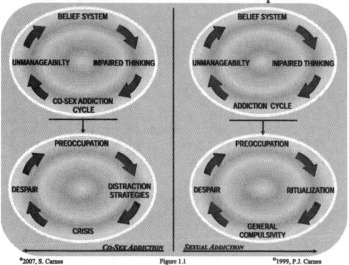

°2007, S. Carnes   Figure 1.1   °1999, P.J. Carnes

The Addictive Cycle
The addictive cycle for sex addiction was originally developed by Dr. Patrick Carnes.[9] Based on Carnes' original model, a cycle for co-sex addiction was developed by Dr. Stefanie Carnes and Cara Tripodi. The original model is briefly described here to serve as a comparison for the co-sex addiction cycle.

The Cycle for Sex Addiction

The Belief System
The first component of the model is that sex addicts have an underlying belief system that they are flawed and will never be good enough. This sense of toxic shame underlies their beliefs about the self. Instead of thinking, *I made a mistake,* the typical addict thinks, *I am a mistake.* This belief system colors their thoughts, behaviors and relationships.

Impaired Thinking
This shame-based belief system leads the addict to partake in distorted thinking processes. Often called "stinking thinking," this is the addictive thinking process that facilitates acting-out behaviors. Thought processes like denial, rationalizations, justifications and distortions are all examples of stinking thinking. Examples would include, *I'm not hurting anyone, I deserve it,* or *No one will ever know.* It's this type of distorted thinking that leads the addict to the addictive cycle.

Preoccupation
Preoccupation is the first stage in the addictive cycle. The addict may be fantasizing about past or future behaviors. This preoccupation can actually take a great deal of time and may significantly impact the addict's functioning. For example, the addict who looks for prostitutes may actually cruise for 20 hours during the course of one week but may actually engage with only one prostitute for 10 minutes. During the other 19 hours and 50 minutes, the addict escapes, medicates and dissociates into a fantasy world. This preoccupation is also a form of acting out. Many addicts can live for hours in their fantasies.

Ritualization
Most addicts have rituals around their sexual acting-out behavior. Ritual behaviors can include grooming or primping prior to acting out, driving a particular route, using drugs, or going to the same hotel room. These rituals become part of the acting out and add to the arousal process.

Acting Out
This is when the addict actually acts out sexually. This might include masturbation, pornography use, engaging in an affair, exhibitionism, anonymous sexual encounters, voyeurism, sexual harassment, phone sex and other behaviors. The modalities are countless, but most addicts have a preferred mode of acting out.

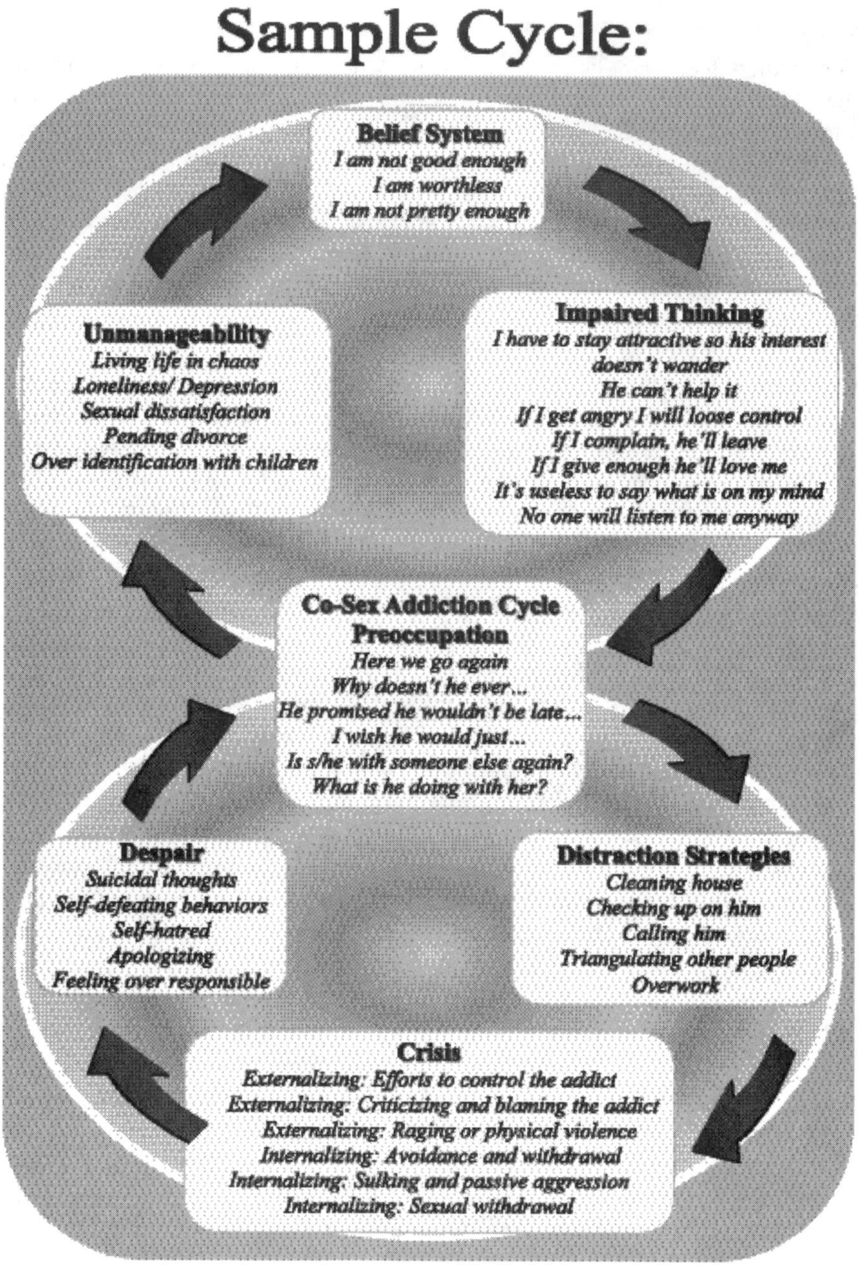

Sample Cycle:

Belief System
I am not good enough
I am worthless
I am not pretty enough

Unmanageability
Living life in chaos
Loneliness/ Depression
Sexual dissatisfaction
Pending divorce
Over identification with children

Impaired Thinking
I have to stay attractive so his interest
doesn't wander
He can't help it
If I get angry I will loose control
If I complain, he'll leave
If I give enough he'll love me
It's useless to say what is on my mind
No one will listen to me anyway

Co-Sex Addiction Cycle
Preoccupation
Here we go again
Why doesn't he ever ...
He promised he wouldn't be late...
I wish he would just ...
Is s/he with someone else again?
What is he doing with her?

Despair
Suicidal thoughts
Self-defeating behaviors
Self-hatred
Apologizing
Feeling over responsible

Distraction Strategies
Cleaning house
Checking up on him
Calling him
Triangulating other people
Overwork

Crisis
Externalizing: Efforts to control the addict
Externalizing: Criticizing and blaming the addict
Externalizing: Raging or physical violence
Internalizing: Avoidance and withdrawal
Internalizing: Sulking and passive aggression
Internalizing: Sexual withdrawal

Figure 1.2   © 2007, S. Carnes and C. Tripodi

Some will have a hierarchy of preferences. For example, using escorts may be number one, phone sex number two, pornography use number three.

Despair
Most addicts feel overwhelmed with hopelessness and despair after acting out. The addict might realize that it was just another empty sexual experience that was humiliating and degrading, and he or she typically feels shame and regret. Usually they are faced with guilt about acting outside of their morals and values and fear consequences to their actions.

Unmanageability
The cycle leads to unmanageability in the life of the addict – and usually the family members as well. The unmanageability usually takes the form of consequences to the addictive behaviors.

Examples include physical consequences such as sexually transmitted diseases, legal consequences, work or financial consequences, or relational consequences. The unmanageability reinforces that shame-based, negative belief system that the addict has about him or herself.

The Cycle for Co-Sex Addiction
The Belief System
The belief system for co-addicts is very similar to that of the addicts. These are the fundamental beliefs you have about yourself. Because many co addicts come from dysfunctional family backgrounds containing abuse and addiction, they often inherit faulty, shame-based beliefs about the self. For example, if you were abused as a child, you were treated as though you were worth less than other people.

You may have internalized that message and incorporated those faulty messages into your belief system about yourself. You may believe that you're not smart enough, pretty enough or talented enough. When the addict acts out sexually outside of the relationship, these beliefs may be triggered and you may experience negative self-talk that includes shame-based messages about the self. This shame-based belief system underlies the impaired thinking of the co-addict.

Impaired Thinking
Impaired thinking includes many different types of thought distortions, such as denial, rationalization, justification, etc. Examples of impaired thoughts for co-addicts include *I deserve to be treated this way. I can't do any better. If I was performing better sexually this wouldn't have happened.* It's essential for your recovery to combat this negative thinking. It's the negative belief system and this impaired thinking that lays the foundation for the co-addictive cycle.

Preoccupation
The co-addictive cycle is usually triggered by an event. Perhaps the addict lost

his job, or you found a phone number in her pocket. He's not where he said he would be, or you caught her in a lie. The types of triggers are endless.

It's common at this point for the co-addict to reflect on every detail of the relationship and have anxious feelings focused on this triggering event. You may be thinking, *Why am I not good enough for her? Why can't he just do...? She said she was going to do.... Why doesn't he listen to me?* This focus on the addict's behavior is called preoccupation and is the first stage of the cycle. You may even experience physical symptoms, such as headaches or an upset stomach.

Distraction Strategies

Distraction strategies are techniques used to cope with the preoccupation and the feelings associated with it. Techniques include distracting yourself with work, cleaning the house, bingeing or restricting with food, checking up on the addict, or talking to others about the addict's behavior. All of these strategies may temporarily reduce anxiety and distract from feelings about the situation. You may feel flooded with emotions depending on the triggering event or, conversely, you may feel cut off and numb to your feelings. Distraction strategies lead into the next stage which is the crisis.

Crisis

The preceding events typically unfold into a crisis in which the co-addict exhibits internalizing or externalizing behaviors. You may find that you struggle more with one than the other, but many partners find that they switch back and forth between internalizing and externalizing behaviors and exhibit both types. Externalizing behaviors involve erupting with anger, usually directed at the addict. The anxiety that has culminated through worry and ruminating is unleashed, and it frequently comes out in an overreactive rush of anger. You may find yourself critical, controlling, aggressive, blaming, raging and self-righteous.

It's important to keep in mind that this reaction is based on justifiable anger. You have a reason to be angry. But by exhibiting externalizing behaviors, your reaction is now part of the problem, which takes the focus off the real issue. Basically, you let the addict off the hook. The blame can now be spread around because you overreacted.

Additionally you may feel guilty about the way you responded, and now you're more likely to forgive the original injustice. This is a trap that many partners find themselves in time and time again. Recovery involves learning how to express your anger appropriately and set boundaries that you can follow through on.

Internalizing behaviors also involve anger, but this type of anger is expressed covertly. Tension and anger can be communicated through many subtle mechanisms in a relationship. Some examples of internalizing behaviors include:

- emotional or sexual withdrawal
- brooding or sulking

- guilt-tripping
- the silent treatment
- passive-aggression
- over-involvement at work or with the children
- being "one up" or better than your partner

Internalizing behaviors can be a huge trigger for the addict's shame and this can be an indirect form of retaliation on the part of the co-addict. These behaviors, while they may be perceived as less caustic to the relationship, are actually equally corrosive to the intimacy in the relationship as externalizing behaviors.

Despair
Typically, the despair stage involves a rift in the relationship. The co-addict may feel guilty, hopeless, self-critical and over-responsible. You may experience shame about the addiction or your response to it. The despair can take many forms, including self-defeating behaviors, depression, anxiety and suicidal ideation. It may even include efforts to make up with the addict, while still feeling frustrated and resentful.

Unmanageability
Living with an active addict creates a lifestyle of unmanageability, crisis and chaos. There's often volatility in the primary relationship, impaired social and occupational functioning, financial unmanageability, and possible physical or legal consequences. Examples include a pending divorce, job loss, depression or anxiety in one or both partners, or over-identification with children. If children are involved, they also become impacted by the chaos in the household.

The addictive cycle for the addict and co-addict is a dance where both participants often respond to one another's dance moves. For example, the co-addict in crisis triggers the despair of the addict, or the acting out of the addict triggers the impaired thinking of the co-addict. Recovery for both parties involves ending this dysfunctional dance and engaging in healthier methods of interacting.

When the addict in your life is facing self-destruction, it can be difficult to look inward. But this introspective focus is critical to your self-care. Identifying co-addictive patterns in your life is the beginning of awareness. Once awareness is achieved, change can occur. Recovery involves letting go of these old dysfunctional patterns, such as caretaking and tolerating unacceptable behaviors.

Taking on the challenge of changing these behaviors is essential whether you stay in the relationship with the addict or not, because these behaviors can be repeated in future relationships. By identifying these core issues, mistakes can be illuminated, and with learning from our mistakes comes empowerment. Allow yourself the empowerment of introspection and accept the challenge of recovery.

Chapter 2
How Do I Handle Discovery or Disclosure of Sexual Indiscretions?

Jennifer P. Schneider, M.D., CSAT

Lorie, 34, is a nurse and mother of two young children. She believed that her 10-year marriage to Todd, an engineer, was good. True, their sex life had decreased recently, but Todd told her it was because he was involved in an important and demanding project at work, and he was usually exhausted by evening. He assured her this was temporary. Lorie's life began to fall apart when she accidentally discovered Todd's secret sexual life on the computer.

A multitude of unwelcome feelings assailed Lorie. She later said,

I felt total distrust in myself, my spouse, and the relationship. I felt betrayed, confused, afraid and stunned. The person I loved and trusted most in the world had lied about who he was. I felt I had lived through a vast and sinister cover-up.

Suddenly, Lorie had a hundred unanswered questions. Should she confront Todd? Where can she get more information? Who is a safe person to talk to about this crisis? Is this the end of their marriage?

Most partners first learn about an addict's sexual behaviors by accident – a friend tells you your spouse is having an affair; you accidentally discover a hotel bill; or you overhear a telephone conversation. Perhaps you read an incriminating e-mail, found a large amount of pornography on the computer, or discovered your spouse having sex with someone online. Perhaps your partner lost his job because he engaged in cybersex at work. Or even worse, he was arrested for some type of illegal sexual activity.

Some people first find out about the addict's sexual activities when the addict reveals them out of fear, believing his or her partner has already discovered incriminating evidence. Another reason is that the addict can no longer tolerate his or her emotions. Perhaps you suspected all along that something was going on, and finally confirmed your suspicions by looking through his or her computer, mail or briefcase. No matter how you discover the sex addiction, this chapter will give you answers to the questions this devastating discovery raises.

I happened to get on my husband's computer and found some steamy letters to several women. I read all of them. Then I spent all morning looking through his computer. I found hundreds of pornographic photos. Some of them looked non-professional, as if those women had sent them to him. Recently he attached a camera to his computer, and I'm thinking he probably sends pictures of himself to those women. I'm appalled, shocked, dismayed, very angry, and I feel very ashamed – both about his behavior and about mine, for snooping the way I did. I'm too ashamed to tell anyone about it. Our sex life in the past has been pretty good, and I just don't understand this. I feel like I'm going crazy!

This reaction is natural and understandable. These days, millions of people are engaging in various forms of sex online, and many of them are now hooked on Internet pornography and other forms of compulsive sexual behavior. Thousands of partners are reeling from this kind of shock. You're not alone.

If you're like most partners in this situation, your first action after discovering these activities is to confront the addict. If your partner agrees he or she has a problem, then a good next step is for the two of you to find a counselor knowledgeable about Internet pornography and sex addiction.

An early part of the counseling will involve a planned disclosure so that you can have a more complete picture of your spouse or partner's sexual activities. Before the disclosure, you need to clarify with the counselor what your goals are.

For example, a positive intent of counseling could be to move toward greater intimacy in your relationship. On the other hand, trying to obtain ammunition to punish, control or manipulate your partner is a poor intent.

You'll also work with the therapist to determine which details of your partner's sex addiction are important for you to know and how these details may affect you.

The counselor will also likely recommend that both you and your spouse or partner join mutual-help programs based on the Twelve steps of Alcoholics Anonymous. Such programs now exist for both sex addicts and spouses, partners and other family members whose lives have been impacted by someone else's sexual behavior.

Later in this book you'll learn more about 12-step programs and their value in recovery from addiction and co-addiction. In the appendix, you'll find contact information for S-Anon and COSA, two self-help fellowships for families of sex addicts. We suggest you contact them and attend a meeting. Through these confidential fellowships you will meet people who can best understand your feelings; these people have had experiences similar to yours, and they have learned how to cope and how to recover.

Feeling like you're losing your mind is common after learning the devastating details behind a loved one's sex addiction. As one man whose wife had been sexual with other men relates,

I couldn't concentrate. I got into two car accidents and did things like putting milk in the cupboard and cereal in the refrigerator. I was afraid I would drive off a bridge or hurt myself using a kitchen knife.

Distraction and depression are common reactions to the crisis of discovery. That is why it's important to get help and support for yourself early on.

My husband is spending more hours at night on the Internet and less time with me. More than once I walked in on him masturbating in front of the computer. Before he closed the screen, I saw he was looking at a nude woman. He seems much more interested in the computer than in making love with me. When I confronted him, he said he's just a normal guy. He doesn't think he needs to change. Where do I go from here?

Whether or not your spouse or partner thinks he or she has a problem, your relationship certainly does. Perhaps your partner would be willing to go with you to a couple's counselor, especially one who understands how online sexual activities affect you and your marriage. If your partner is unwilling to go to counseling, go alone to figure out what your options are.

I recently discovered my husband was having an affair. He says it's over now and he's willing to go to counseling with me. I keep asking him for more information about her and their relationship. He's balking, but I feel driven to know everything. I can't stop thinking about it.

Partners often initially ask for complete disclosure. This is a way for them to:

- make sense of the past
- validate their suspicions about what was happening in the relationship - suspicions the addict often denied
- assess their risk of having been exposed to sexually transmitted diseases, to financial disaster and to shame
- evaluate their partner's commitment to the future of the relationship
- have some sense of control

No matter how many details you know about your partner's acting out, the ultimate choice to change his behavior lies with him or her, not with you. Having more information won't give you more control.

On the contrary, sometimes too much information can cause you additional problems. You may end up obsessing even more about your partner's behavior. Intrusive thoughts about the addict can cause additional pain. If you know "they" ate at a particular restaurant, you may never want to go there again.

One woman who learned her husband had had sex in their bedroom insisted on replacing the bed. If you know your husband and his affair partner did a particular sexual activity together, you may find yourself obsessing about them when you and your husband share that activity.

Two women who now wish they had been told less comment,

I created a lot of pain for myself by asking questions and gathering information. I have a lot of negative memories to overcome. This ranges from songs on the radio to dates, places and situations. There are numerous triggers.

I wanted every detail. I thought that would help him with shame, and there was safety in knowing everything. Looking back on it now, I wouldn't have asked for such a detailed disclosure or insisted on complete honesty.

Twelve-step members caution against giving "free rent in your head" to images that may be difficult to erase later. Consider carefully what information you need rather than ask for "everything."

How much information should I ask for?

Couples who have been through the painful process of disclosure have provided us with some guidelines about what to tell – and what not to tell. In brief, even though it may be painful initially, it's a good idea to ask for the broad outlines of all the significant compulsive activities. Addicts may be tempted to leave out some damaging material, often because they fear their partners will leave them.

This can be a big mistake. If a partner believes she or he has come to terms with the addict's sexual activities only to learn at a later time about other sexual behaviors, this can result in a major setback, destroying whatever progress the couple has made in their relationship. Staggered disclosures can make it very difficult to rebuild trust. One co-addict explains,

There were several major disclosures over six months. I was completely devastated. He continued to disclose half truths, only increasing my pain and making the situation worse. Each new disclosure was like reliving the initial pain all over again. I wish the truth had been disclosed all at once and not in bits and pieces.

Another adds,

Disclosure came in parts during the first year. I felt immense pain and anger. Part of that was not being told. I felt lied to and didn't trust any part of the relationship.

The lesson here is that although giving and receiving a disclosure is a painful process, it's best for the relationship if the addict doesn't keep any big pieces for later disclosure.

You also need to know if there have been any sexual activities that put you at risk of sexually transmitted diseases. If this has happened, both of you should be tested, and this may include repeat testing. Until then, if you choose to be sexual with your partner use condoms for protection. Having to use a condom is likely to elicit negative memories and feelings, but this is better than risking infection with a dangerous sexually transmitted disease.

As to what types of details are appropriate to ask for, this depends on the particular circumstances. For example, if the person your partner had the affair with is someone you know, it may be reasonable for you to know this person's identity. If your spouse was having an affair with a co-worker, you will need to know this; you and your spouse will have to work out, often with the help of a counselor, how your spouse can limit contact with this person. On the other hand, it is best not to ask for details about sexual activities, such as locations, because this information often causes more pain.

I can't help feeling that a lot of this is my fault. My guilt and shame make it hard for me to talk about this with other people. What can I do?
Co-addicts often feel excessively responsible for other people. You probably like to have control of situations. Unfortunately, the flip side is if things don't turn out the way you want, you feel responsible, that it was your fault. When the problems are of a sexual nature, there's extra shame attached to them. As one co-addict recalls,

When my husband first recognized he was a sex addict, I felt a lot of shame. He went around telling his friends, which just made me want to sink through the floor. I was sure they would think I hadn't been a good enough sex partner. I thought, if only I'd lost more weight or dressed differently, or even cooked him better meals, he wouldn't have needed those other women. I kept thinking it was my fault.

Unfortunately, this attitude can keep you isolated at a time when you need support from others. One of the advantages of involvement in a self-help group is that being with other people who have similar feelings and experiences will help defuse your shame. Some group members will have been working on their own recovery for some time. They will truly understand your situation and won't blame you. They will help you sort out how you may have contributed to the problem, but they will also help you see that you had no control over the sex addict's behavior.

What is a formal disclosure?
The first information you receive about the addict's sexual activities usually comes to you with no warning. In other words, this is not a planned disclosure. Your initial reaction is likely to be shock, dismay and anger. You may threaten to leave. You may ask a thousand questions. If you're lucky, you will subsequently have the opportunity to participate in a formal disclosure in which you will hear from your spouse and ask your questions.

This should be done in a safe setting – in the office of a knowledgeable therapist (or perhaps in an inpatient setting), after preparations are made to ensure the best possible outcome.

The formal disclosure is preceded by several individual therapy sessions, some with you, some with your spouse or partner. The addict will be taught to disclose with integrity – to reveal the information while taking responsibility and avoiding blaming others. Usually the addict receives help writing an "amends" or "I apologize" letter to you, in which he or she lists the ways his or her behavior has hurt and affected you. It includes an offer to answer any of your questions about the past. Since rebuilding trust has a great deal to do with how serious the addict is about recovery, the early sessions will emphasize behavioral changes as well as a commitment to work actively on addiction recovery.

You also may have individual sessions with the therapist to prepare you for the disclosure. The therapist will discuss your role in the "dance" of the addiction, which is not the same as being responsible for the addict's actions. You will also discuss what information is useful for you to have. If you want to know all the "gory details," the therapist will work with you on understanding why this may not be in your best interest initially.

Some therapists will agree to plan a session in the future – say in three months – at which time you'll have the opportunity to learn additional information, such as details about the acting out. The therapist will also encourage you to become involved in 12-step recovery.

The therapist will likely ask you to think about and write out the following items, which will be the basis for discussion during the disclosure session:

1. Make a commitment to yourself to use the disclosure as a way to start the healing process for yourself. You can decide if you want to work on the relationship after you have heard what the addict has to say. Part of working on yourself is acknowledging your fears about the situation.
2. Acknowledge that knowing only part of the truth hurts and that being in limbo contributes to the confusion, fear and anger.
3. Write a letter of anger about what you do know. Identify all the ways the addict's behavior has had an impact on you.
4. Write a boundary letter about how you want things to be different. Review the letter with your therapist or 12-step sponsor, and then read it to your partner.
5. Formulate any questions you have and what type of information you want to know.
6. Identify where you have made threats that represent your fear that you are not good enough and that you seek validation primarily through your spouse.[1]

The formal disclosure may take up to two hours or more. The therapist will monitor your reactions and that of your spouse to prevent the session from breaking down into acrimony or shutting down. Many couples consider this session to be a turning point in their relationship, an opportunity to begin to establish a healthier marriage. For some the disclosure will reveal it's time for the couple to begin new lives apart from each other. Regarding the timing and extent of disclosure, after two years of recovery from co-sexual addiction, one woman advises,

Do the disclosure soon and in the safety of a supportive environment, such as a therapist's office. Be fearlessly honest, but not detailed. Be willing to share without regard to consequences that might affect your honesty. Try to understand your partner's feelings without judging them or closing down. Realize you are valuable and lovable, regardless of what anyone says or does. Look at being honest as a gift you give yourself. You can say, "That's who I really am." Give others the choice to decide to like you or not, to be with you or not.[2]

I've heard that disclosure is a difficult event. What are its consequences?
Yes, disclosure is a difficult event. Disclosure of affairs or other sexual acting out is likely to cause you pain, as well as shame, guilt, anger or depression. At first you may distrust everyone, fear abandonment, lose sexual desire, or even become physically ill.

Other potential consequences include loss of self-esteem and the decreased ability to concentrate or to function at work. The addict may feel guilt, shame, anger, and fear that the partner will leave. The disclosure may, at least initially, damage the couple's relationship even more, or it could result in separation or divorce. The disclosure may also damage the addict's relationship with his children or friends.

Facing these negative consequences can make addicts reluctant to admit their behaviors to their partners. However, addicts need to remember that, in the long run, it's the behaviors not the disclosure that led to the negative consequences.

Even without disclosure, it's likely that sooner or later the same outcomes would take place. If disclosure has only negative effects, it's unlikely that couples who have been through the experience would recommend it to others.

Yet, when 164 addicts and partners were surveyed months to years after disclosure, 96 percent of addicts and 93 percent of partners felt it had been the right thing to do.[3] Both groups reported significant positive aspects of disclosure. For addicts, these included:

- honesty and an end to putting on a false front
- an end to denial
- hope for the future of the relationship
- a chance for the partner to get to know the addict better
- a new start for the addict, whether in the same relationship or not

The positive outcomes for the co-addicts who had heard the disclosure included:

- clarity about the situation
- validation they're not crazy

• hope for the future of the relationship
• finally having the information necessary to decide about the future

One of many women whose husbands had covered up their behavior by casting doubt on their wives' emotional state relates,

One of the most helpful things about the disclosure for me was that it confirmed my reality. My husband had repeatedly told me how crazy and jealous I was. Over time I had started believing him. Finding out I had not misread the situation helped me to begin trusting myself, that I wasn't as crazy as he had said or as I had thought.

Despite her pain, another woman felt the disclosure could be the start of a better marriage:

It was the best and worst day of my life. I knew for once that he told the truth at the risk of great personal cost. It gave me hope that he could grow up and face life's responsibilities. It was the first time his words of love and his actions were congruent. I felt outraged and sick, yet I also felt respected and relieved. It gave me hope for our relationship.

In the past, I've threatened to leave should my partner have an affair or even get involved sexually with someone online. How likely are couples to split up after discovery or disclosure?
Threats to leave are a common, easily understood reaction to the shock of learning that your partner has betrayed you with another person. Many partners have some suspicions about the addict's behavior long before the addict admits the secrets. Some of these partners confronted the addict and threatened to leave, others said nothing.

But once the partner discovers the acting-out behavior, the majority do threaten to leave or end the marriage or relationship. However, only a few do separate, and in a study of addicts and co-addicts, half of those who separated eventually reunited.[4] Of those partners who threatened to leave but didn't, half changed their minds because the addict became involved in recovery work; the co-addict did so as well, and both went to therapy and worked out their problems. Sometimes the addict sought treatment because of the partner's threat to leave; other times it was because of other consequences the addict experienced.

For the remaining group of partners who didn't leave, despite threatening to do so, the reason was primarily out of a fear of abandonment, the study showed. Some co-addicts have childhood wounds which result in a great fear of abandonment. Life without the addict may seem too difficult. They may conclude that living with the pain of the addict's acting out is better than living alone. They may be moved by the addict's promises and decide to give the addict another chance, threatening to leave "if it happens again." Some partners feared confronting the addict. A minister whose wife had online and offline sexual partners stayed with her because he felt he needed to maintain a certain image before his congregation, and he didn't want to subject his children to a divorce.

Couples who stay together and get involved in addiction recovery have to simultaneously work on individual and couple recovery. This is more complicated than focusing on your individual recovery. Sometimes, especially if the couple doesn't have young children, one or both partners may feel it's easier to separate. Sometimes the co-addict feels so much pain, anger and betrayal that a period of separation is helpful while she or he works through the emotions and issues.

If you're thinking about separation, it's a good idea to discuss it with your counselor or support group. What are your motives? Are you threatening to leave to force your partner to attend therapy and 12-step meetings? Or do you feel you need the separation for you? If you have children, how will they be affected? In general, it's advisable not to make major decisions in the early days, unless you need to leave for your safety. So think about it, get input from others, then make a decision based on what's best for you, not what the affect will be on the addict.

Should we get disclosure over with early so we can get on with rebuilding our relationship?
The first thing you need to realize is that disclosure isn't a one-time event – it's a process. In a survey of 164 recovering sex addicts and partners, 59 percent of addicts and 70 percent of partners reported there had been more than one major disclosure.[5] Sometimes the initial disclosure was incomplete because the addict deliberately concealed the most damaging or shameful behaviors, or he/she minimized the number of partners or episodes of acting out.

You need to recognize that some addicts may not initially remember various behaviors, especially if their addiction included multiple episodes or different types of activities. Or the addict may have been intoxicated or on drugs and does not remember particular events. In other cases, the addict may not have realized that revealing a particular behavior would be important to the partner.

Additionally, addiction is a disease of relapse. Even if your partner is actively working a recovery program, he or she may have a slip or relapse. It's quite possible that there will be additional behaviors to disclose in the future. As part of your therapy after the initial disclosure, you and your spouse or partner will need to work out guidelines for how to manage any additional information that should be revealed.

It's a good idea to think through the possible types of information and make plans. For example, new information about sexual behaviors that preceded the initial disclosure is likely to be less traumatic to the partner than information about relapses. Co-addicts may be able to make a clear distinction about acting out that took place before the addict got into recovery, and may be able to accept additional information about that period of time without major upset.

When recovering co-addicts were asked what information they wanted to know, the most common replies related to the addict's sobriety status. A wife with seven years of recovery from co-addiction says, "If he loses his sobriety, I would want to know when and how and what he plans to do about it, so I can act accordingly." Another type of information co-addicts want to know about is specific behaviors which might have legal consequences. Yet another recovering co-addict expresses,

I want to know if he's engaging in sex outside the marriage, because that affects my health and our commitments to each other. I don't want to know his addictive thoughts. I appreciate when he can share the inner pain he feels. This helps me understand and forgive.

If significant additional disclosures are necessary, it's a good idea to do so in a therapy session. When co-addicts were asked what they would like therapists to know, they most commonly expressed:

- a desire to feel empowered
- to be the one to decide how much to be told
- a wish they had sought or received more support from peers and counselors at the time of disclosure.[6]

Contrary to some co-addicts' fears, planning for subsequent disclosures is not an invitation to relapse. It's like a fire drill – it will prepare you for an eventuality that you hope won't happen.

At our first formal disclosure my husband insisted he told me all the big pieces of his acting out, but over the next two years he told me some other things. How can I trust him?
The most common reason for this is probably a slip or relapse. Addiction is a disease where there is always a risk of relapse. As part of your early counseling, it's a good idea to discuss strategies for dealing with any slips or relapses the addict may have in the future. Some situations that many co-addicts decide they would want to know about include: sexual behaviors that put them at risk of STDs, sexual activities involving other people, or sexual behaviors that will impact the relationship.
On the other hand, the couple may agree that minor slips are best processed by the addict with his or her support group rather than with you. One co-addict recalls,

One day my husband came home rather grumpy. He explained, "I saw a really gorgeous woman on the street today, and I found myself feeling resentful of you. I was thinking, if only I wasn't still married to you, I could get something going with her." Well, this made me resentful! I told him, "Joe, it really isn't helpful for me or our relationship for you to tell me this. Next time please spare me and instead discuss it with your group.

Another understandable reason for a late disclosure is that during the initial disclosure your partner may have forgotten some pieces. Addicts frequently have an extensive history of sexual acting out and may not initially recall everything. Also, the addict may at first not have thought that some behaviors were important enough to mention to you, but further along in recovery, may have realized that you need to know these things. A co-addict gives an example:

One evening, after my husband I had been in recovery for over a year, we were having dinner with an old friend of his, and my husband told him what he thought was a funny story about a prostitute he'd been with a couple of years earlier. I was furious! When we were again alone, I immediately confronted him. "How come this is the first I'm hearing about this? I thought you told me everything important" He said, "I did so many things back then that I'm sure there will be others in the future that will come out. I can't do anything about my past, but I can assure you that since I've gotten into recovery, I haven't done anything untrustworthy." After I calmed down, I found his statement reassuring.

When you receive new information about events that occurred before the initial disclosure, don't jump to conclusions about your partner's trustworthiness or lack thereof. In addition to the content of the disclosure, think about the meaning of the fact that he's telling you now. It may be that he recently realized that there was another secret that he'd rather not have between you because he's committed to your relationship and your future together.

My spouse is the one with the compulsive sexual behaviors. My spouse is the one who needs fixing. I'm the one who was lied to and betrayed. So why do you and others keep saying that I should go to a 12-step program and counseling?

When a person's compulsive sexual behaviors come to light, most partners feel like innocent victims – they were betrayed, manipulated, deceived, put at risk of contracting a serious disease. But it's never that black and white. For one thing, being in a relationship with an addict is usually hard on the partner. You may have sensed your spouse's emotional withdrawal. Perhaps you wondered if he or she wasn't being honest about certain activities. Your partner might have blamed you for some of your couple problems, saying you're too busy, too overweight, too involved with the kids, uncaring about how hard he works, or that you ask too many questions.

As things get more out of control, partners of addicts increasingly try to control the situation or to please the addict. Some get angry. Some become junior detectives, looking for clues to explain the addict's behavior. Some change their appearance, even going so far as to have cosmetic surgery. Your self-esteem is likely to suffer. You may feel rejected. By the time discovery or disclosure happens, you also need help.

In response to being in a relationship with an addict, some partners cope by developing their own addictions or compulsive behaviors. Some become addicted to alcohol or prescription drugs. Some become workaholics, compulsive housekeepers, or overly focused on their children. Some overeat or become bulimic. Others get depressed. If you have any of these problems, you need to reach out for help immediately.

In addition, you may have brought your own problems into the marriage. Couples choose each other for a reason. Studies have shown that many sex addicts and co-addicts come from similar types of families – families that have rigid rules, want to look good, and aren't very emotionally involved with each other.[7] In these families, the children's emotional needs weren't met, often because some type of addiction was present whether it was chemical dependency, sex addiction, workaholism or eating disorders. The parents were too involved with their addictions to really pay attention to the kids as people or consider their feelings.

In your family of origin, you may have become a people-pleaser, someone who ignores his or her own needs and helps others, someone who doesn't talk about feelings. You may have presented a successful face to the world, while inside you might have become someone with low self-esteem and self-doubt. You may have experienced abandonment in childhood and are still so afraid of abandonment that as an adult you're willing to tolerate unacceptable behaviors rather than risk being alone. You may have grown up with a set of beliefs and behaviors, called co-dependency, that still govern the way you respond to other people. Your spouse was likely a good fit for you – someone who needed you, someone you could help.

In addition, both sex addicts and their partners often come from families where there were sexual issues. Perhaps no one talked about sex in your family. On the other hand, you may have been sexually abused or there may have been a heightened awareness of sex. Many co-addicts, even before marrying a sex addict, have come to believe that sex is the most important sign of love. This makes them the perfect partner for a sex addict, who usually believes that sex is his or her most important need. In other situations, some women who were sexually abused are not interested in sex; they are "sexually anorexic" or sexually aversive. A spouse who isn't very interested in sex with them seems like a good fit for a partner who feels the same. But the sexual anorexic often doesn't realize the reason her partner is not intimate with her is because of his other sexual outlets.

When you start to look at your own issues, one of the first things you'll be asked to do is to review your own past relationships. Have you had a previous spouse or boyfriend/girlfriend who was sexually compulsive? Abusive? Emotionally detached? Having a pattern of unhealthy relationships is a strong sign that you need to explore the factors that have led you to make the choices you've made in your relationships. A co-addict in recovery relates,

When my husband began attending a 12-step group for sex addicts, he suggested I attend S-Anon, a group for co-addicts. I was incensed. It was bad enough he had put me through the pain of his betrayal. Now I was supposed to get myself fixed! I didn't think there was anything wrong with me. But in order to please him, I went to the meetings. It didn't take me long to recognize that I was a co-addict – that I had felt responsible for his happiness, I had given him all the power for my happiness, and I took the blame for the problems in our marriage. I also recognized that most of my previous relationships were with addicts of one sort or another. It wasn't an accident that I had chosen him.

The bottom line is chances are excellent that you, too, have unresolved issues that can be helped by attending a 12-step program and attending counseling. Consider this an opportunity to help yourself become a healthier and more well-adjusted person.

You need to develop clear boundaries about what behaviors are acceptable and which are unacceptable to you. You will learn to clarify what you need from a partner. You need to become sufficiently comfortable with yourself that you can make a real choice about staying or leaving a relationship, knowing that you can have a good life alone. If you stay, it should be because you choose to rather than from unhealthy dependency.

Chapter 3
Is this Going to Get Better?

Stefanie Carnes, Ph.D., CSAT and Cara Tripodi, M.S., CSAT

My world has been turned upside down. I can't even remember the ride home after our "disclosure session." I felt like I was in a haze for a week, just going through the motions. All of the information is just starting to come together for me. I fluctuate between wanting to forgive him and filing divorce papers. I have always been the "stable" one in our relationship and, recently, I feel like I'm going crazy.

– JoAnna, 43, after learning her husband had been exhibiting himself in parks.

My life is falling apart since learning about my partner's sex addiction. When is the pain going to go away? Am I going to get better? Is it normal to be so upset?

The pain you are experiencing is normal. Learning your partner is a sex addict is devastating and life-altering. The betrayal triggers a myriad of emotions. Feelings of anguish, despair, anger, hopelessness and shame may threaten to overtake you. This time feels surreal, and you may be wondering, *Where do I go from here?* The shock and crisis brought on by this newfound reality may have you feeling alone and in unchartered territory. You may not know where to turn.

Although your situation feels unique, it's important to know that there are many people like yourself who have traveled this path before you. They have come through it stronger, more knowledgeable, and even grateful for what the addiction has done for their lives. Many of them followed a similar course of transformation that is outlined in this chapter. Their decision to enter recovery only came once they were forced to face the inevitable: that their lives were out of control from living with an addict and they needed help. True transformation and lasting change can only happen when a personal decision is made to face your own pain and no longer hold others responsible for what brought you to this place.

Partners of sex addicts commonly demonstrate six stages of personal growth and development. These stages were initially developed by Dr. Patrick Carnes.[1] His research focused on sex addicts and their partners. He followed 99 partners of sex addicts over five years as they progressed from finding out about the addiction to integration of this in their lives.

These stages were compared and contrasted to the progression of sex addicts from crisis to long-term recovery. For a discussion of the differences in these two populations see Chapter 4.

These six stages will serve as a model to help guide you through a rough and necessary journey toward your healing and recovery. There are aspects of the stages that will best describe you today. But the stages are also meant to give you a practical set of steps involved in recovering from this crisis in your life. Most important, the stages help you see that you are not alone and that things can improve. The Stages of Recovery for Partners of Sex Addicts are:

- The Developing Stage/Pre-Discovery
- Crisis/Decision/Information Gathering
- Shock
- Grief/Ambivalence
- Repair
- Growth[2]

How you experience the stages of recovery will depend on many factors, including your personality, any medical or psychiatric diagnoses such as depression or addiction and past losses. If you have experienced losses or betrayals, or have suffered abuse or trauma in your background, you may find it more difficult to move through these stages. All these factors will play a role in how you process your pain, and will influence the timing of when and how you advance through the six stages.

You may find one stage more challenging than another, and you may even stay in one stage for a longer period of time. Conversely, you may move through other stages more quickly. You might confront a new crisis or challenge which may pull you back into an earlier stage, such as a triggering event like the anniversary of discovering your partner's addiction or an old cell phone bill that reminds you of when you found out about his/her addiction. These triggers can conjure up old feelings that you believed you had resolved. Similarly, you may see yourself vacillating between two or more stages at once.

The Course of Recovery Over Time

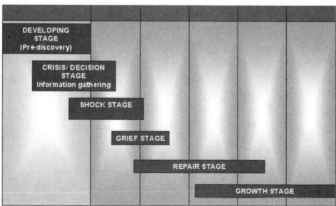

Figure 3.1   ©2007, S. Carnes and C. Tripodi

The Stages of Recovery for the Co-Addict

The Developing/Pre-Discovery Stage

The developing stage is the period of time prior to knowing there was a problem or before discovery/disclosure. You may find during this stage that you were either completely in the dark about the addiction, or had some suspicions but were not fully aware of the extent of your partners sexual acting out. During this stage, you might try to keep the peace in the home and hold an idealized view of the relationship.

For example, one spouse states, "I just wanted us to be the perfect family. I wanted that dream family that I never had, so I unconsciously overlooked problems." When problems do arise during this time, you may be quick to blame yourself or define the problem as a relationship issue.

If you were completely in the dark about the sexual acting out, you may have had a hunch that something wasn't right with the addict. You likely experienced the unmanageability of the addiction in other areas of life, such as parenting, finances, work and intimacy. Because life was increasingly unmanageable, you may have found yourself attempting to control the other areas of life, such as work, the children, the household, etc.

Conversely, you may have known about certain aspects of the behavior, like pornography use, but had no idea about the extent of the sexual acting out. When you accidentally found suspicious information you might have overlooked it or believed the addict's convincing explanations. Your gut may have been telling you one thing but your mind told you another. You sensed that something was wrong, however, you didn't have the information to back it up. Instead you questioned yourself and would give your partner the benefit of the doubt. This may have even resulted in you questioning your own self-worth.

During this stage it's common to tolerate behaviors that others would find intolerable. This may include verbal or physical abuse, lack of availability, emotional distance, and lack of functioning in many areas of life. You may have found yourself caretaking to a fault. Unconsciously, you may have minimized the addict's behaviors, and covered up for them by making excuses or concessions despite your better judgment. You may have found yourself defending the addict, and believing the addict's words over his or her actions.

Another way you may have tried to address the problem was through couples counseling. If you sought marital therapy after learning about your partner's sexual addiction, it's likely that you found the focus was on stabilizing the coupleship and not on separating out your partner's behavior from the relationship issues. Many partners have been frustrated by couples treatment because the focus was often on both parties, rather than focusing on holding the addict more accountable and seeking recovery for the addiction which needs to be treated first.

Core Characteristics of the Developing/Pre-Discovery Stage

- believing tall tales
- tolerating and normalizing unacceptable behavior from the addict, such as verbal abuse, dependency, unavailability, mood swings
- self-doubt such as second guessing, not trusting gut feelings
- having hunch something isn't right
- seeking couples therapy
- unmanageability
- loss of values, morals, or beliefs deemed important to keep peace with your partner

The Crisis/Decision Stage

During this stage, the façade of the secret life of the addict has been exposed, and reality and disillusionment is beginning to settle in. As in any life-altering crisis, how you respond has a lot to do with your personality and if you suffered from prior crisis in your life. This means that if you are someone who has experienced frequent losses, then you are apt to be more reactionary than someone who has not. The old responses get reactivated and add to your distress. In addition, the duration of the addict's behaviors, the types of behaviors engaged in, and length of time of the relationship will also influence how you respond to the fallout of discovery/disclosure.

If you are someone who withdraws from crisis, you will find that you want to avoid knowing about the addict or sex addiction in general. You may act as though nothing has changed and try to keep up with your normal responsibilities. Or if you are someone who is more action-oriented, you will find yourself seeking honesty and accountability from the addict, despite the fact that a part of you cannot trust what she or he says.

Due to the broken trust, you may find yourself checking up on your partner or playing detective to determine if he or she is still lying and acting out. In fact, you may find yourself doing these behaviors when typically you are not someone who snoops or even wants to, but you find you are compelled to look for things. You may ruminate or obsess about the addict, his or her whereabouts and seek to review the details of his or her behavior repeatedly.

Much of this in an attempt to examine what happened and to come to terms with how you didn't figure out what your partner was up to before the discovery. You may be replaying the past in an attempt to capture how you could have prevented it from happening or confronted it sooner. All of these action steps are in response to being lied to and are a strategy to ward off the painful realities you are beginning to experience as a result of the betrayal.

For some partners, the crisis stage is a time when you want to hurt the addict. You do things to catch him or her in lies, like having secret e-mail accounts to track online activity. You may even seek to retaliate by finding a sex partner or contact the affair partners and act out your anger at them. These actions only further the crisis phase and keep you in a dance of confrontation and avoidance of your own pain.

The crisis stage is a crucial time in learning to care for yourself. The most resilient partners are able to gain perspective and establish a plan of care for themselves. Empowering yourself by seeking information and taking action is a beginning step in developing your voice and directing the course of your life. You may be motivated to seek answers to how you found yourself in this predicament.

This includes learning about sex addiction by reading, attending 12-step meetings or educational seminars; considering treatment options in the form of individual, group therapy and psychiatric consultation; and seeking legal and financial consultation. Establishing concrete resources helps compensate for the feelings of powerlessness that may threaten to overwhelm you.

Core Characteristics of the Crisis Stage

- a catalytic event occurs: you discover or are disclosed to about your partner's duplicitous behavior
- information gathering
- taking action/making decisions, such as sending the sex addict to treatment or joining a 12 step group

The Shock Stage

The crisis and shock stage often overlap, and for some may even happen simultaneously. During the crisis you learned about the behaviors, gathered information, and perhaps responded by making decisions. Shock is how you responded emotionally and spiritually to the crisis confronting you.

The upheaval during the shock stage can last for months and at times years. Variables that predict how long your are in these two stages depend on your response to the crisis and how your partner does or doesn't progress in recovery. Feelings of betrayal are overwhelming and mistrust of the addict reaches its peak. You seek honesty and accountability from the addict even though he or she has become untrustworthy to you. Despite this, you want disclosure of all previously concealed information or believe there is more when you have been told that there isn't. You don't know what to believe and you suffer from a multitude of reactions.

You may have periods of numbness, contrasted by times of upheaval and conflict. At times, you may find it easier to avoid the feelings. However, despite that strategy, there are often many feelings lurking underneath the surface that arise during times of conflict such as anger, resentment, pain, shame, hostility and hopelessness. You may experience crying spells, depression and even thoughts of suicide. You might begin to question your worth. One spouse states,

I began to wonder what he was getting from the other women that he was not get-ting from me! I tried to dress sexier to win his sexual interest. In hindsight, I wish I had just taken care of myself instead of worrying about his needs.

Understandably, you will have tremendous self-doubt and will need outside sup-port to help you validate your pain and challenge some of your thinking. Living in an addictive system is about secrets and isolation from others. Recovery becomes about letting others into your world and learning new behaviors and choices that were previously unavailable to you.

Core Characteristics of the Shock Stage

- emotional numbness or avoidance
- feelings of victimization
- suspiciousness
- terror about slips, future relapse
- distrust
- conflict
- feelings of despair
- anger, hostility, self-righteousness, blame and criticism

Grief and Ambivalence

One of the most important aspects of moving through your pain is recognizing and experiencing your grief. Acknowledging your pain and sadness is essential to moving past feelings of anger and betrayal. At the core of betrayal are feelings of pain, sadness and rejection. Anger is also often considered a secondary emo-tion to pain and sadness. So grieving is one of the central processes allowing you to move through your anger and feelings of betrayal. The wounding you have experienced cuts to the very core of your heart and soul, leaving you feeling shat-tered. Allowing yourself time to grieve the many losses during this time will help propel you into the next stages of repair and growth.

Distinguishing grief from self-pity is important, too. You may believe that feeling sorry for yourself is a waste of time and an indulgence that should not be tolerated. But grief is essential because it is that most private area of yourself that allows you to own your pain on a deeper level. Acknowledging, *Hey, I have been seriously wronged and I hurt is important.* It helps you stop intellectualizing of the problem and move into your own core feelings of loss, betrayal and sadness. It also allows you freedom from focusing on what the addict is or isn't doing which will assist you in connecting with your authentic self. Some of the losses you will experience are:

- loss of the dream of your relationship
- loss of self
- loss of relationship as it once was

- loss of emotional safety
- loss of sexual safety
- loss of financial stability
- spiritual vacancy: e.g. "where was God?"

During this period you may feel a deep sense of ambivalence about the relationship. When the wound is exposed and the healing is occurring, it will be difficult to think of reconnecting with your partner. You will question, *Why should I open myself up to this kind of pain again? How do I know he won't act out again? I want a guarantee that he'll never slip.*

You may contemplate separation, divorce, and have fantasies about how life would be without the partner or wish something would happen to him so you wouldn't have to go through this pain anymore. You may also find yourself attracted to someone else or imagine what it would be like with someone new without this addiction. Alternatively, the idea of being attracted to anyone right now may repulse you and conjures up tremendous fear and mistrust.

One of the significant gifts that comes from this stage is the gift of self-awareness and introspection. Instead of focusing on the addict's needs and wants, you begin to focus on your own needs and wants. Your self-care typically deepens during this time. This is an essential shift to make in the healing process because without focusing on yourself, you will not move forward into the next stage of repair.

Core Characteristics of the Grief and Ambivalence Stage

- grieving losses
- feelings of depression
- ambivalence about the relationship
- increased introspection and focus on the self
- less focus on the addict's behavior and more on your own

Repair

For many partners, it can take years of shock and grief before healing really starts to solidify and they move into the repair stage. Repair is marked by increased introspection and less focus on the addict's behavior. Although you continue to hold the addict accountable for what he did to you, you have moved toward greater responsibility for your own happiness. You know you need to be treated respectfully and honestly by the addict, but you see that how others treat you stems from your own self-worth.

You may also start to make the connections between your past during this stage. For example, you may consider how your family of origin impacted your choices and influenced your adult actions, especially in your relationship with the addict. This may include focusing on themes from your past, such as abandonment, abuse and neglect.

Many partners deepen their spirituality at this time. Their 12-step program deepens and becomes more fruitful, or religious ties strengthen or are changed for a new one that best reflects the internal transformations that have occurred.

In the 12-step fellowships there is a phrase found in the *Alcoholic Anonymous – Big Book:* "You will experience a new freedom and a new happiness."[3] This is when some of that new freedom begins to manifest. Coping skills and social support systems become stronger. Secrecy and isolation are replaced with solitude and companionship. Self-defeating behaviors often diminish. Overall, your deep pain and turmoil subsides and a more relaxed, introspective self emerges with a stronger voice.

These changes are reflected in your relationships as well. You will have a better understanding of the addiction and the addict's behavior, which places you in a stronger position to evaluate the relationship. You have a clearer picture about the addict's sexual acting out and the boundaries you need to keep yourself safe. You believe the actions, not the words of the addict, and you don't live in denial of the addiction or the addictive behaviors. You are able to hold the addict accountable with boundaries and are better at following through with them.

If you have doubts about the addict's recovery, you are likely to protect yourself. You are able to see red flags and confront them effectively. If you become re-traumatized by relapses or divorce, you openly seek additional resources to handle it. You are also more emotionally prepared to make the decision to leave the relationship if indicated. If the addict is in recovery, and your relationship is progressing in a healthy way, you may explore trust and intimacy that is deeper than before.

Core Characteristics of the Repair Stage

- introspection
- decision-making stage about the relationship
- deeper insight into causes of your co-addiction
- family of origin themes examined and integrated
- prior losses more fully grieved
- increased strength and coping skills
- boundary setting
- emotional stability

Growth

The final stage is growth. This stage involves continued self-transformation. One of the hallmarks of this stage for partners is letting go of feelings of victimization and replacing it with resiliency. You may discover a way to make meaning out of your suffering.

Gratitude for the addiction and the opportunities for self-actualization that it has provided occur here. The addiction was a catalyst for change and you responded to it. The many challenges you faced elevated you to a higher level of well-being, and you experience peace and greater appreciation for the work that you had to do in confronting this challenge.

You turn outward, not in a caretaking sense, but in a genuine desire to pass on what was given to you. Your compassion for other people's pain reinforces your commitment to healing. You can now realistically check your motivations and can catch yourself when you fall into old self-defeating patterns. You have integrated what you learned about your family of origin and are able to apply these insights into all areas of your life. If you find you are trapped in old patterns of behaviors, feelings or attitudes, you have choices now that seemed unavailable to you before. Those choices allow you to seek additional help in tackling any problem that presents itself.

You find you have more clarity and vision for your future. You no longer live in a denial of what life should be, rather you accept what life is and flexibly address problems that used to scare you. Intimacy is something you can reasonably address, respecting the limits of yourself and your partner. With your increased self-confidence, you will likely experience successes in other areas of you life, such as work, parenting and spirituality.

Core Characteristics of Growth

- decreased feelings of being victimized by the addiction
- focus on issues not directly related to the addiction
- communication skills and conflict resolution styles explored
- awareness of your role in the dysfunction of the relationship increases
- acknowledgement of gifts the addiction has brought to your life
- ability to be present and fully focused on other areas of life

Frequently Asked Questions

Below are frequently asked questions for spouses or partners that are on this journey into recovery. As you read them, you will see some of these stages reflected in the questions.

I had no idea! How could I have been so duped?

You may have been completely in the dark about the sex addiction, or maybe you had a hunch something was not right with the addict. Or you might have been concerned about your partner's sexual behavior, but you minimized or overlooked the seriousness of your concerns telling yourself, *At least she isn't going outside the relationship* or *All men do this.* This may have quieted your doubts for a time, but the problems never seemed to go away. In fact, maybe they got worse, increasing your sense of concern and catapulting you into this current crisis in your life where you can no longer deny what's really going on.

You were duped because your partner needed you to be in the dark in order to support his or her secret lifestyle. Sex addiction is insidious. It can mask itself in many different ways and can keep a partner deluded into thinking something is not what it appears. It manifests itself in a multitude of ways, such as financial unmanageability, relationship impairment, neglect of parenting responsibilities, reduced occupational functioning, or mood irregularities on the part of the addict. The fact that you didn't know about the addiction is a reality. Your partner wanted to distract you from the real issue of addiction; denial allowed him or her to continue uninterrupted in the sexual indiscretions.

Addicts deflect, manipulate, criticize and blame others for their problems to keep others from knowing what they are doing. Even if you suspect something, they will deny your truth and convince you otherwise. Over time, your doubts about your own reality may have gotten the best of you, damaging your self-worth. Addiction precipitates selfish behavior and the addict did whatever he or she needed to at the time to get what he or she wanted. Lying to you and coercing you to believe things that were not true are part of his or her attempt to get what he or she wants, disregarding you in the process.

Like the story *Little Red Riding Hood,* the young girl thought the wolf looked, smelled and spoke like her grandmother but, in reality, it was the wolf in her clothing on the prowl to hurt the girl. Just like this story, you have been deceived and nothing will change that truth. How you prevent that from happening to you in the future requires you to examine those areas of the relationship that were problematic to you. Were you apt to assume responsibility for problems, telling yourself that it was somehow your fault that the addict was behaving in a certain way? Did you find you overcompensated for his or her responsibilities at home, financially, with childcare or chores?

For instance, did you support him financially and emotionally when he or she was laid off from work only to find out later that your partner had lied to you about why he or she lost the job? Perhaps you then discovered the real reason was poor work performance because your partner was staying up late to view pornography. You may have found yourself bailing your partner out by making excuses for absences, when you didn't know where he/she was. Or maybe you rescued the addict with financial support. Did you feel indebted to your partner because he or she paid the bills and provided you a comfortable lifestyle that afforded you the time to work on your career or raise kids? Did this mean you would take on more of the blame for the problems and, in this way, quiet your suspicions and doubts? Undoubtedly, you experienced the chaos and unmanageability of the addiction in your life only you didn't know that's what it was at the time.

These examples are common experiences for partners of sex addicts. In a healthy relationship, it's normal to give your loved one the benefit of the doubt, and make assumptions and concessions to your partner. Holding a positive image of your partner and the relationship are also helpful ways to thrive and grow together. But in addictive systems one person, usually the partner, is being taken advantage of by the addict. This creates an imbalanced and unhealthy environment.

Addicts take more than is rightfully their share in a relationship. Therefore, applying normal adaptive beliefs and supportive assumptions to your partner in this type of system backfires because the addict is not interested in your well-being when caught in the throes of the addictive lifestyle. Changing these chaotic patterns starts with you. What you were doing was not working. Begin to own and evaluate how you were treated in the relationship. Start to rely on your own intuition and to challenge the beliefs, attitudes and feelings that you have had in the past.

You will be greatly assisting yourself by piecing together the manifestations of the addictive behaviors, those areas that were a problem in the relationship prior to discovery/disclosure, and the ways you accommodated to or managed those issues. Utilizing a support system is useful in putting the pieces together and in practicing new attitudes and behaviors.

I feel so despondent about this, yet I cannot stop thinking about it. Will I ever get back to normal?
After finding out about your partner's sex addiction, it's typical to question whether life will ever return to what it once was. Because you have suffered such a deep injury that cuts to the core of who you are, your pain will be extensive and repairing these wounds will take a long time. Furthermore, if these wounds in any way replicate prior painful experiences from your past, your pain will be more complex and confuse the process of your recovery.

How your pain may be expressing itself is through preoccupying thoughts about the addiction. Due to the fact that the betrayal of trust was so severe, the intrusive thoughts often center on the unfaithfulness of your partner. It's common for partners to ruminate about issues directly or indirectly related to this broken trust. Some of the ways this will express itself include:

- promises the addict made
- the sexual behaviors he or she engaged in
- his or her whereabouts
- his or her use of time
- his or her attitudes towards you
- the addict's behaviors (e.g. following through on their commitments)
- the trustworthiness of the addict
- the addict's sexuality (is he or she acting out again?)
- should you stay or leave the relationship?

Ruminating about the addict's behavior is part of the fallout from the crisis and it may be difficult to stop without help. Ruminating serves as defense mechanism for self-protection. It also may reduce your anxiety and keep you from feeling other deeper feelings related to the addiction. This is a stage you're experiencing and you'll get through it. You may find this takes a great deal of emotional energy and the duration of this stage commonly can last from one to two years.

Don't give up. Having a positive vision of yourself in the future will help you move forward. It will allow you to gain a sense of control over your life. If you find you're feeling stuck in this phase, try to direct your own healing. Become a partner to yourself. How would you want to be treated by others at this time and begin treating yourself this way.

Seek out mentors who have overcome difficult trials in their life and allow their experiences to strengthen your resolve. The more you recognize that you're deserving of a better life, you'll become a stronger advocate for your own healing. Own the reality of where you're at today. You will not always feel this way, but you will learn from it if you can open yourself up to the growth that this pain is offering you.

I'm afraid he is going to act out again. What can I expect?
Unfortunately, addiction is a disease of chronic relapse. It's realistic for you to be concerned about relapses, especially in early recovery. However, differentiating between a relapse and a slip are helpful in defining your non-negotiables.

Non-negotiables are those behaviors which you are not able to tolerate in relationship. You will learn about setting non-negotiable boundaries in Chapter Five. There are differences between slips and relapses. A slip, such as masturbating, can be less offensive to you than a visit to a strip club. In fact, you may not even see masturbation as a problem.

What is important is how the addict responds to his or her lapse. Those critical decisions will tell you more than the actual behavior. So if he or she is scared and immediately seeks help through his or her sponsor, group or therapist, that tells you this is a possible learning opportunity. If it deepens his or her insight into the causes of the behavior, then it's possible that it can be a learning experience. If, however, he or she minimizes it and doesn't increase his or her program in some way, or if you have to tell him or her to, then that will be a sign to you that he or she may not be approaching his or her program seriously enough.

Gathering data over time and comparing it to the list of non-negotiables you have established will help you in managing any slips and relapses. The differences between slips and relapses, in time, will not matter to you if the addict cannot maintain a continuous period of abstinence, which may force you to make a decision about the relationship.

Rebuilding shattered trust in a relationship requires reliable behavior over time. This is the only way to regain trust. After months or years of the addict being accountable, working a program, and doing what he or she says he or she is going to do, then your trust will be restored incrementally. Until then, it's normal to feel doubtful and suspicious, especially in this early stage of recovery.

I find my feelings are all over the place. One day I am angry and the next I am sad. How come I can't trust what I feel from day to day?
Confronting the painful truth that your partner is a sex addict propels you into experiencing countless emotions. You are embarking on a transformation that brings with it many challenges. One of the most complex challenges you will encounter is tolerating the various feeling states you will go through in your

recovery. Below are common feelings associated with experiencing the loss of the relationship as you knew it:

- grief
- ambivalence
- anger
- sadness
- loneliness
- abandonment
- fear
- shame

The shock of this discovery sets off a cascade of changes to your body, mind and spirit. It is crucial that you take the time and seek out supportive avenues that allow you to have the freedom you need to heal. In this way you are becoming better prepared for the next stage, which is acknowledging your losses and re-examining who you are going forward.

I really don't know that I want to be with a "sex addict," even if she is in recovery. I don't know who she is anymore and this isn't what I signed up for! Why should I stick around? What's in it for me?
Most partners experience a period of ambivalence about the relationship. There is so much shame attached to the disease of sex addiction, you think it would be just easier to leave the relationship behind. Making your ambivalence clear at the early stages of recovery is important for the relationship. *I'm not all the way in this relationship and I'm not all the way out* is an honest way for the addict to know exactly where you stand. This gives the addict an opportunity to "walk the walk" of recovery and recognize that the relationship is on thin ice and that he or she needs to put recovery first.

Whether you decide to stay or leave the relationship, finding out your partner is a sex addict presents growth opportunities for you. If you stay, the intimacy in your relationship with the addict can deepen through the recovery process. You will learn that the behaviors your partner engaged in, although unacceptable and offensive to you, was a form of escape and coping. Underneath the sexual behaviors lies a person who has used a false sense of self to keep you from truly knowing who he or she is.

If your partner takes on the responsibility of recovery you have a chance to have a true relationship built on a foundation of honesty. If you chose to leave the relationship you will also be challenged to grow in many ways, such as living on your own and possibly renegotiating another loving relationship.

Either way it will be important to assess what led you to being in a relationship with a sex addict and to begin to make connections to how this relates to your own interpersonal and familial issues. Even though this is a painful experience, you're going through this for a reason and there are lessons you will take from it.

Why should I forgive? I am so angry about what my spouse did. Shouldn't he ask for my forgiveness? I want true remorse, not "I'm sorry"! When will my spouse get how he hurt me?

Wanting your partner to "really get" how he or she hurt you is a normal wish but may be futile. Don't stop believing this is important for you. However, in early recovery there is very little available for you because all the energy your partner put into his or her addiction must now be directed toward his or her own recovery. In some ways you may be similar to two ships passing in the night. For a period of time you will be wrestling with your own distinct issues that, for now, can't be fully understood by the other. The addict can no more understand your need for remorse than you can understand what it's like for him to not act out for 30 days.

It's more important to pay attention to his or her actions about recovery, because recovery becomes the stepping stone for deeper amends to those the addict has hurt and that will come with time. The addict may make many promises, but it will be the cumulative actions in support of challenging his or her additive thinking and behavior that will give you small vestiges of hope about his or her growing capacity to experience remorse. Further in recovery, you should expect – in writing or with the presence of a trained professional – an acknowledgment of what he/she did to you, and the addict should listen as you explain how he/she hurt you. This will further honor your need to right the wrongs done to you.

Forgiving the addict prematurely is a common problem for many partners. Perhaps your religious beliefs encourage forgiveness and you feel that you "should" forgive. You may have been taught or saw in your family that you shouldn't hold someone accountable for their transgressions. Alternatively, you may feel sympathy or pity for the addict. Realistically, however, forgiveness takes time. It is essential for you to grieve your losses before being able to forgive. There are so many losses you will confront – the loss of the "dream" of your relationship, what you thought you had; the loss of trust with the betrayal; possible financial losses; or losses in social stature and relationships.

Not only does your sadness need to be adequately expressed and acknowledged, but also you will need time to heal. Grief takes time. This is an inevitable emotional response, and the last thing you need to do is put pressure on yourself to forgive before you are truly ready in your heart.

Finally and most important, you will need to forgive yourself. Many partners blame themselves for being unaware of the problems in the relationship, for accepting the unacceptable, or not challenging things sooner. You will find that your self-criticism may be the hardest obstacle to overcome before you can forgive the addict.

All the attention you give to yourself in your recovery will actively move you toward self-forgiveness. This will eventually allow you greater freedom to forgive but only after you reach a level of self-acceptance.

My husband says he is in recovery, but his behaviors do not always reflect a recovery lifestyle. I continue to hold him accountable, and set boundaries with him, and he follows through about 50 percent of the time. I am fed up. What should I do?

This behavior is referred to as "riding the fence" or demonstrating behaviors and attitudes that indicate partial recovery. The addict may be trying to convince you that they are working a strong program, when in fact they are not. You may know on some level that the addict is not fully engaged in recovery. As you get stronger, you may become more willing to set boundaries and follow through with them, hold him or her accountable, and be assertive regarding your needs in the relationship.

If you believe that what you are witnessing is true, verify your data. Common ways to do this are to ask your partner to share your concerns with his or her support network and to follow up with you about it. Next would be to discuss it with your support system and create some options that will help you decide what to do next. Check the behavior against his/her words and notice how he/she responds to you emotionally. Each of these data points allows you to be an informed participant in your life with an addict, protecting you from becoming victimized by the addiction. This will help to ensure that you do not have to experience again the shock of finding out about behaviors unknown to you.

One of the most common motivators for recovery from sex addiction is the potential breakup of a relationship. It's important to realize, that you have more power than you think you do. Sometimes the addict needs to experience "rock bottom," which may be the loss of an important relationship before being willing to embrace recovery. When addicts are faced with their consequences they often experience the desperation they need to be motivated for recovery. In many instances it comes down to timing. Are you willing to wait until he or she "gets it" or hits bottom? Or will you have already moved on? This is a very personal choice and one only you will be able to make.

What does my family of origin have to do with this? How did I get here?

You may be questioning how your family background contributed to your choice to be in relationship with an addict. Addictions travel in families and are passed on through generations. Most likely, you were raised in an addictive family or a family organized around a particular family member's needs. You may have learned that chaos and secrecy were part of normal functioning within a family.

When you got older, it's possible that you sought out mates who replicated aspects of your childhood. That familiar feeling was comfortable. You developed a tolerance for this kind of relationship in your family of origin. For example, you may have learned to expect less and then began to seek less from a partner. By accepting little in the way of your needs, you have duplicated how you were treated by your family by tolerating less than you deserve. You may be able to readily identify the connections to your family of origin. Or they may be more subtle and may require more work to see parallels to your current situation.

52

Whatever your situation, it's essential to your growth that these connections be made. Only when the unconscious is made conscious, will you find the capacity and insight to alter the course of your life. Having the courage to look at old hurts and challenge dysfunctional messages from childhood, creates a new pathway of choice and freedom for yourself. Believing you deserve better out of life and personal relationships is a huge step toward gaining empowerment.

Again, it's vital to realize that no two partners will experience these stages in the same way. By examining these stages, you may recognize yourself on the journey to recovery and be reassured that this will get better over time. You may be currently experiencing one of the more difficult stages of recovery from co-sex addiction, but this will pass and you will move into a more peaceful stage of introspection and growth.

While considering these stages, don't judge yourself harshly or try to force yourself into a future stage. Every partner goes through the stages at his or her pace. Hopefully, reviewing these stages will provide you some peace of mind that the crisis will not last forever, and growth and insight are the inevitable gifts you will receive through this experience.

Chapter 4
Should I Stay or Should I Go?

Patrick J. Carnes, Ph.D., CSAT

Modern physics shows us that once two molecules touch each other they have a relationship forever. Mating is similar. Three basic neural networks exist in our brains that involve sexuality. First, there is basic lust in which there may or may not be any attachment. Second, there is romance which has a cycle of four to seven years. And finally, there is a neural pathway that is about companionship and mating which when it serves us well, keeps reactivating sex and romance.

So deep is that mating response that one of the great pioneers of family therapy, Carl Whittaker, once quipped that we are "never divorced, we simply add marriages." Many clinicians become wary when they hear the phrase "soul mate" because it is a term romanticized in the media. The implication is that soul mates are exempted somehow from the everyday struggles of real intimacy and commitment. Therapist witness daily how deep, enduring and perplexing these human-mating attachments can be.

Multiple attachments are sitcom fodder. They build on the difficulties of multiple ex-spouses, step-parents and reluctant siblings. We see stories in which kids attempt to reunify their divorced parents, or the converse in which the children of remarried parents attempt to destroy the new union. We are moved by the *Sleepless in Seattle* scenario, and shudder at *War of the Roses*. Our media simply reflects our new realities as humans.

When our neural networks around sex evolved, life expectancy was less than 30 years not 80. In those times, the focus was on survival. Our longevity and abundance creates choices. We have reached the cultural conclusion that one does not have to stay in a relationship that is dysfunctional or worse, destructive. The price we pay is the poignancy of moments such as when three spouses appear at the funeral of someone they were married to, each lost in their private sorrow.

Our abundance and longevity create another set of problems called addictions. To live with an addicted loved one is heart wrenching. To live with a sex addict adds profoundly to the pain and confusion, because the very foundations of the relationship and one's life are attacked. Because so much deceit is involved, co-addicts become distrustful of their own perceptions. They ask how they could not see this problem in the making. They cannot believe anything the addicts say, and this creates unbearable anxiety.

Thus, a co-addict can go to extraordinary means to find out the truth, turning life into a malaise of obsession that, at times, exceeds the preoccupation of the addict. They hate who they have become and will do anything to stop the pain. The easiest apparent solution is to leave.

To abandon the relationship at this point, however, is akin to having a broken bone and not setting it. Broken relationships require attention as well. Failure to attend to this self-care can be crippling to future relationships. And if there are children involved, problems are inevitable. Whether you go or stay, it makes no difference. Mending will be required. And as painful as it is, there will be less pain and more effective healing when the fracture is dealt with as soon as possible.

The decision to stay or go calls for the deepest personal wisdom. Wise people seem to be able to suspend their feelings and dark thoughts, even in the midst of crisis, to see clearly their best options. This presence of mind is very much in keeping with 12-step wisdom. In the 12-step program, the key to serenity is having the wisdom of knowing when to act and when not to act. This time-proven approach is articulated so well by members of Al-Anon who recommend, "Nothing major the first year."

The Problem of Mismatched Stages

One of author Melody Beattie's funniest observations is that "seldom does everyone get into recovery on the same day."[1] Therein is one of the greatest challenges to a couple's life in recovery. Not everyone "gets it" at the same time. A preceding chapter outlines specific stages that co-addicts typically experience as they enter recovery. The stages are:

Developing Stage: Co-addicts start to understand that addiction is present in a loved one and that something has to be done.

Crisis Decision Stage: Co-addicts realize they simply can no longer tolerate the problem.

Shock Stage: Co-addicts adsorb the reality of how bad things have gotten and deeply engage in therapy and the recovery process.

Grief Stage: Co-addicts profoundly understand their losses and pain throughout life and specifically how the addicts' behavior fits the larger patterns.

Repair Stage: Co-addicts reconstruct how they interact with themselves and those around them.

Growth Stage: Co-addicts experience a new depth in their relationships and a new level of openness and effectiveness.

The problem is the addict and the co-addict usually move through these different stages at different times. Working through the stages takes three years or more. This allows the time for the brain to grow new, functional neural networks.

Plus, there is a host of skills and an array of knowledge to be mastered. To illustrate this, the following examples of Jeff and Fran shows how a recovery mismatch can occur.

Scenario One

Fran, the co-addict, is significantly ahead of Jeff in the recovery process. She has known for some time that he has not been himself. She had discovered the various ways he had been unfaithful, but she now has a good therapist and joined a 12-step group. In her recovery, she has gone to workshops and intensive experiences to add to her understanding. She sees how overlooking the obvious has been a pattern in her life. Her father's alcoholism kept her family in chaos, and she married a "high-maintenance" man. Plus, her early sexual experiences made sex at times difficult. She was at her best when there was crisis. Her biggest realization is that if she had not married Jeff, she may have married someone like him. She knows she has as big a problem as Jeff does.

Jeff, however, is still sorting out whether or not he is an addict. He knows he has done a lot of sexual acting out and that he has hurt Fran. Yet, he is not ready to stop all forms of acting out. He fears, in some fundamental way, that he will lose his sense of who he is if he totally surrenders. He goes through the motions of attending meetings and has visited with a therapist, but all he basically wants is to calm down Fran. He vows only to do behaviors that keep him off her radar. Unintentionally, he postpones the inevitable painful feelings that await his acceptance that he is a sex addict.

Fran intuitively knows that he is stuck. He has not grabbed the lifeline of therapy the way she has. So she decides that he will never change. She has tolerated behavior she should never have tolerated. She decides to initiate a divorce, which sets up another problem – eventually she will have to face her own feelings. More than anything she wants a shortcut through her fear, shame or anger.

The Course of Recovery Over Time

Scenario 1

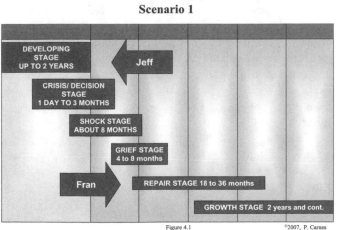

Figure 4.1   ©2007, P. Carnes

Scenario Two

In this scenario, Jeff has a head start because he got into trouble at work for his sexual behavior. He knows that his problem is profound and there is wreckage everywhere. His 12-step meetings are like deep drinks of water for a parched soul. He is excited at what he discovered in recovery. His company sent him to inpatient treatment, which stripped away all the pretenses and lies. He was raw and really needed his wife to be part of all that was happening to him. He also started to understand his wife in a whole new way.

There was so much she needed to know, so much hurt she has not been able to make sense of. He knew her family and could see how all the pieces came together. He could see what a difference all this learning could make in her life and in their marriage. She, however, elected not to come to family week. Instead, she informed him she was talking to an attorney.

For Fran, you simply could not put the words addiction and sex in the same sentence. She was stuck with four kids, and the request to take a whole week away from home for behavior that was not her fault seemed to be more of Jeff's self-centered thinking. She resented deeply that all they had worked for was now in jeopardy.

Further, some of her friends knew of Jeff's problems at work and offered to talk. She found the gestures embarrassing since she had nothing to say. No one could really help her now. She had learned a long time ago to do things on her own, and here again she was forced to handle everything. To Fran, it was simpler to go on alone. Only now it would be like having one less child.

Fran actually went to Jeff's therapist and was outraged. There is simply no excuse for what Jeff did. The idea that she needed help was beyond insulting. She walked out of the office vowing never to see one again. It was just a way to make money like anything else. When she walked out of therapy, Fran literally walked out on herself. The therapist was kind, but Fran felt attacked. Fran would not let anyone close to her, because to open up to another would reveal to herself wounds that were unbearable. It was easier to be critical and outraged.

Like all grief, anger and denial are closely linked. We push away with a vengeance those who could help us. Fran only trusted her children because she felt safe with them. She failed to notice that having a husband who was like a child replicated the same unhealthy reverse dependency. Further, these children will grow up, and these same issues may be repeated in their lives.

Jeff finally acquiesced to talking to the divorce attorney. There seemed to be no way to help Fran. The more he tried, the more her anger escalated. He realized that he had to let her go.

Part of the wreckage of what he had done was a tipping point. It was a trauma that had activated Fran's deep family wounds. As she lashed out at everyone, he felt sad for what he had done, but he felt even worse that she had decided to banish him from her life. Ironically, he had never been more aware of his deep care for her.

The Course of Recovery Over Time
Scenario 2

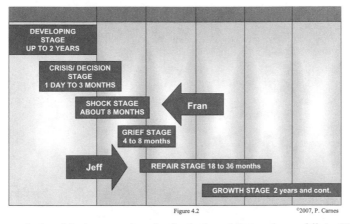

Figure 4.2   ©2007, P. Carnes

Leaving a relationship is an option for both the addict and co-addict. However, leaving the relationship before the couple has a chance to understand each other and the illnesses of addiction and co-addiction is the tragic loss. Like the Greek heroines and heroes, the problem of hubris – or believing that you are different from other mortals – is a pride we can ill afford. Yet both addicts and co-addicts are vulnerable to it.

Eleanor Payson writes in her book *The Wizard of Oz and Other Narcissists* that both the addict and the co-dependent become "self-absorbed."[2] In that state, neither addict nor co-addict fully appreciates how they impact on others. With recovery the preoccupation with self falls away and there is this discovery: We are no different than other mortals – including our partners. Like the Greeks we reclaim our humanity by giving up our pride.

Scenario Three

Consider a third scenario in which Fran and Jeff both make it to the pain stage. Something amazing happens when you see the pain of your partner. Many co-addicts talk about how they recommitted when they saw the sorrow of the addict. Similarly, addicts report losing the characteristic ambivalence they had toward their partners when they see their spouses' heart-wrenching pain.

Key to this process, however, is that both persons usually recognize, with remorse, their respective roles in what happened. Each partner – whether addict or co-addict – discovers his or her unresolved grief over the losses that occurred prior even to meeting his or her partner. All the blame and critical judgment toward the current partner was, in part, a defense against earlier hurts. The irony, of course, is that choosing the current partner has deep roots in the earlier wounds as well. In that emotional environment deep personal change occurs. The addict and co-addict also become aware of how much they appreciate the other.

The Course of Recovery Over Time

Scenario 3

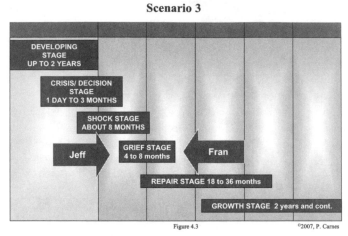

Figure 4.3   ©2007, P. Carnes

Recovering Couples Anonymous has an exercise that therapists have used for years. Each person is asked to make a list each week of the behaviors that have made life more difficult for their partners. They also make a parallel list of what they appreciate about their partners. Done sincerely, there are few dry eyes in the couple's presence as they share.

In many ways, this shift away from blaming your partner to taking responsibility for your own part changes everything. The most volatile, difficult relationships can be transformed by this level of integrity. And each person discovers the truth of the "wisdom" encapsulated in the Serenity Prayer: *God, grant me the serenity to accept the things I cannot change, courage to change the things I can, and wisdom to know the difference.* We cannot change our partners. The only thing we can change is how we respond in our new truths.

This process is not easy. It is truly a road less traveled. It requires the support of many, therapy, and the 12-step process. As the denial wears off, understanding grows and the pain is accepted. Plus, there is so much information about family functioning, child abuse, trauma, addiction, co-addiction, and brain functioning to know. As in any disease, there is much to learn.

We are reminded again of the insight behind that Al-Anon aphorism, *nothing major the first year.* Here is the bottom line: There is about 18 months of learning to make it through the initial stages. At the beginning, however, you simply do not know what you do not know. So each partner has to risk. There is no guarantee that the relationship can be restored. First of all, there is relapse to be concerned with. Second, some couples, after they become healthier, realize their partnership was never a good match. Sometimes couples reach this point, divorce and then remarry. There are no guarantees. By going through the process, however, you minimize damage, learn about your part, and are informed about what the stakes are. You give yourself the gift of an informed decision.

Whether you stay or go, the processes will involve pain. You will need help from your therapist and your partner. Your therapist can be expected to bring the knowledge and skills you need. Your partner will bring history, perceptions and perspectives you will need to hear.

I cannot imagine trusting like that again. How do I risk like that? Can I shorten the time? Can I do the work without involving my partner?
When co-addicts become self-absorbed, they want immediate gratification and they want long-term guarantees. The process of healing begins when they abandon the need to control how healing happens. Core to the process of codependency is anxiety. Remember that both addicts and co-addicts come from the same type of family structure. They tend to come from "disengaged" families in which bonding has been disrupted. Intimacy in these families is undermined by complex rules systems which create fear of abandonment. Rejection and pain create a chronic state of anxiety and intolerance of intense feelings.

They also tend to come from "rigid" families which have rules about "keeping the peace." Avoiding conflict, keeping appearances, and sacrificing personal needs all serve to keep the lid on the anxiety. Mostly "growing up" has failed to teach them how to take care of themselves, tolerate life's inevitable challenges, and to be calm when facing difficulty. Basically they have lost their integrity because they will do anything "expedient" to keep the peace. They will do anything to keep the peace externally so everything looks good to others. They will do anything to keep the peace internally so they do not have upsetting feelings.[3]

Divorce looks good to both addict and co-addict because it is expedient. Blaming everything on the spouse keeps the outside looking good because you can say, "It was my partner's fault." Divorcing provides a short retreat into denial and anger, so that internal grief is held at bay. While divorce is often complex, at first it seems a simple way to disassociate oneself from chaos and pain. What most therapists witness is that divorce intensifies the very worst aspects of both partners. The adversarial nature of legal battle tends to intensify obsession with the activities of the partner and proving that the partner is wrong, deceitful or even pathological.

The great irony in using divorce as a way to escape the inevitable grief is that it creates more. So much of the addict's life was spent proving something that was not true. Proving, for example, that the partner's fears were not grounded in reality is common to most addicts in relationships. Everything is fine. Similarly, co-addicts will spend so much emotional energy to prove that the addict is not telling the truth.

Thus, at times co-addicts will go to such extremes they lose contact with reality. They make accusations that are not true so others start to dismiss them as overreacting or exaggerating to make a point. Or they go to great lengths to prove to others that there are no problems in the family. They cover their partner's trail. Again, everything is "fine." Most recovering people, however, learn this fundamental rule: As soon as you are in the "proving mode" you are in trouble.

Here is reality. Divorce is an adversarial process. Litigators are champions at "proving" their sides. It pits former lovers against one another. Issues around children and money dramatically escalate the very worst aspects of this illness. In the midst of the divorce process, it is hard to achieve the perspective, detachment and process critical to healing in recovery. Further, because passions are so high, things may be said and done on both sides which create more wreckage, deeper wounds and inevitably more collateral damage to others, including children.

More losses are created when people divorce before they learned about addiction and co-addiction because they have not processed their own part in their addictive dynamics, and they have not acquired the basic skills necessary to negotiate good relationship decisions. They have taken a long drink in the river of high drama, intensity, grievance and obsession. Many years later those who have divorced without the insights of recovery realize they may have created unnecessary pain for themselves and others. Further, they guaranteed, in their righteousness, that they would repeat certain relationship patterns. The lesson here is: You can be right, but you may not learn nor will you heal.

Consider Carol who married the same type of abusive addict three times. Each time she told friends that she "had learned her lesson," although she seldom was clear about what the lesson was. Each time she married she was confident that she had made an improvement, that this husband would be a better match. Each marriage, however, was worse than the last.

Finally, she sought therapy, and an astute therapist helped her find a 12-step group. The timing was important because all three of her children had different fathers, and all three children were acting out in different ways. Once Carol started to connect with women in recovery she learned how much she was missing in not having good relationships with other women. She did not date anyone for more than a year. She became much more skilled at handling her emotions and realized how growing up in an anxiety-filled home had affected her. One day her therapist asked her to summarize what she had learned so far. Here is some of what she wrote:

I learned early to take care of others. It was a way to assure I'd have a place in the family. With men I would be attracted to the flawed and the hurt. I would seduce with my kindness. While I was willing to be Supermom to everyone, I was stubborn about letting anyone help me. I spent decades pushing help away. I overlooked stuff that was obvious to everybody else. I did not want the relationship or my life to be upset anymore than it was.

I learned about "negative intimacy" when I kept story telling about people who had wronged me. All I was doing was keeping them around in my head. I am a drama junkie. My life and the people I picked to be in it were all about my addiction to stress. I misused anger. I used it to bully people and to be controlling. I did not use my anger to empower me or protect me and my children. By being so perfectionistic I put my shame on everybody else. I cannot tolerate not knowing what is going to happen. My anxiety has made me so controlling I drive away those I love. I avoid conflict by having conversations in my head – but not with the person I need to have them with. My kids have seen through all the ways I have pitted them against their fathers. That is one of the biggest mistakes I made.

When asked by her therapist what her greatest source of grief was, she surprised herself by saying,

I watch my first husband now when he is with our child. He is a good father and he is in a good marriage. He is happy and successful. And he has a good recovery. For years I lived in resentment thinking of him as a hypocrite. Now I understand that anger really covered my being sad. The woman he is with has my place. I wished I had learned all of this stuff years ago.

If we return to the three scenarios outlined at the beginning of this chapter, we now can see the advantages of both partners committing to a recovery process and tabling major decisions until recovery has gained traction. Partners who both have committed to the process have new tools to mend what is broken. In many ways, they realize that two abused kids found each other but did not know how to make a relationship work. Now they can make an adult commitment to each other. If it is clear this relationship does not make sense, then they have tools to separate without the volatility and dysfunction they brought into the relationship. They can, for example, create a good, effective parenting relationship.

To discard the opportunity of having your partner in therapy, even if the relationship is untenable, closes off very important information about yourself and the relationship. There is essential debriefing that must happen. It is more than a therapeutic autopsy. Many life issues can be resolved to the extent that the future becomes a much more functional prospect. Nothing is sadder than when one or both partners opts out of this important reality. Recovery groups are filled with people who have a more difficult task of doing therapy because their partners refuse to be part of the recovery process.

What my spouse did is unforgiveable. Since I know I am going to divorce him, why should I go to treatment with him? Is an immediate divorce ever called for?
Situations do exist in which immediate divorce is appropriate. Threats to life, serious crime, further exploitation, financial and legal complications – the list of good reasons seems to be endless. Some situations are simply intolerable. Leading the list is when the addict continues to act out sexually. If there is clearly no effort toward recovery, there should be zero tolerance. In the original *Alcoholics Anonymous - Big Book,* they refer to the person who constitutionally could not commit to the process. All addictions have people who are not able to do what is necessary. For families it is a profound sadness. It is one of the great

sources of sadness for addiction professionals as well. And it is the life or death part of this disease.

Ultimately there are five levels of realities that partners of sex addicts have come to grips with. These realities are:

• The hurt and betrayal you feel is real.
• Addiction truly exists.
• The codependent plays a role in active addiction.
• Co-addiction is a mental health disorder which is separate from the addict's problem.
• Addictions have also damaged the coupleship.

First, no matter what the context is, the hurt and betrayal you feel is real. To learn of your partner's behavior is traumatic. Worse, most partners have a history of deception, abuse and exploitation. Thus, most often the wounding is reopened. This alone is a cause for deep therapy. This therapeutic work is best done by people who have experience with trauma and addiction because they often are inextricably connected.

The second reality is addiction truly exists. Addiction is a brain disease. We are decades behind other branches of medicine in understanding and researching how addictions work. We are even further behind in explaining it. Sex addiction now has enough research to place it in the category of addictive behaviors.[4] We know all addictions are considered a disease of the brain. Co-addicts must stop and consider, if their partner was diabetic or had Alzheimer's, how would their disease be regarded? It is a difficult reality to accept a disease in which the behavior is so hurtful.

With help co-addicts start to appreciate that part of their reaction overlooks the disease part of the problem. Remember, the disease of sex addiction is treatable. The elasticity of synaptic connections in the brain are remarkable in their ability to shift given time and the right treatment. Yet making this shift to understand sex as an addiction is so much harder than other mental diseases like Alzheimer's or depression. For the family, this requires help and education.

The third reality is that the codependency plays a role in active addiction. Most co-addicts discover they have actively been a co-participant in the process of the sex addiction. They learn about ways they have shut down intimacy, failed to hold their partner accountable, or become very controlling, been difficult and unavailable – again another endless list exists about how the problem evolved.

Therapists have long used the metaphor of the electric blanket with two controls. When the controls get mixed up, one partner gets cold and turns up the heat and the other turns it down. With the controls jammed to the extreme, both get the opposite of what they want. The way out is to reverse the controls and simply be responsible for your own side. In partnerships, the switching of the controls requires a great deal of help to do.

The fourth reality is that co-addiction is a mental health disorder which is separate from the addict's problem. We use terms like love addict or relationship addiction or traumatic bonding to describe situations in which a person cannot let go of a partner who is destructive to oneself or others. The bottom line is that co-addicts also have compulsive behavior which manifests in how they attach to others. This compulsive attachment is a disorder of the self in which the neural pathways of the brain are altered.

The result is the co-addict has difficulty determining what is normal in a relationship. Noted neuroscientist Louis Cozolino, suggest that codependence is rooted in "stress addiction" because of trauma.[5] When noted researchers speak of addiction to the trauma, the world is full of examples. Just think of ones you know:

- spouses who stay in battering situations
- employees who cover for abusive bosses
- sexual abuse victims who work as prostitutes
- battered boys who become mercenaries
- congregations who cover for exploitive pastors

People who stay in threatening circumstances recreate a neurochemistry in their brain in which they will do everything to maintain a destructive relationship. When a therapist says, "that man is your drug," it is more than a figure of speech. There is good science behind it. Fortunately, there are great resources of help in Al-Anon and codependency groups for sex addiction, such as S-Anon or COSA.

When we put the prefix *co* in front of a word related to addiction – as in co-addict – we risk implying that the co-addict or codependent has less of a problem than the dependent person. In alcoholism, for example, research has long shown the spouse to be so traumatized there often is more disturbance than in the alcoholic. We are quite sure that is true for co-sex addiction as well. The greatest irony is the spouse actually needs more help than the addict, but rarely is it offered to the extent that it is needed.

The fifth and final reality is hard to grasp but probably the most important. When both the addict and co-addict figure out they must have a grounded recovery for themselves, they realize that addictions have also damaged the coupleship. Recovering Couples Anonymous describes it this way: There is my recovery, your recovery, and our recovery. This is the famous "three-legged stool" of couples recovery.[6] Taking recovery to a relationship level is critical to the whole system of recovering. True healing occurs when partners collaborate to care for the relationship they have.

Thus, the couple looks at how they have been powerless over their own dynamics, they look at the ways they have damaged others together, and they explore the additional healing processes necessary to a successful relationship. In a long-term study of recovery from sex addiction, the couples who attended this level of recovery faired the very best.

Five Levels of Reality Acceptance

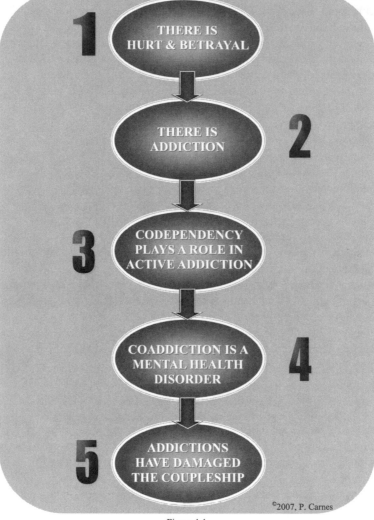

1 **THERE IS HURT & BETRAYAL**

2 **THERE IS ADDICTION**

3 **CODEPENDENCY PLAYS A ROLE IN ACTIVE ADDICTION**

4 **COADDICTION IS A MENTAL HEALTH DISORDER**

5 **ADDICTIONS HAVE DAMAGED THE COUPLESHIP**

©2007, P. Carnes

Figure 4.4

The bottom line to all five realities is acceptance at each level of reality means therapy is necessary. Once you accept these realities, questions about immediate divorce become more clearly defined. Part of recovery means no longer tolerating situations which are intolerable. That remains true even if you have to proceed alone in your process. Continuing abuse, physical jeopardy and sexual acting out would be examples of such a threshold. However, bear in mind the difference between behavior that is intolerable and behavior that is unforgivable.

Often times when situations emerge, they are so beyond comprehension that the partner sees them as unforgivable. When spouses learn about children conceived with others outside of the marriage, that other families exist, or even sex has occurred with another family member, the issues seem insurmountable. Yet, recovery history is filled with stories about how these situations get resolved. In short, when things are intolerable, it is about boundaries. When it is about forgiveness, discerning what to do truly requires more time and diligence to sort out.

Whether the behavior is intolerable or unforgivable, you should still go to family week or any other learning opportunity that presents itself. Recovery requires that you learn as much as you can. Whenever the co-addicts talk about issues, bond with others or learn new skills, they actually start to grow new, more functional neural pathways in their brains.

Further, it is heartbreaking to see partners opt out of the therapy process, when clinicians know there is information they do not have which could absolutely change their understanding of everything. Often this comes in the guise of the addict not having told the partner. And much of it has not to do with sexual behavior. The addict did not know the significance of the information. Or they felt the spouse already knew. Therapists cannot help because they cannot break confidentiality, and addicts will not reveal them if the partner does not show up to a safe environment so these issues can be aired. Almost every therapist has been in the bind of knowing that people are making decisions with insufficient data and there is nothing that can be done until people are willing to talk.

Given the scarcity of resources, it's important for couples to utilize all the inpatient and outpatient resources that are available. Building a recovery requires diligence. Not to do so usually means poor decisions about staying or leaving. Read everything you can find. Go to 12-step meetings. Find a good therapist who has been trained to help people coping with sex addiction issues. Find intensive workshops and group experiences around co-addiction issues. If you find yourself really desperate, seek inpatient treatment.

However, you simply must build a support network with people who understand this problem. They become the consultants who help you keep perspective, pass on critical tools you need, and give you the care you need and deserve. Ultimately they will also be the reality checks you need for good decision making. Most co-addicts will admit that, on their own, their decisions have not been good. That is because they attempted to do it without help, without all the information and without the tools they need.

So how do I make the decision to stay or leave? How do I know I have done enough to take this step?
Let us assume all of the above is in place. You have excellent support by people who are experienced in the problem of sex addiction. You have taken sufficient

time to let the dust settle and the brain to start to shift to a higher level of functioning. You have done enough therapy and recovery work to deeply accept the five realities of co-sex addiction. You have been proactive about learning about the disease. You have incorporated 12-step principles and practices into your life. To make a decision, there are some things you must remember.

Core to co-sex addiction is the erosion of a sense of self. This fact is why therapists may suggest a therapeutic separation. By living some months separately, and doing therapy, a couple can do what clinicians call *individuation*. This means the partners get a new take on what it means to be responsible for only themselves. Part of the goal is to develop enough ego strength to negotiate a new relationship.

This strategy is scary for couples, but it reveals so much and can be really useful. It illustrates a critical task necessary for making a decision about staying or leaving. Recovery means being able to discern what is right for you. You do not have to go through a therapeutic separation to learn that, but many still have the learning to do. The habits of being with someone are so ingrained, a dramatic change may be necessary to see how easily the self is lost.

One of the tests for an intimate relationship is answering the question, *Can I be most myself in your presence? Can I be creative, funny, vulnerable, productive, strong, weak, flamboyant, shy or even smart? Can I couple any of those words with sex and romance? Can I be tough, forgiving, generous, spiritual, intuitive, graceful, clumsy, lazy, self-indulgent and disciplined? Do I feel equal, successful, attractive, encouraged, trusted and believed? Can I be fully as competent as I can be and not have my partner disappear? Do I feel challenged? Can I be accountable and hold my partner accountable? Is it OK to make a mistake? Does our time together really seem to matter?*

There are many ways to discern if one can be most oneself. The more fundamental issue implicit in the question is: Are you willing to risk yourself with this person? Intimacy really comes down to what you bring to the equation. And happiness stems from what we bring to that table called intimacy.

There are two decisions on the table. The first is the choice to be in relationship. A committed relationship is a way of life which requires much of the partners. And it is has little to do with who you are with. This commitment has more to do with how much you have grown up, learned skills, developed integrity, understood your own limits, and healed your wounds.

From a therapist's perspective, people's unhappiness is often of their own making. To be an adult, especially with children, work responsibilities, and the nightmare of addiction, it is a difficult context to discover you still have growing up to do. For some the best choice is to take the time until you know you are really ready to be in a relationship.

The second choice is to whom you are willing to commit. Two things make the choice of who you successfully choose to commit to – after the initial rush of sex and romance wears off. When intimacy boils down to its essence, physical characteristics, such as breast size or an athletic build, become tangential. The size of the bank account becomes irrelevant. The level of learning, while important, pales by comparison. Ultimately these two issues make or break successful intimacy. First, these relationship qualities truly matter:

- Does your partner freely admit their mistakes?
- Do you feel safe enough to readily admit yours?

Nothing lasts without those basic qualities of integrity. Everything else – sex, romance, success – goes through that filter. No long-term intimacy can survive without this essential sense of our own limits.

Second, psychiatrist Carl Jung long ago pointed out that the most important part of any relationship is the willingness to share the darkest parts of ourselves. It is critical to good parenting. Children need to understand that their parents struggle in life. Otherwise, unrealistic expectations create shame in children. Similarly, no primary relationship survives without the full disclosure of self. Again there is this great irony that shame is reduced by telling the most shameful things about ourselves. When partners keep secrets from one another, they invariably introduce shame into the intimacy of the relationship. So the second key issue is:

- Can you share the darkest part of yourself?
- Can you hear about the dark side of your partner?

Being vulnerable doesn't require that the partner fix anything but rather witness the strength and courage it takes to be an adult human being. In the movie *Shall We Dance*, Susan Sarandon stars as a suburban wife who hires a private detective to find out about her husband's secret life. She learns that her husband has secretly been taking dance lessons. While he hasn't been unfaithful, he did have a secret life. The private detective clearly wants to use this discovery to become involved with her, so he asks her why she stays with this man. She responds with one of the best statements of what it means to be in a relationship with another: *Because we need a witness to our lives.*[7]

There are a billion people on the planet. What does any one life really mean? But in a marriage, you are promising to care about everything. The good things, the bad things, the terrible things, the mundane things. All of it – all the time, every day, you're saying, "Your life will not go unnoticed because I will notice it. Your life will not go unwitnessed – because I will be your witness."

All relationships are challenges. The ultimate test of human life is making a successful long-term relationship. It is part of life's refining process that calls us into being better people. Family therapist Carl Whittaker once observed that all relationships are a struggle. It is simply a matter of finding the best "struggle" you can. Many times we find it is the one we are already in.

Chapter 5
How Do I Set Boundaries and Keep Myself Safe?

Cara W. Tripodi, LCSW, CSAT

Boundaries can be one of the most confusing – yet freeing aspects – of healing from your partner's sexual addiction. Learning to identify, define and act upon boundaries will take a tremendous amount of focus as you navigate the unchartered territory of recovery from sexual codependence.

Boundaries function along a continuum from healthy to unhealthy and from flexible to inflexible. They involve your physical, emotional, spiritual and sexual self. Boundary development starts in childhood and continues throughout your life and is reflected in the cultural, social, familial and religious affiliations in which you were raised. They also influence how you relate to yourself and those around you. Children raised in environments that were flexible yet predictable learn that what they say matters and that the appropriate limits will be adhered to. If a child is taught to be respectful of others, for example not to interrupt when someone is speaking, he learns to expect the same from others. If that is violated, like if a friend were to steal from him, he has a healthy level of upset and expects his caregivers will support his feelings and explore possible actions regarding the offense to him.

When boundaries are unpredictable, rigid or abused in families, problems around self-definition arise. For example, if you were raised with a father who was an alcoholic, you may have learned that drinking was more important than his relationship with you. If your brother physically abused you and no one intervened to protect you, you learned that your physical safety and emotional needs didn't matter. These types of experiences can leave you vulnerable in your intimate relationships because you didn't learn that your needs mattered or that when your safety was jeopardized that anyone was there to protect you. Developing these types of dysfunctional boundaries often leads to high tolerance for unacceptable behavior in your relationship to the sex addict.

Boundaries are critical to your recovery from your partner's sexual addiction. You will find that they will become a cornerstone for lifelong change and help to redefine the direction of your life and the relationship to the sex addict. They can also be the most difficult part of the healing process. You will make a lot of mistakes as you attempt to challenge old patterns of behavior with yet untested but more adaptive ways of relating to the sex addict. Realizing that you are living with an addict shakes the deepest parts of your identity, and setting and enforcing boundaries will become an essential part of how you manage your recovery going forward.

Do I have a right to set boundaries with the sex addict?
In the early stages of recovery, it's essential that you know you have the following rights in relation to the sex addict:

- to not tolerate any unwanted sexual advances
- to expect a commitment of recovery defined by actions: such as 12-step meetings, individual and/or group psychotherapy
- to set boundaries and expect they be respected
- to not accept sexual acting out, such as no viewing of pornography, no contact with sex partners
- to not to be victimized again by the sexual behaviors
- to not be lied to or deceived

Highlighting these rights underscores the injustices done to you by your partner's addiction. You may find that in defining these rights that you have various reactions. You might believe you are wrong, controlling, or rigid for setting limits. You may have been told this by your partner which left you feeling further doubts about your perceptions. You may feel conflicted between who you have been versus how you need to respond to the crisis at hand. Changing your thoughts and behaviors is bound to elicit those types of feelings and judgments. That is normal, as are your concerns and needs for limit-setting with an addict.

In order to implement your boundaries, it's useful to thoughtfully consider your needs and discuss your ideas and plans beforehand with trusted individuals who understand your situation. If the addict's duplicitous behavior extended over years, the severity of the violation will be greater, especially if you confronted the addict but your suspicions were repeatedly denied or explained away. If the sexual behaviors you've learned about are a recurrence of other previous indiscretions, then your level of mistrust will be further magnified. If the behavior is illegal, you may face greater social, legal and financial consequences. It is important to recognize that your partner deceived you and violated your trust and no excuses need minimize this reality.

You may think, *She didn't mean to hurt me, or He did this because of how he was raised,* but these rationalizations, although they may be true, may sidestep you in setting the necessary boundaries for yourself and your partner. Making a commitment to developing healthier boundaries will help protect you from being victimized by the addiction in the future.

Boundary work is a fundamental step in your recovery. You will need a lot of practice in identifying and respecting your boundaries. Your partner's addiction brought you here, but it's up to you how you handle this going forward. The choice to heal and transform your pain into meaning is one worth making. A step in protecting yourself is to not minimize the damage from the addiction. The pain will lessen in time but much depends upon how you care for yourself and face the difficult task of learning better ways to communicate your worth to yourself and others.

What happens if the addict doesn't respect my boundaries?
In the first few years of recovery from sexual addiction, you'll need to create very specific, definable boundaries, also referred to as non-negotiables. These will help you establish a foundation of security and predictability and should be specific to behaviors or situations relevant to your circumstances Non-negotiables can range from determining the need for additional boundaries with the addict to grounds for ending the relationship. Some examples of non-negotiables include:

- No sex outside the relationship.
- Internet access at home is to be regulated by a monitoring program.
- Money spent over_____ must be discussed beforehand.
- Recovery must remain consistent.
- No viewing pornography.
- No masturbation.
- No contact or alone time with prior acting-out partners. This can include e-mailing, phone calls, text messaging, secret bank accounts, cell phone numbers, or e-mail addresses.
- No verbal abuse.

Defining your non-negotiables can be immediate or can happen over time. Either way, establishing boundaries and following through with the stated consequences will help you become more consistent and allow you to be clearer in what you can and cannot accept in your relationship to the sex addict. For example, if having sex outside of the relationship is a non-negotiable and the consequence is separation, how will you respond if you learn he went to a strip club? Does that equate to sex outside of the relationship? If so, are you prepared to act upon your stated non-negotiable?

Be prepared to have a list that best defines the parameters of your boundaries and consequences if a boundary violation occurs. Be careful and think through the excuses you might tell yourself that may communicate a mixed message. If you say one thing but do another, think through how that will affect you and the sex addict. Most addicts avoid and displace responsibility for their actions. Many rebel against rules meant to limit their behaviors and avoid accountability. This can be especially prevalent in intimate relationships where accountability is most likely to be expected. Limits you set can activate defensiveness and reactivity, which in the past may have caused you to compromise and acquiesce to the demands of the addict.

If you're not prepared to act and want to take a wait-and-see approach, it's understandable. It's even advisable because many of the addict's behaviors may fall into gray areas and you may be uncertain as to what is or is not acceptable for you. It's better to wait before establishing boundaries than to set them and not be prepared to follow through. Understanding your non-negotiables will advance your own healing process because you will gain knowledge and clarity for yourself which will help you when confronted with addictive behaviors and attitudes.

If you learn that the addict has violated one of your non-negotiables, culti-vating a practice of "gathering data" will help. When a problem arises, like a slip with masturbation or an unexplained phone bill, first allow yourself to experience your reactions and seek safe people to talk to about what happened. If you con-front your partner with the information and you're still not satisfied with the response, do not discount your feelings and perceptions. Instead, enlist a detached stance similar to an observer to the situation. See how many other issues arise over a period of time that gives you pause and triggers suspicions. Review and compare the information pertaining to the infraction to other evidence gathered. Does the behavior match other aspects of the addict's actions and attitudes with you or others? Some questions you might ask include, *How is he or she treating me emotionally? How invested in recovery is he or she? Do words and actions add up consistently?*

Taking these steps doesn't mean avoiding or denying your concerns, rather these steps help you act from a place of preparedness. Confronting your doubts and your concerns makes you an active participant in the facts facing you and allows you to act rather than react.

Practicing an observer stance can conjure up feelings of impatience or fear of being duped again. You may believe you are avoiding the suspicious behav-iors, when in fact you are actively addressing issues in a new way. Threats or ulti-matums haven't worked in the past and learning newer ways to handle situations that used to confuse you is difficult in the beginning. By pacing your responses, you allow yourself time to gain perspective in an objective way, which distances you from personalizing the behaviors and empowers you to act in more effective ways. The addict acts out because of difficulty in relating to life in a responsible and adult fashion – not because of who you are. By delaying your response you build confidence in enforcing boundaries and in asserting your worth as a person. You find you are better able to make choices. "I'm not going to take it anymore!" is no longer a meaningless threat but an action you are prepared to take to create greater safety and predictability in your life.

How are boundaries different from controlling?
In early recovery they often do not feel all that different. A basic distinction has to do with intentions. Boundaries are about self-care and serve as a means of self-protection. Setting a boundary begins with you. Controlling is "other focused" and is centered on managing the outcome of someone else's behavior or attitudes. A few questions can help in discerning your intentions when questioning your boundaries:

- For whom is the boundary intended?
- What is the desired outcome I seek?
- Am I protecting myself or trying to change the addict's behavior?
- What am I trying to achieve?
- Do my actions and words match?

Often in early recovery the boundaries you set will involve external controls. For example, choosing to live apart after learning about the addiction, having separate bedrooms or a no-sex contract are examples of boundaries with external controls. In distinguishing the difference between controlling behaviors versus establishing boundaries, examine your motivations pertaining to the circumstances. For example, you may decide an appropriate boundary is sleeping apart from your partner if you find out that he has lied about attending 12-step meetings. If you are establishing the limit to retaliate and make him change, this would be control. In the early stages of recovery, establishing safety should be your number one goal. You can't attain a higher level of emotional growth until there's stability in your home. Your physical, emotional and spiritual safety was jeopardized as a result of your partner's sex addiction. You may not know what you need initially, but as time goes on the parameters will become clearer to you.

If your partner spent hours isolated in her basement office "working," and you later learned it's where she spent time viewing online pornography, then having the computer moved to a neutral space, even if it is you who moves it, can be seen as controlling. In reality, it's not. The goal and the intended outcome you are seeking is primarily for yourself. You are saying through your action that pornography is not acceptable in the home. Moving the computer to a more open space in the home acknowledges the impact of the addiction on you and the need for safety in your home as you define it. A desired secondary or simultaneous gain is that the addict will stop the behavior and change. However, what motivates you to set the boundary is to regain control over your life and to limit the toxic effects of sexual addiction in the home.

Emotionally believing in yourself despite what your partner tells you will be a hurdle in your boundary development. Typically addicts respond to demands for accountability with accusations that deflect responsibility onto others, most likely you. Labeling you "controlling" saying you are "managing his/her recovery" are common ways addicts may try to manipulate you to avoid your requests for change. These types of comments can make you doubt yourself. It's imperative that you listen to yourself and seek guidance from supportive people in these matters. Trusting yourself by learning to explore and implement new behaviors will help foster healthier boundaries.

Is it OK to tell my close friends or family? I feel so alone and want those close to me to know.
The discovery of being involved with a sex addict is like stumbling upon a rude and unwelcomed guest in your home. It's there, you want to get rid of it, and yet the memory of this intrusion is always with you. Upon first learning of sex addiction, the shock and devastation you experience is overwhelming. Like any other life crisis it's normal to want to talk about the crisis. You're tempted to turn to those who know you best; yet afraid to tell them because you're too embarrassed and ashamed about your partner's sexual behaviors. Sex is a taboo topic for much of society. Sexual indiscretions can be a far less tolerable topic. Little is still

known or talked about regarding the compulsive use of sex, much less the disorienting impact it has on families. You're angry and hurt, yet may not feel comfortable talking about your partner's sex addiction with those closest to you. Who is appropriate to tell? And how will they respond? The following list offers some considerations to keep in mind as you ponder disclosing to others.

What is your motivation?

Is it to retaliate against the addict for having done this to you or for your own emotional support? It may be hard to distinguish your motivation, particularly in the beginning. For example, if you've been with a partner whose mother has always been critical of you, your first instinct may be to tell her. In this case, you would be trying to validate your pain at the cost of the addict's relationship with his or her mother. Perhaps the addict hadn't planned on disclosing the information to family members. This may become a non-negotiable to consider if acting out continues. One option in addressing this non-negotiable is to have the addict tell his or her mother or another mutually agreed upon family member.

Safe vs. unsafe people.

Imagining the future is a good way to decipher if someone will be supportive or judge you down the road, especially if you reconcile with the addict. Consider how this person will react. Will he or she hold it against you? How will their reactions impact you? Will they tell you to leave the relationship making it harder to know what to do for yourself?

Long-term ramifications.

You want to be sure the person you tell is someone who will keep your confidences. What you say now isn't something you can take back in two months or two years, so weighing your decisions against the long-term ramifications are factors to consider.

Prepare what you will say.

Depending on the person, you may want to modify the details. With one person you may be more open yet with another person less so. Write out what you will say. This prepares you for any unwanted questions you may feel compelled to answer. Give the scope of the problem but not necessarily the graphic details. For example, "John and I are in therapy because John discovered he has an addiction that has become out of control." Or "I learned some devastating news about Sally and I am in a lot of pain. I'm not comfortable talking about the details at this time, but would greatly appreciate spending some time with you for support."

Inform the addict of your intentions.

During this time you will find your needs are very different from the addict's. The need to tell others can be a boundary for you. Talk to your partner and let him or her know who and what you plan to share. If your partner doesn't want you to share information, work toward a compromise in terms of when, how much and who to tell. For the addict, telling others about the behavior is shaming. If confiding in someone close to you is part of your healing and not as retaliation for the pain your partner's behavior has caused you, then your partner's reaction can be considered a consequence of his or her behavior. For example, telling the addict, "Because of your behaviors I plan to let_____ know."

Sometimes the boundary can come in the form of you wanting him to tell someone. Upon learning about her spouse's addiction, one woman told her husband that he needed to tell one close friend and call for professional help by the end of the day. She expected this of him because she didn't want to be the only person carrying his secret. Because she had little understanding of his addiction at that time, she was scared he might do something to her. She was shocked that this part of him existed, and her motivation in doing this served as a form of self-protection, not as a form of retribution.

You may be embarrassed and don't want anyone close to you to know what you're going through. That's your choice. But keep in mind that talking to at least two people, including a therapist, will help you move through the various stages of healing. Sometimes partners find they absolutely don't want others close to them to know. If that describes your situation, consider why you're feeling so strongly about this. Does your partner or spouse's addiction somehow reflect on you? If so, it may be you are internalizing some of his or her behaviors and feeling responsible for what he or she did, as though you could have prevented the addictive behavior. Perhaps you fear others may judge you. Exploring some of these themes with a therapist will help you sort through your internal boundaries and define where your issues end and the sex addiction begins.

What happens if I can't uphold my boundaries?
"I say one thing and then do another!" "I told him no sex for a month and then the next week I wanted to have sex with him and he said no!" "What's wrong with me?" "I have said the same things time and again and nothing changed; she still did what she wanted. Why should I believe I can affect change now?" Learning you were living with someone who violated your trust has given you opportunity for change. You're in a transformation of finding your own voice. Trying it out and living by your own words are two entirely different things.

If you've been violated, seeking recourse is up to you. Emotional recourse can come in the form of setting limits you haven't established before. No longer subjecting yourself to your partner's behavior means going to any length to look at those areas where you compromised yourself. Most important, that means backing up what you say. Your words may not change much, but the internal conviction by which you speak followed by a plan for follow through will alter the course you're on.

Give yourself permission to be in a process of change rather than an event. The event was learning that your partner is a sex addict. The process of change will be lifelong. In the early stages you may have had a hunch that the addict was up to something. Boundary failure often occurs in the beginning of recovery because there's confusion between new behaviors versus old ones. Further along, boundary failure occurs because old beliefs about yourself complicate your ability to trust yourself – what you say is what you mean. Seeking the understanding from others who share and support your change process will help you gain perspective on those roadblocks.

You will often make the mistake of focusing on words rather than actions. You've been accustomed to listening to the addict's explanations, rationalizations or promises. Pay attention to the inconsistencies between the addict's words and actions and challenge these inconsistencies. Remember the concept of observer – notice what you think or feel about the situation. Reevaluate and slow down how you communicate with the addict. Pointing out inconsistencies may trigger defensiveness. Be prepared for how you will respond in this instance. Remember that it will take practice to communicate differently and effectively and you will not be perfect.

You have listened to the addict at the expense of yourself. Commit to yourself that your needs come first. In the beginning this is difficult because you cannot yet integrate the addictive part of the partner you knew. Recognizing the ways you were manipulated, cajoled and persuaded is how you learn to separate the addict part from other aspects of who he is as a partner. Your capacity to forget the pain caused by the addict will become more understood in time. Until you become a better judge of the addictive aspects of your partner's personality, you need to remember that you're vulnerable because of your lack of understanding of addiction. The first step is to go easy on yourself. Remember that boundary development is a learning process. *Learn* about boundaries. *Commit* to the hard work involved in developing boundaries. *Apply* a "trial and error" approach. It's essential to long-term growth. *Take the time* to learn where your boundaries were porous within the relationship prior to the discovery of sex addiction. Begin to apply new ways to prepare and follow up on changes for yourself. Be curious and observe what worked and what didn't. Talk to others. Don't do this alone.

How do I keep from reacting in extremes like kicking my partner out, threatening divorce, or yelling in front of the kids, so I can make choices that are best for me?

In the beginning you may feel compelled to act on your feelings or thoughts about leaving. In fact, you maybe tried leaving or asked your partner to leave. You'll likely feel pressure from others to end your relationship as though that would end the emotional turmoil you're in. Or you may be determined to make it work. The questioning goes on and on, often with no resolution. Most therapists suggest you make no significant life changes during the first year of recovery. This initial time period will feel long and often very open-ended, but it affords you the necessary time to sit with the myriad of feelings without having to act on them. Making a decision to not act is an action. Just because you're not making any significant life changes doesn't mean you're doing nothing. You are actively engaged in a process of discovery necessary for your well-being. Attending to your own pain, recovering from the trauma in a safe place, and allowing yourself to witness whether your partner is able to commit to recovery will move you forward if you allow yourself the time to heal.

Delaying major decisions can be valuable, even for those where the damage may be too great. If the acting out was too pervasive, extreme or involved damaging consequences you may feel almost certain you cannot re-enter the relationship. However, investing in this initial time period does not deny your certainty, rather it allows you to process all the losses associated with the relationship while not getting distracted or caught up in the decision-making involved in ending the relationship. By acquiring skills and implementing tools you will be better prepared to enter a relationship with another partner. All of these steps take time and attention. You have had an attachment to someone important to you and giving yourself the time to disengage is acknowledging the depth of this bond. Allow yourself time to grieve and heal. Boundary development is an essential tool in this process, and will better equip you in all future relationships.

Defining, acknowledging and implementing are all separate yet intertwined steps in boundary development. How you were raised – and the messages you received about your self-worth and value in relationships – have played a large role in how you entered into a partnership with someone with distorted sexual and intimate boundaries. Recognizing how your needs were not being met prior to discovery and disclosure will assist you in looking at your own impaired boundaries. Learning how you allowed your partner to mistreat you in the past and establishing non-negotiables for the future, sets into motion a new and solid foundation of self-discovery. You are worth it. Taking the time to heal from the pain of sexual codependence will give you a freedom you've never really known.

Chapter 6
What About My Sexuality?

Omar Minwalla, Ph.D., CSAT

When it comes to sex addiction and sexual compulsivity, there is tremendous focus on the addict's sexuality. This makes sense because, after all, it is the sexual acting out of the addict that in many ways characterizes the problem and is one of the targets of treatment. Often, the addict's sexuality is perceived as "the problem." Therapists, sponsors, support groups, couples and the addict, all pay close attention to the addict's sexuality.

However, seldom does the spotlight spin around and shed light on the sexuality of the partner or spouse of the sex addict. In all the effort to help address the addict's problem, the sexuality of the partner or spouse is most often conspicuously minimized, neglected and ignored. Rarely does the partner's sexuality become a focus of clinical attention or discussion and, when it does, it's most often in the context of couple's treatment – in attempt to help the couple become sexual in the later stages of the recovery process. Since the majority of partners are female, one of the reasons for this is the still-prominent patriarchal dynamic of neglecting female sexuality and rendering it unimportant and illegitimate. It also reflects the clinical field's squeamishness and avoidance of female sexuality, including sexual and gender-based victimization.

What happens to the sexuality of the partner or spouse of a sex addict? What type of impact does sex addiction have on the partner's sexuality and what can he or she do to address this impact? This chapter aims to address some of the ways that your sexuality, your sexual sense of self, sexual psychology, and sexual functioning may be impacted and wounded by the sexual addiction and its consequences. In addition, a treatment model is proposed to help partners embark on a sexual-healing journey and reclaim aspects of your sexuality in the context of sex addiction. This is designed to speak to you directly as a partner.

The Sexual Trauma Model
As one begins to understand the sexual symptoms experienced by partners of sex addicts, the symptoms are strikingly similar to the symptoms known to occur from sexual trauma, such as rape, sexual assault, sexual abuse and molestation. When we look at well-established symptoms of sexual trauma and abuse, partners of sex addicts can identify with many or all of them. Many experts hold a new emerging perspective that partners of sex addicts experience a form of sexual trauma.

Using this model, the partner's symptoms, reactions, and what is otherwise perceived as "erratic behavior" may be understood as symptoms of trauma, including sexual trauma. These symptoms, when ignored, only serve to exacerbate them. These symptoms may be similar to those seen in post-traumatic stress disorder (PTSD) and rape trauma syndrome (RTS). Working from a trauma model, the partner's symptoms are understood and framed as natural and expected responses to trauma – a way of coping and trying to adapt and survive. This perspective respects and validates the partner's sexual wounding and victimization and, most important, emphasizes the importance of looking at his or her sexual symptoms and healing them.

When we shift our thinking and perception to include and acknowledge the sexual trauma that you may be experiencing, your reactions and symptomology make much more sense. This perspective also helps the professional address the issues at hand in a way that will more likely lead to healing and change – helping you to move through your wounding rather than remaining stuck in your pain.

It's also known among professionals that one of the most challenging aspects of recovery for addicts and their partners is regaining a sense of sexual health. Even when some of the emotional and relational aspects seem to have been worked through, confronting and addressing the sexual aspects of healing often go unaddressed. The sexual trauma model may help explain why sexual healing and finding healthy sexuality can be so challenging for partners and couples in recovery. If symptoms of sexual trauma have been ignored, finding healthy sexuality as a couple can be a near-impossible task. Underneath the attempts to regain intimacy and sexual pleasure lay trauma wounds that are open and still bleeding. Again, the trauma perspective helps the journey of sexual healing in that it specifically acknowledges any sexual trauma and makes imperative the need to address and attend to the specific sexual symptoms as part of treatment toward sexual health.

Sexual Wounding

The process of discovery can clearly have many consequences: psychological, emotional, relational and spiritual. One of the dimensions of your experience that's often impacted, yet frequently unacknowledged, is your sexuality. Of course, simply avoiding your sexuality doesn't make the impact any less. It simply leaves many partners impacted by the addiction to either address these issues in isolation with little support or ignore them altogether. Silence, however, only perpetuates the symptoms.

Sexuality fundamentally impacts the core of our psychology and sense of self. This is why the impact on your sexuality cannot be compartmentalized and left ignored without it affecting other aspects of your life, along with your healing process as a couple. It is vital for you to acknowledge, validate and address how the addict's sexual acting out affected you. It's additionally important for the addict to recognize the impact of his or her behavior on your sexuality as well.

Every partner is impacted differently by the addict's sexual acting out. Some may experience few sexual symptoms. However, others experience a greater effect on their sexuality. It's imperative that every partner or spouse struggling with these issues go through the process of assessing their sexuality and recognizing any wounding in this area.

This chapter discusses some of the ways your sexuality can be impacted. Much of this discussion is based on qualitative research, where partners describe their experiences in their own words. Not every type of sexual wound will be described here and many may not apply to every partner. However, this chapter will give you awareness that, indeed, many partners of addicts do experience sexual wounds that are significant, painful, and clearly indicate the need for attention and healing. The types of wounding described here are based on the sexual trauma perspective.[1]

As you read them, take time to reflect on the ways you identify with the experiences of other partners, and try to become more aware of your sexual wounds. Remember, you are not alone and many partners out there share in your pain.

Why do I avoid, fear, or lack interest in sex?
One of the most common sexual wounds that you may experience, particularly early in the process and often immediately after discovery or disclosure, is a type of sexual shutting down and sexual aversion. The idea of sex is painful and overwhelming. You may no longer feel pleasure or have any interest in sexuality.

I couldn't masturbate for at least a month or two after disclosure.

I can't imagine ever being sexual again. I have no interest.

I feel dead sexually. I couldn't care less whether I have sex again.

I fear sex in the future. I don't think it's just because I've been with the same man for 16 years and am no longer youthful. I think it has a lot to do with how my sexuality has been impacted by the sex addiction.

Specific behaviors that you once enjoyed may become aversive and may produce anxiety or fear.

I never again performed oral sex. Possibly it was the submissive nature to it. Or it was just me pleasuring him. I never wanted to do that for him again. Possibly because I could so easily imagine all the other mouths, bought and paid for, that had performed that little service before. It took on the feeling of service, rather than intimacy. I just refused to go there again.

I still feel sexual. I still want to engage in sex. But I know I will never feel as sexually free as I did before I became involved with my sex-addict husband. I'll always be leery about what lies beneath, possibly feeling that there is always darkness, shame, hidden secrets associated with a man's sexuality.

Why does sex feel like an obligation?
Many partners describe approaching sex as an obligation. In these cases, you're not engaging in sex because there's an internal desire or motivation, but rather because you feel that you "have to." Often what's behind this is the idea that if you are not sexual with your partner, he or she will act out. If you don't attempt to satisfy his/her sexual needs, then your partner will get them met elsewhere.

This may translate into having sex when you don't feel like it. Given that you may not have been educated on the nature of sexual addiction and the underlying causes, it's understandable that you may assume, erroneously, that you can control the addiction through your sexual behavior or that the addiction has to do with your sexuality.

All along, I had thoughts that if I just went along with everything he wanted sexually then he would get better...I ended up doing things that disgusted me.

I thought that if I gave him enough sexually, he would stop acting out. When he entered recovery, I would feel obligated to be sexual with him when he wanted to even if I didn't want to, because I felt if he was abstaining from all sexual stimulus outside of our relationship, then I owed him sexually. But this made me feel resentful because it was not what I wanted and I still feel unsafe.

Why do I engage in compulsive or inappropriate sexual behaviors?
Sometimes you may find yourself engaging in sexual behaviors or activities that you would otherwise not want to or that are incongruent with your comfort level or value system. Again, this may have to do with obligatory demands you may feel, and you may believe that your partner's sexual acting out is dependent on your sexuality. You may also be using sexuality in a compulsive manner, in that you use sex as a way to medicate your pain caused by the addiction. This may then leave you feeling your own sense of shame as a consequence of using sex as a way of coping – creating your own cycle of compulsive sexual behavior.

While it's understandable to think that a partner's sexual acting out could be curtailed and controlled by giving him or her more sex or the type of sex that he or she seems to seek in his acting out, it's critical that you come to recognize that your sexuality is independent of his or her sexual acting out. Dependence on problematic sexual behavior and arousal is not about you or your sexuality – it's about the addict's underlying psychological and emotional dynamics. Using sex to try to control or "help" another person doesn't constitute healthy sexuality.

I found myself becoming more sexual and willing to engage in behaviors I didn't like.

I felt pressure to comply with his sexual desires...that if I acted like a porn star, he would like me and not act out.

I felt obligated to wear lacy or sexy underwear even though I hated the way it looked under my clothes. I hated wearing the underwear, especially when I would wait up for him to see it and he wouldn't come home until 2 a.m. I felt unwanted by the one person I wanted, and powerless to please him. Now I am resentful of the years of dressing the part, and regret that because of how hurt I still feel about it.

Why do I experience negative feelings such as anger, disgust or guilt with touch?

You may find it challenging to experience touch, particularly sexual touch, in a way that's pleasurable, comforting or loving. Instead, you may fear touch, find it aversive and feel uncomfortable with being touched. This is particularly significant when we consider how important touch is to human functioning. Touch is a basic need; thus, demonstrating how you may be feeling a type of wounding on the most core and basic level of human experience.

I feel disgusted by the idea of sex and a man's body. I am scared of physical contact.

I recoil from touch now. I just don't want anyone touching me anymore. I am damaged.

I can't imagine what a passionate kiss feels like anymore. I cringe when he attempts to embrace me – even platonically.

Why do I have difficulty becoming aroused or feeling sensation?

One possible symptom experienced by partners is a lack of physical and sexual responsiveness. Sensation may be experienced as diminished. Arousal, orgasmic response and the ability to lubricate may all be impacted on some level. It makes sense that when there are so many psychological and emotional disturbances occurring that the physical body will also be affected.

I definitely had difficulty becoming aroused and feeling sensation. I wasn't sure if that was a factor of the sexual trauma, or what was lacking between my husband and myself.

I have been unable to experience any type of sexual pleasure or intimacy for a very long time.

I didn't feel anything anymore…it was like I was numb.

Why do I feel dirty and contaminated?

Some partners describe feeling dirty and contaminated. The disgust the partner feels toward his or her partner's behavior is often projected onto the self. The addict's behaviors are seen as dirty, and she/he perceives herself as dirty. By being associated with that which you feel is disgusting, you have become contaminated as well.

I feel dirty and disgusting and objectified. I feel crazy for thinking and feeling that way.

I feel dirty, marked and scarred.

Obviously, this includes more than just a perception of being contaminated; it includes anxious fears of actually contracting a sexually transmitted infection.

I not only feel dirty and contaminated, but I worry about becoming infected with a disease.

My health is hugely at risk. I am terrified of HPV, AIDS and other STDs.

I feel angry and anxious because I have to use a condom with my husband. I can't trust that he's clean and doesn't have a disease and this is supposed to be the man I trust the most. I feel like he's dirty and I am too for being with him.

Why do I feel emotionally distant or not present during sex?
The experience of feeling detached and not present is common among partners of addicts. There's often a part of you that feels unsafe, suspicious, untrusting and uncertain about the presence of your partner. You may wonder if she or he is fantasizing about other partners or pornographic images, or if your partner is enjoying sex with you. There's often a part of you that's still wounded, hurting and in considerable pain. It makes sense that you may be unable to be fully present under these conditions. You may be preoccupied with anxiety about an STD or if your partner has been acting out again. You may be focusing on your own sense of inadequacy, feeling preoccupied with your body image, and whether you are arousing your partner.

I felt detached from my body. I dissociated.

I feel emotionally separate from him and have a really hard time being present when trying to be intimate. I panic when he won't look at me and wonder where his mind is.

Why do I experience intrusive or disturbing thoughts, images and flashbacks?
Experiencing intrusive thoughts or images is common and highly disturbing for some partners. You may discover images on the computer or in videos that become firmly etched into your visual mind. These can often be of a highly

graphic nature because contemporary pornography has become highly intensified and diversified. Particularly as an addict's pornography addiction escalates, he often will find himself looking at increasingly more intense sexual imagery and content – often moving into domains such a rape scenes, extreme torture, bestiality and child pornography. Many partners often have little exposure to pornography. If exposed to the extreme content found in an escalating porn addiction, discovering such images can have a shattering and horrifying impact on your psyche.

This is particularly so when you have little knowledge of how porn addiction works and the reasons for increased intensity among addicts. Because men tend to be more visually sexual, a female partner with little exposure to porn will be even more impacted by graphic sexual imagery. It's difficult to let go of such disturbing images, because the psyche has a way of noting material that is highly emotionally and psychologically charged. Akin to a rape victim's flashbacks of the traumatic event, graphic images can be experienced in the same way and can significantly impact sexual functioning.

The intrusive and disturbing thoughts and images were some of the most difficult experiences post-disclosure. For more than a year, I was haunted by all kinds of pornographic images involving my husband…during sex, in dreams, or just in the course of my day.

Intrusive thoughts are the most apparent way that I have been scarred by this, the most compelling symptom of trauma. I had my own sexual fantasies and thoughts, but what goes through my mind now doesn't really feel like my own. It feels like something forced into my psyche against my will. It's very disturbing. It's something I still contend with two and a half years later.

I also experience a type of flashback and I wonder if I don't have something akin to PTSD. Certain behaviors of his, arguments we had, moments of doubts I had about his veracity, these would trigger thoughts and images accompanied by a rush of adrenaline and all that goes along with that.

I can't make the flashbacks stop. I see him with prostitutes all the time in my mind. I see reminders every minute, every day. I'm exhausted from all the symbolism.

Why do I have trouble establishing or maintaining intimate relationships?
One of the most painful and wounding aspects of the addiction dynamic is the breakdown of trust in a relationship. Without trust it's almost impossible to create a healthy and stable intimate relationship.

While distrust works on all levels of a relationship, it certainly impacts sexuality in a relationship. Since healthy sexuality most often requires vulnerability, the lack of trust will often impact your ability to fully relax during sex and will significantly impede your ability to enjoy the experience.

Furthermore, many partners come to view the addict's sexuality as fundamentally compulsive and unhealthy. The lack of trust in the addict may leave you feeling that it is simply unrealistic to expect your partner to stop acting out. This can often leave you feeling hopeless about intimacy and relationships in general. You may experience a feeling of resignation. You may reason that it is better to stay with the addict that you already know, rather than investing in a new relationship that may ultimately lead to similar pain.

I feel a general distrust of men and what they really think and feel about women.

I began to fear that all men act out using pornography and obsessively fantasize about other women, and as a woman, if I wanted a romantic relationship with a man, I have to tolerate it. The idea of that being true is so unbearable, it makes me want to never have a relationship with a man again.

It's hard not to think of all men as being unable to control themselves if tempted. I question whether all men think of women as being only sexual objects. Are all men this sick inside their heads?

I am unwilling to have sex with my husband or any man. My trust was destroyed and I cannot put myself in harm's way mostly physically and somewhat emotionally.

Why do I experience vaginal pain or orgasmic difficulties?

The impact of discovering a partner is sexually addicted can go beyond "sexual shutting down" and diminishing sexual response and sensation. It can actually create psychosomatic sexual symptoms such as vaginal pain.

I have been unable to achieve orgasm for a long time, and for the past few months when I am kissing him and would normally become aroused, I instead have aching (and sometimes sharp) vaginal pain, which also used to happen whenever I would catch him acting out or think about sexual things he had done.

During the period after he expressed sexual dissatisfaction (during his acting out) but before initial disclosure, I experienced painful cramping with intercourse. The crampng lasted for hours after the intercourse. This symptom did not occur during the period of sexual activity after initial disclosure and then formal disclosure.

Why do I experience body image issues?

A common outcome experienced by partners is body-image concerns and an increased sense of insecurity about physical attractiveness. In a culture where most people, particularly women, carry insecurities and concerns about physical appearance and body image, you may experience a heightened sense of inadequacy about your body. Whatever issues you may have had prior to the addiction, they are often exacerbated and intensified. You may become preoccupied with evaluating and criticizing your body, your sexuality, and your sense of attractiveness. If you once felt confidence and enjoyed your body, you may suddenly find yourself doubting your appearance and feeling inadequate.

I felt like damaged goods. I didn't want to look at my own body. I felt detached from my own body. I had trouble even looking at myself naked.

Feelings of self-consciousness about my body would overcome me during times I was trying to be free and sexy.

I have felt detached from my body, disgusted by it. I have felt unattractive, fat, ugly, insecure, and like I must be inferior to other women for them to have captured his interest.

I asked him about my vagina size. I never used to give this stuff a second thought, but now I wonder.

Among the body image concerns that you may experience, specific sexual and genital image issues may appear, resulting in significant negative consequences on your overall sexual functioning, sexual self-esteem and sexual health.

I had never worried about whether or not my vagina was tight enough before, but now I do.

Knowing that every pornographic image or prostitute he looked at undoubtedly had large, and most likely, enhanced breasts, my small breasts, which I had always thought had appealed to him, seemed flaccid and spent to me. Unappealing and limp after two children, I never really enjoyed him touching them again, and that had always been a part of my pleasure in love-making.

After learning of his desire that I have bigger breasts, I went through a period of wondering whether I owed it to him to try to enhance them. Mostly I felt angry that my breasts were deemed less than desirable. I used to spend a lot of time comparing myself to the sexual ideal he described.

Why do I feel secrecy and shame?
A common problem experienced by partners is the shame they feel and the embarrassment that the addict's problem is sexual in nature. This may leave you isolated and silent about your pain. Due to the fact that sexual addiction is still a relatively new diagnosis and lacks the legitimacy of alcoholism as a disorder or

problem, sharing that your partner is a sex addict with others leaves you vulnerable to the misconceptions and myths that exist regarding sexual addiction.

Many spouses fear, for example, that their partners will be automatically perceived as pedophiles and they will be judged for staying in the relationship. The impact this has on your sexuality is that it leaves you hiding secretly with your sexual wounds, afraid of reaching out to others for help or support.

I have difficulty sharing information about his addiction with friends because I am embarrassed and afraid of what they'll think of him and me for being with him.

I felt like damaged goods. I thought about how others would view me: "Oh, she couldn't satisfy him sexually." I felt marked.

Why do I feel responsible for this victimization?

As mentioned, shame and secrecy often accompany your symptoms. Like many victims of sexual trauma, there's a feeling of somehow being responsible or in some way having contributed to the addict's behavior. You may struggle with notions that you caused the addiction and see it as a reflection on you. You may have been encouraged to take responsibility for your part in the addictive processes in the relationship. This might lead to self-blame and confusion about your role in the addictive process.

We are told that we are codependent and contributed to the problem. I find myself asking if I had been less emotional, if I had been less volatile, if I had been more emotionally in control, this would have enabled him to work his program better. He's done a number on me in terms of putting so much blame on me. It's hard to sort through it all.

Therapy, books and support groups – they all ask us not to blame ourselves, but we are also told that we contributed to the problem. This is something I am trying to work on.

I have a hard time getting away from the idea that this addiction has something to do with me.

What are the indicators of sexual abuse?

To further explore how you, as a partner of a sex addict, may have been abused sexually and to appreciate this perspective, it may be useful to review author Wendy Maltz's four indicators of sexual abuse.[2]

Again, you may consider your own experience and in what ways you can identify with the following indicators:

1. **Were you unable to give your full consent to the sexual activity?**

He has never touched me without consent or forced anything on me. But in lying, he has robbed me of my ability to consent with full awareness of the truth, because had I known about the sexual addiction, I never would have consented to a sexual relationship.

2. **Did the betrayal involve the betrayal of a trusted relationship?**

It's very traumatic to find out that the decisions I've made in our relationship, (including entering it and becoming attached in the first place), and the way I've felt about my partner hasn't, in large part, been based in reality, but in deception.

3. **Was the sexual activity characterized by violence or control over you as a person?**

I feel like I've had my sexuality stolen from me, and that even as an adult, I've had very little say about what happens with and to my body and what kind of sexual relationship I will have and what my partner is allowed to do and bring into our bed.

I feel as if my sexuality has been ripped from me and I wonder if I'll ever be able to have sex again.

4. **Did you feel abused?**

I have been raped and molested in the past...and I have done some healing around that. This too feels like a rape, but even worse – because I know and love this person. He is my husband.

I feel that I was sexually abused and that I suffer from post-traumatic stress syndrome. I have flashbacks regarding the prostitutes.

Targeting Sexual Trauma Among Partners of Sex Addicts

Working within the sexual trauma model, it's important for partners to acknowledge any symptoms of sexual trauma or wounding and to address these symptoms. Of course this can be a painful process, requiring patience, insight and a tremendous amount of effort and courage.

Current clinical interventions often don't include the partner in the initial stages of the addict's treatment. As a partner, you may feel that the problem is the addict's and therefore, understandably, resent the idea that you may need professional help. Most current models of treatment focus primarily on the addict;

if the partner is included, it may only be in the context of couples work during later stages of treatment.

In the cases where the partner does engage in his or her own work during the initial stages of treatment, the focus is typically on issues related to codependency. This emphasizes learning to draw boundaries, self-care, getting out of the victim role, and gaining support through 12-step groups such as COSA or S-Anon. When trauma or victimization is addressed, it's typically limited to the emotional and relational betrayal and trauma, which is obviously critical and important. Integrating the sexual trauma perspective expands treatment to include additional emphasis and focus on the sexual wounding. Your need for healing becomes emphasized and your own need for professional help should be explained in a way that helps you appreciate your wounding and need for self-care.

As a partner, it may be helpful to consider integrating some of what's offered into your own recovery journey. One of the first aspects of healing as a partner impacted by sex addiction is to recognize that the need for some individual therapeutic work that is done independent from your partner. Due to the potentially traumatic nature of the wounding that occurs sexually, it's imperative that you first address some of the sexual wounding on your own, on your own terms, before trying to be sexual with your partner or another person.

Abstinence/Sex Vacation

I recognize myself in the symptoms listed above. How should I approach my sexuality in early recovery?

One thing to consider early in the beginning of your healing journey is taking some time out to heal. This means permitting yourself to take a break from being sexual and allowing yourself some time to adjust and process the consequences of the addiction in your experience – the emotional betrayal, the change in your perception of the relationship, the hurt of having been lied to. You may feel pressure to be sexual – that if you don't, your partner will act out. You may find yourself wanting to help take care of your partner's needs at the expense of your own. Both reactions are unhealthy.

You may also feel compelled to be sexual in order to comfort and reassure yourself that the relationship is still viable and your partner still loves you. You may use sex as a way to medicate and comfort your pain of the addiction. This too is unhealthy. Many partners are relieved when they are given "permission" to abstain from sex. You can let go of the pressure and feelings of obligation and attend to your wounds without sex becoming a distraction and confusing your healing process.

Don't let your partner or anyone else, including a professional, pressure you into the idea that you need to be sexual before you're ready. Whether you're going to remain in your partnership with the addict or move on, taking some time out to heal your sexual wounds is important to healthy sexuality. If you remain in a partnership, it still makes sense to first concentrate on repairing the emotional betrayal and focus on creating a basic level of relational and emotional intimacy before being sexual. It doesn't make sense to work on sexual intimacy with your partner until there's an adequate level of trust and intimacy in the other areas of the relationship – whether it's emotional intimacy, work intimacy, spiritual intimacy, communication intimacy, or aesthetic intimacy.

Reclaiming Sexuality

One important part of healing is to make a conscious, internally driven decision to reclaim your sexuality. While those around you may encourage and want you to heal on the sexual level in light of your partner's addiction, it's ultimately critical that you find a place inside yourself that wants to heal and make a commitment to a healing journey. One way is to articulate the specific ways you want to heal your sexuality. Some examples include:

- I want to develop a more positive view of sexuality.
- I want to stop thinking about my partner's acting out during sex.
- I want to be able to say no to sex when I don't want it.
- I want to be able to appreciate my body.
- I want to be able to share my sexual desires and needs with my partner.
- I want to be able to believe that my partner's acting out was not about my inadequacy as a lover.

Make sure they are specific and realistic. Always recognize that healing is an ongoing process – progress not perfection.

Sexual Assertiveness - Finding your sexual voice

Another critical aspect of healthy sexuality is the ability to negotiate and be assertive, to communicate and make sexual negotiations, to protect yourself, and to draw sexual boundaries. You should educate yourself on why this may be a challenge and why many of us find it difficult to own and assert our voices, particularly in terms of gender dynamics and damaged boundaries from trauma. Being able to communicate, particularly about sexuality, becomes vital in the healing process and may take practice.

When will I be ready to be sexual again?

One of the most important aspects of the healing process is asking yourself if and when you are ready to be sexual with someone else. As a partner of a sex addict, you have hopefully educated yourself, come to know some of your sexual wounds and have done some work on them, and found support. Part of healing is reaching a place of willingness to be vulnerable again sexually. It's only at this point in your process that you should engage in couples sex therapy.

Couples Trauma-Targeted Sex Therapy

Couples sex therapy, for couples recovering from sexual addiction, should acknowledge and process the sexual wounding and any trauma experienced by the partner. This requires the addict to take full responsibility for his or her actions and the consequences of the behavior on the partner. If this doesn't occur, he/she will have trouble finding appropriate empathy and understanding the partner's symptoms and reactions.

It will also be difficult for the couple to be able to negotiate sexual boundaries and communicate honestly if the addict doesn't fully appreciate the sexual wounds of the partner and how it may be impacting the sexual experience. For example, if the partner needs to stop because he or she is feeling averse to the lover's touch, the addict needs a framework and prior discussion of why and what this is about – in order to deal with this reaction in an optimally healthy manner.

Another important aspect of sexual recovery for a couple is learning and practicing how to communicate sexually. After being able to draw boundaries and reclaim your assertiveness, it's important to communicate vulnerability with your partner. One helpful exercise is for each partner to share a list of likes and dislikes. They may share a sexual fantasy. Couples are often amazed at how little they really ever communicated or knew about their partner when it comes to sex.

Recovery is a Journey

Recovery from the sexual trauma of discovering you partner is a sex addict is a journey. It requires willingness for self-exploration, honesty and openness. It can be painful as the wounds are acknowledged, but it's important to grieve about your experience with other supportive people. Reclaiming your sexuality will be an essential element of your healing.

Chapter 7
What Can the 12 Steps Do for Me?

Mavis Humes Baird, BFA, CSAT

When many people hear the word "addiction," alcohol addiction is typically the first thing that comes to mind. First recognized as a disease by the American Medical Association in 1956, it was described as a "primary, chronic, progressive, family disease." Since that time, we have discovered all addictive disorders have a family component and create similar symptoms among family members. "Addiction as a family disease" means it runs in families and it affects the whole family. Addiction is often passed down from generation to generation. Researchers have established a genetic component as well as an environmental one.[1]

Much like alcohol addiction, sex addiction is a devastating disease and all members of a family are impacted. As a partner, spouse or family member of a sex addict, it's crucial you take the time to recognize the many ways the addict's behaviors has affected your life. Simply leaving the relationship without seeking the healing you need could affect your future relationships. You need to surrender to your own recovery process.

Anyone who is close to an active addict becomes affected to some degree. Just like in families of alcoholics, most partners of sex addicts come into the relationship with particular traits and vulnerabilities that make them more likely to get in – and stay in – relationships with sex addicts. Thus, you are more easily drawn to – and less aware of – the addictive cycle than someone from the general population. In other words, you have more denial, more tolerance, and more attraction to addicts. It's not uncommon for co-addicts to report getting out of one relationship with a sex addict, determined never again to let the disease into their lives, only to find the same addictive and co-addictive patterns reappear in future relationships.

Twelve-step programs are a major part of any comprehensive relief from the effects of addiction. Much like Alcoholics Anonymous and Al-Anon's Twelve-Step programs – where addicts and loved ones can attend group meetings geared toward healing by working through steps – so, too, can sex addicts and their spouses, partners and family members. This chapter will discuss the various programs and their differences, how meetings work, and the vocabulary you're likely to hear when attending meetings.

Which meeting should I attend?
The 12-step programs designed for spouses and partners and other family members of sex addicts are called COSA, Co-SLAA, SRA-Anon and S-Anon.

(Contact information for these groups are located in the Resources Pages.) All four adhere to the Twelve-Step system created by Alcoholics Anonymous. Each of the above programs was formed as a counterpart to one of the 12-step programs for recovery from sex addiction. In accordance with what are known as the Twelve Traditions of these fellowships, each operate autonomously, and although they may cooperate with each other, they are not affiliated with their counterpart fellowships or with each other.

What are the differences among the fellowships?
There are some minor conceptual differences between these fellowships, but all adhere strongly to the 12 Steps, 12 Traditions, and the spirit of recovery. The biggest differences tend to be more pronounced among the counterpart programs for sex addicts. The primary importance for co-addicts is in understanding and observing the etiquette of whatever group you're attending.

One difference is how some of the programs define sexual sobriety. SAA, SCA and SLAA all instruct their members to come to terms with their own individual patterns of compulsivity. As they learn to face their particular patterns, addicts will recognize which sexual behaviors are compulsive and problematic for them, and those behaviors become the ones they need to abstain and recover from. They recognize that members have differing patterns of compulsivity among them, so each member identifies his or her own personal sobriety plan.

In contrast, SA and SRA give one across-the-board definition of sexual sobriety. Sexaholics Anonymous has drawn some attention for its stand against homosexuality. Its texts classify any form of homosexual sex, even within a committed monogamous relationship, as acting out addictively. Therefore, the only sexual sobriety for homosexual members is sexual abstinence. Sexual Recovery Anonymous defines sexual sobriety as:

Sobriety is the release from all compulsive and destructive sexual behaviors. We have found through our experience that sobriety includes freedom from masturbation and sex outside a mutually committed relationship.[2]

In ruling out all forms of masturbation and all non-committed sexual activity, some therapists believe SA and SRA may be giving its members the messages that one's experience of healthy sexuality is dependent on having a partner, and that sex can only be non-addictive as part of a committed partnership. Sex educators and sex therapists express concern that these definitions could limit the development of responsible sexual awareness. They point out that monogamy and commitment to a relationship do not necessarily equal sexual health.

On the other hand, many addicts and their families find the sobriety definitions in those fellowships to be reassuring and clear-cut, and they are fearful of an open-ended process for finding one's own definitions, as practiced in SAA, SCA and SLAA. Since these sexual sobriety definitions are tools of the addict's recovery plan, they are not part of the counterpart programs for family members.

At the time of this writing, S-Anon had developed a more extensive service structure and more active meetings than COSA. Some cities have COSA meetings; others have only S-Anon. Some rare cities are fortunate enough to have both. Both fellowships maintain a website, national help lines and e-mail outreach.

Can I attend the same meeting as the addict?
By attending your own meetings, geared toward support for you, you will see addiction is a family disease. You will also come to understand the nature of addiction and recovery for the addict and yourself. Some family members either don't see a need for their own recovery program, or want to attend the same meetings as the addict.

By attending open meetings of the addict's fellowship, you may learn to see the nature of the disease in others as well as coming to understand the nature of addiction and recovery for others. Being introduced to recovery in this way sometimes helps you to recognize your own need to recover. However, there is also a danger. Many partners struggle with obsessing about the addict's recovery. Attending the addict's meetings can reinforce your focus on the addict's progress or lack of progress, which would impede your recovery to co-addiction.

Additionally, most addicts find it unbearably distracting to have their family members with them in meetings. One reason for this is that it focuses their attention more on worrying about what you are thinking, rather than on relating to the message being shared. Therefore, the general guideline is that it's best for the family members to only attend open meetings of the addiction fellowships where their family members will not be present. In some cases, the addict will feel relaxed enough to invite you to one of their regular meetings, but this is not the norm and family members shouldn't expect such an invitation. Their fellows will most likely not have their own family members with them so you would likely be the only one.

Special recovery events such as conventions, learning days, couple retreats, or pre-planned dinners are more acceptable times to share directly in fellowship with the addict and their support systems. Once you've had your own program of recovery firmly in place for a while, you may find that attendance at occasional open 12-step meetings for sex addicts enlarges your perspective in a healthy way, especially in balancing your sense of compassion for the addict with your own need for self-care and safety.

What is anonymity?
Anonymity is a spiritual principle of all 12-step fellowships. It's practiced in a variety of ways. First, members usually identify themselves by first names and last initials only. Anonymity serves to take the focus off of what members' roles, responsibilities and status may be in the world, and puts the focus on your equal footing as fellow humans. No matter what their differences, all members are suffering the same condition, and all need peace and healing.

By challenging all its members to put their societal identities and roles on a shelf before they come in the door, 12-step fellowships establish a new basis for belonging and status. If you have qualified to belong to the group, you have earned your seat and no one can remove you. In that sense you are all equals. Anonymity also serves to protect your identity. Because of the societal stigma surrounding addiction, many addicts and their family members choose to keep the addiction a private matter.

How do I identify myself during meetings?

Members of the 12-step fellowships have developed a practice of self-identifying their conditions every time they share. You may not have a magic wand to wave and make the whole thing just disappear, but you can learn to recognize the disease for what it is, and learn to put the blame where it belongs – on the disease itself. By seeing the disease for what it is and reminding yourself regularly, you break through the negative and shaming messages and labels you may have received. As you face the true nature of your condition, it is natural to feel shame about it or worry what others will think.

In our society, addictions are stigmatized. There is a lack of recognition and understanding of addictive and co-addictive disorders. So at first, you may not think terms such as addict or co-addict are acceptable terms; you may see these words as more negative judgments and labels. As you learn to recognize the symptoms for what they are and to separate from the active disease process, your understanding of the terms will change.

Because COSA recognized that their members had a variety of preferences for how they identify themselves, they came to a consensus as a fellowship to accept all the terms. Here's a short list of acceptable terms:[3]

- co-addict
- co-sex addict
- codependent to a sex addict
- sexual codependent
- codependent sex addict
- sexual co-addict
- addicted to a sex addict
- adult child of a sex addict
- sex addiction family member
- partner of a sex addict

Also, the letters COSA are not an acronym but stand on their own.

Do I have to speak during the meeting or can I just listen?

Some meetings have a custom of screening newcomers to make sure you're not in the wrong type of meeting or you meet a requirement to be allowed to attend. The only requirement for membership is that you have been affected by someone else's sexual addiction/compulsive sexual behavior. If they do screen new members, one or two members will most likely speak with you privately. Once you join the meeting, you don't have to speak or even introduce yourself. Some meetings have a custom of going around the room and introducing everyone by first name only, or going around in turn to allow each member time to share if they so choose. It's always OK to say, "I pass" when it's your turn.

What if I'm a male co-addict and the 12-step meetings for co-addicts in my town do not allow men?
Unfortunately, there are not yet as many men who are active in co-addiction recovery as women for a variety of reasons. Fortunately, due in great part to the growth of the Internet and COSA's recent commitment to recognize men suffering from this disorder, there has been a greater influx of male members, and more continue to join the program as men create support networks and establish quality co-addiction recovery.

If your town's only local COSA, S-Anon, Co-SLAA or SRA-Anon meetings are women-only meetings, try writing to them. Explain why you'd like to join the meeting and ask them to consider changing their membership policy. Or consider starting your own meeting and invite members from the women's group. Some will likely want to support your efforts. Also, check each fellowship's website to see if they address the topic. Due to the small size of the fellowships at the time of this writing, you may need to look for long-distance support groups and attend annual conventions or retreats.

I'm embarrassed and afraid I might see someone I know.
Sex addiction is a disease and not a moral issue, despite the fact that it sometimes leads to moral decay. Recovering people as well as addiction professionals have campaigned to correct the cultural stigma of addiction in general. This stigma especially applies to sex addicts and their families. The risk of being shunned by members of your community is real. Those who you see inside the meeting are also there to seek help. Family members who have been scared to attend meetings report experiencing relief to finally find a place that welcomes them and enables them to become a part of a group that understands them and has experienced similar situations.

Understanding Addiction Terms
There are many new words and phrases you will learn on your road to recovery. Some may be familiar to you while others seem confusing. Understanding these concepts is crucial to your recovery.

What is powerlessness?
This 12-step concept, along with several others, has often been misunderstood and misrepresented. The 12-step fellowships teach that by surrendering to the disease and accepting its existence fully, one can begin to find the strength to

recover from it. Accepting that you are powerless doesn't mean you're hopeless and hold no accountability. Rather, it's the serene acceptance that you have no control over addiction, and when you embrace that notion it provides clarity and empowerment for your own recovery to work on the things that you can change.

One old phrase that describes this is "being my own worst enemy." Another is "needing to learn to get out of my own way." These phrases refer to the tendency to revert to the old, self-destructive, addictive or co-addictive thought patterns and behaviors. These slogans point to the 12-step belief that addicts and families alike, when fully suffering from their diseases, can become similarly invested in willpower and control as the answer for every problem.

Your attempts to maintain control – whether it's controlling your own acting out, your partner's acting out, or other challenging aspects of your life – rarely works in the long run. In reality, as you cling tighter to your attempt to control the addict and other aspects of your life, the more people rebel against you and take advantage of your "good will."

It is confusing because some of your efforts to control others do work some of the time. Twelve-step members recognize that while you may have great justification for your behaviors, as they play out over time they eventually become quite obviously self-defeating and compulsive. Both addiction and co-addiction are chronic forces that work against your health and your sanity. The addicts and co-addicts who eventually surrender and experience a sense of peace have come to accept the incurable yet treatable nature of this disease.

The 12-step programs for co-addicts all recognize the need for ongoing recovery from your own compulsive condition. They also teach that these diseases are both very treatable on an ongoing basis through application of recovery principles including the 12 steps. The existence of millions of recovering people with balanced lifestyles proves their success.

What is detachment?
Detachment means learning how to step back and see the big picture. With practice, detachment allows you to separate yourself from your own reactions in order to make better choices. Newcomers often misunderstand the recovery concept of detachment to mean, "the ability to no longer care" or "the ability to cut yourself off." Detachment is actually a spiritual response to the problems of an addict. After all, you didn't cause the addiction and you can't cure it. What you can choose, however, is your response. When dealing with addiction, the fact is, often the very best response you can offer is one of measured calmness. Addicts take notice when you stop screaming, crying and overreacting.

Why are these recovery concepts so difficult?
Some recovery principles are not easy to internalize or use on an ongoing basis. Fortunately, ample evidence exists that these principles work beautifully in confronting the family disease of addiction. At first, many of the principles of recovery may seem contradictory. It has often been said that the 12 steps are simple but

not easy. Let us add that they are deceptively simple. On closer examination, however, you will see that these principals are actually paradoxical.

Here is an example: When an addict admits his powerlessness over sex addiction, he may for the first times in years feel a sense of relief and hope. The principles of recovery often seem counterintuitive, especially when you are first looking for black-and-white answers. Primary examples of this are "powerlessness," "detachment" and "putting the focus on yourself."

Twelve-step fellowships talk about the aspect of addictive and co-addictive disease that feeds on your natural human instincts. *Alcoholics Anonymous – Big Book* and *The Twelve Steps* and *Twelve Traditions* describe the disease as feeding on one or more of your human drives.[4] As the disease takes hold and begins to progress, it seems to satisfy something missing within us. As the disease progresses further, however, it actually rewires our brain's neural pathways, driving us into increasingly compulsive behavior. When you try to break free of the addictive pattern, your very instincts will convincingly urge you against it and your defenses will rally.

The *Big Book* describes the addict's belief that the problem lies with the outside world and other people. Addicts believe that it is other people that need to change, not them. Addicts handle their relationship problems much like a director would manage a play, the actors and various elements. If all these externals could be corrected or adjusted, the addict's illusion is that he/she would be satisfied. Co-addicts report the same outward-focused beliefs and effort to manage their feelings. Both suffer from a disease that uses defenses to block the afflicted from their own internal integrity and equilibrium.

How can I ever hope to break free from this depressing nightmare?
Twelve-step fellowships teach that the natural spiritual state of the individual can be restored to a condition of core integrity. With maintenance of the supports and practices needed, spiritual awakening can be maintained over the long term. To do so, that restoration process needs to be repeated and adjusted frequently. It's a lot to learn and allow, and it takes time, desire and commitment.

In this awakening, you'll be able to achieve and maintain a balanced sense of awareness and a connection greater than yourself. Mentally, you'll come to know open-mindedness, calm and clear thinking, and even excitement about your future. You'll be able to consistently practice positive communication with a balance of restraint and expression. You will learn to channel your rich and unique experience of your own inner knowing to contribute creatively to the world around you. You will become able to operate from a place of compassion, gratitude and humility without setting yourself up for ego crashes. You will come to know your life purpose as you develop the ability to choose and to act – instead of react. You'll come to value your various emotional states, know how to take care of yourself emotionally, and learn more about yourself from the lessons and messages your emotions bring you. You will develop a unique sense of your place on the earth and a practical, grounded outlook.

Why do 12-step fellowships work?

The three primary elements of 12-step healing identified by Alcoholics Anonymous are unity, service and recovery.[5] The concept of unity is captured in the spirit of fellowship between members.

Members often gather at a local diner for conversation and plan other recovery-centered family activities and outings. The concept of unity is captured in the 12 Traditions, and in the principles of inclusion, anonymity, equality and interdependence.

You are a member when you say you are. The common problems and solutions you all share is what's relevant, not who you are and what you do out in the world. You need each other in order to recover. The strength of the group bond and of inclusion is crucial. The "higher power" of recovery lies in the act of surrender. All are welcome.

The concept of service is captured in every aspect of the structure of the fellowships. All members are expected to do service, even newcomers. Newcomers are often grateful for the opportunity to complete a useful and unselfish task. It helps them to break their obsessive focus on the addiction and makes them feel like a part of the solution.

Members' service positions are volunteer tasks. Many service positions are simple, such as setting out chairs before a meeting. Others are more complex, such as chairing a meeting or helping create a public service announcement.

Twelve-step fellowships have vast decentralized service networks. It's a challenge to learn the inner workings, customs and policies, and how much they vary from one meeting or one area of the country to another. The skills learned over time for participating in business meetings and the spirit of cooperative service are some of the same skills required in healthy, sober relationships. These include skills such as safe communication, mutual respect, finding win-win solutions, healthy decision-making, progress not perfection, "minding your own business," and singleness of purpose.

The concept of recovery is captured in the ongoing action of listening to each other share your progress on a daily basis, working the 12 steps, and applying recovery principles to your daily living, one day at a time. The power of learning to see yourself, past your own subconscious defenses, and the ability to change inside lies in part to listening to other members' stories of recovery.

Change occurs as you work the steps and pass on your growing awareness through service and supporting others. Members support each other through speaking at meetings, sharing their stories of recovery, giving out phone numbers or e-mail addresses for times of distress, and sponsoring other members. These are not considered service positions; these are a part of step work and "carrying the message."

Anthropologists, psychologists, physicians, treatment specialists and recovering people themselves have studied the experience of 12-step recovery to analyze its success formula.

They have identified several major healing components:[6]

- the single purpose of the sharing of mutual help to address the disease
- the single focus on the disease and its recovery
- the power of the group and the magical and ancient power of storytelling[7]
- the power of repetition and a concrete structure
- rigorous honesty and "reality checks" with yourself and with others who have been in similar places
- resolution of the contradictions in one's personal beliefs and commitment to place your trust in and live according to those beliefs
- the spiritual tools, slogans and processes

How much work does recovery involve?

The 12-step goals cannot be achieved by our intellect alone. They are better absorbed by making the effort to try them through a series of repetitive actions and experiences. In this way, learning the steps can feel rather like learning to ride a bicycle. Actually, recovery is more like riding a variety of bicycles as a remedial treatment for a degenerative muscle condition. When we accept the chronic nature of the underlying condition, we begin to understand the metaphor of bicycle riding differently. Recovering addicts – as well as recovering family members – don't do as well when they live life without these tools.

While a bicycle is usually built for one person, the nature of working the steps is relational. With the 12 steps, people often need the witnessing, acceptance, love and direction from others in order to truly see how to apply the principals to each new situation. Therefore, the wisdom and safety of the steps continues to unfold and is revealed as one applies them to life's challenges – one day at a time. People do get the hang of working the steps, and they experience that same sense of freedom and balance that one feels on a bicycle.

How do I "work" a program?

The most typical way to get started is to join one of the 12-step fellowships, attend meetings at least weekly, and get to know other members. As you acclimate to the lingo and customs of the group, you'll observe how others are "working the program." While the meetings hold a range of cultures, educational levels, socio-economic backgrounds, and political, sexual and religious orientations, attendees are all family members of sex addicts who have been through situations similar to yours and can relate to what is happening in your life. In fact, it can be comforting to realize that the range of symptoms of co-addiction is the same even for different types of people and personalities. It can help you see the illness for what it really is.

The basics of working a program include attending meetings, collecting phone numbers from members, establishing a routine of calling them for regular check-ins, learning how to apply the slogans, and reading the literature. The emphasis is on establishing a daily routine that helps ground you in recovery principles so that you can start responding to your daily challenges from a balanced and serene frame of mind.

As soon as you can, start collecting phone numbers and calling other members to build up your "recovery support system." Once you're acclimated to your surroundings, establish a regular habit of meeting attendance and practice of other recovery tools. The next challenge is to find a sponsor and begin working the steps.

Both COSA and S-Anon have published literature containing step study questions. They also encourage their local groups to hold structured step meetings on a regular basis, and both hold retreats and conferences on working the steps. COSA provides step study supports online and via e-mail. (You can view the 12 Steps of Sex Addicts Anonymous at the back of this book.)

Working the steps in any 12-step fellowship begins with learning the general meaning of the step through a series of readings, discussions and listening to others. Second, you complete a series of contemplations and written exercises, which will help you begin to integrate the step into your awareness. As you progress, you share your work with a "sponsor" or support group. Gradually you'll be able to apply the step to various situations or circumstances in your life.

Because someone else's addictive disease is intrinsically a part of a co-addict's condition, you may sometimes feel as if you have to do double the step work in order to get and stay sober from your active co-addiction. First, you must come to terms with your powerlessness to control somebody else's addictive disease.

Therefore, the first step represents the process of realizing and accepting the truth that you cannot control someone else's disease any more than they themselves can. Getting treatment for the disease is not the same thing as controlling it. There is still a wildcard component to it, where it can flare up without anyone catching on until it's fully active again. Alcoholics Anonymous refers to the disease of alcoholism as "cunning, baffling and powerful" – and sex addiction certainly shares these qualities.

Like other family members of sex addicts, you will find that not only are you powerless over your loved one's condition, but you suffer from your own condition. In spite of your best efforts, you also have no lasting comprehensive way to remove sexual compulsion from an addict's life, nor can you keep in remission on your own. Second, you must work the steps to determine your own degree of co-addiction. You will need to accept the truth of your loss of control over your own life.

Fully facing a first step in any 12-step program usually brings about waves of feelings, including anger and resistance. The resistance manifests in a variety of ways. A strong desire to blame the addict is one of the most common ways that co-addicts resist recovery.

Another common form of resistance is insisting that you're right. You may indeed be right, and you also may close off your awareness to a range of points of view from each person's perspective. This resistance can be a natural part of your recovery, but if you are aware of it and continue to reach out for support, you will be able to work through it as it arises.

Will the 12 steps teach me about boundaries and accountability?
The 12 steps develop our awareness and give us an appreciation for developing new, healthier boundaries. The steps also provide us with a system of accountability, which allows us freedom from the effects of sex addiction and co-addiction in our lives. Consistent accountability over time will help you keep your bearings – with your thoughts, feelings, actions and decision-making. As you work the steps, you will develop your boundaries naturally.

For example, as you absorb the full significance of the first step, you'll begin to find your center, sometimes for the first time in your life. As the gifts of healing continue along with your stepwork, you'll probably develop a sense of gratitude for your recovery. That gratitude will become a part of the foundation for restoring health to your spirit.

What is a sponsor?
A sponsor is like a big brother or big sister in the program – someone who is further along in recovery and can pass on what she or he has learned. A sponsor is also someone you can turn to for special guidance in working your steps and someone who will be a listener. As you start to build your support system, you'll usually find someone you connect with. Most meetings will also have brochures with tips on choosing a sponsor

Will finding a sponsor be difficult?
Due to the recent epidemic of Internet sex addiction and because 12-step fellowships for family members of sex addicts are still small, the influx of newcomers is often greater than the availability of members with the time and experience to be a sponsor. In these isolated or newly forming areas, members either seek long-distance sponsorship or practice co-sponsorship, which is supporting each other to do stepwork and taking turns. In these cases, it's best to also plan day-long step workshops or attend fellowship step retreats to experience more seasoned messages of joy and healing.

Do the 12 steps help with couples' issues?
The 12 steps can help couples in a variety of ways. Working the steps allows addicts and co-addicts to find freedom from acting-out behaviors, clears up distorted thinking, balances emotions, and allows development of vulnerability and communication skills over time. Both members of the couple may occasionally want to speed up the couples healing in order to relieve their sense of losing control or get past deep feelings of guilt, remorse, or fears of loss or abandonment. Other times, couples – or one member of the partnership – will try to avoid the couples work out of fear, anger, shame or combination of mixed feelings and insecurity. Typically, the compulsion of co-addiction will drive you to want to

work on your partner's recovery, or at least on the coupleship more than your own recovery. Therefore, each partner should focus on their individual recovery first. Once individual recovery is stable, you may want to consider attending Recovering Couples Anonymous (RCA). In this fellowship, couples gather to apply the 12 steps to strengthen and nurture their relationships.

How will my religious beliefs be affected by working the program?
Contained within the steps are many commonly practiced spiritual principles. What makes the 12-step programs unique is their focus on the particular conditions its members face. The 12-step programs do not adhere to any particular religion, but welcome you no matter what beliefs you have. They are for use by all people who suffer from these conditions. People of all backgrounds have a right to recovery.

The 12-step fellowships focus on establishing and maintaining recovery from a progressive illness. They also teach that your condition has probably disrupted your spiritual footing, and that your recovery will need to include sorting out all your various beliefs, not just your religious ones. You will not be expected to change your religious beliefs unless you feel the need to do so. You'll be shown respect for your beliefs and learn to respect the beliefs of other members who may have beliefs different from your own.

Some members of 12-step fellowships do not believe in God and never see a need to change their minds about that. They learn how to practice the recovery principles from that perspective. The 12-step fellowships view each member's religious beliefs as a private matter. All members work the second step by identifying whatever it is they believe will restore them to sanity. They then start working the second step by learning to put their faith in those beliefs.

Because 12-step fellowships encourage members to develop a relationship with a God of their own understanding, all members can find a way to interpret the use of prayer and meditation in a way that works for them. Some 12-step members think of prayer and meditation as the practice of sacred attitudes, such as wonder, gratitude, humility and contemplation. Others believe in a fully traditional religious prayer life. Still others gradually change their beliefs as they maintain their recovery by seeing what works for them.

What if I don't feel a connection with my group?
COSA, S-Anon, SRA-Anon and Co-SLAA all agree that the nature of the disease varies from person to person. One may become addicted to their partner, to their partner's sex addiction or recovery, to the drama of the conflicts with the partner, to the hope of rescuing their partner, to all of these, and so on. The experiences, personalities and behaviors of the sex addict in a co-addict's life will vary from person to person. Yet you will find that by focusing on the commonalities you will find the most healing.

You may not like everyone you meet at a 12-step meeting, and you will see people in varying states of health and functioning. It's important to remember that everyone is there for the same reason and may be in a great deal of pain. When we can't offer a shoulder to cry on or a kind word, we can practice not adding to others' troubles and steer clear. You can ask others to do the same for you. You can practice learning about boundaries among your peers as part of implementing the same boundary practices you will develop with loved ones.

While you will find no one member to be perfect, as you develop your interdependence with the group as a whole, you'll discover it frees you and allows you to find your true self. Asking for help will no longer have to wait until it becomes a desperate act, but can become a simple and well-deserved tool to use on a daily basis.

This is not to say that you would be encouraged to lean on others for things you need to learn to do for yourself. Program members generally will not feel comfortable lending you money, getting in the middle of your conflicts, or providing for you. They will, however, provide plenty of support in the form of encouragement and guidance.

Over time, you'll be able to recognize a true sense of balance and equilibrium. When you're working your program consistently over time, you'll learn how to sense when the balance is off, and often will know what to do to restore yourself, including reaching out for support.

Relapse and Recovery

Many co-addicts who find solid long-term recovery say they initially doubted that they had a need for a recovery program. Others learned about recovery concepts, glimpsed the nature of their own condition, started to work a program but didn't fully grasp the seriousness of their condition and they dropped out of recovery.

Once the crisis stage lifts or the addict is no longer in their lives, many co-addicts believe the problem is gone. Many co-addicts say they created an illusion that they were in solid recovery – only to realize later that they had been relying on the strength of the addicted partner's recovery to carry them as well. These co-addicts admit their focus had remained on the addicted family member's recovery and on the coupleship recovery, rather than on their own. Some found a new relationship to believe in, never completing their own recovery from co-addiction.

Some co-addicts' commitment to recovery is conditional on the addicted family members' ongoing recovery. When the addict stops working the program, so does the co-addict. Many co-addicts report periods of feeling fully committed to this new path, then relapsing, sometimes for unknown reasons.

Losing the connection to a recovery program is often a reason for relapse. Often it is only in hindsight, seeing the resulting return of unmanageability and further progression of codependency, that many co-addicts can recognize a relapse for what it is.

When we first meet family members learning about recovery, many are focused on their belief that the addict will probably never maintain recovery. It's ironic that in actuality, the number of family members who find recovery is much smaller than the number of sex addicts in recovery, even though estimates show that for each addict there exists an average of five family members affected.[8]

Contrary to what you might expect, attendance in each of the family 12-step programs is much smaller in number than its counterpart program. The 12-step program with the highest numbers of registered groups and largest service structures are COSA and S-Anon. At the time of this writing, the numbers of groups in COSA and S-Anon are in the hundreds for each of those fellowships. In recent years, Co-SLAA has dwindled down to about a dozen surviving groups. SRA-Anon exists in only a handful of cities and has less than a dozen meetings in total existence. Even when a solid set of weekly meetings and sponsors are available, most family members do not stay connected to their 12-step program.

In areas of the world and parts of the United States where these 12-step fellowships are not yet developed, new members need to increase service work or even start their own meetings. Either way, the numbers of family members who will only try a handful of meetings is higher than almost any other type of recovery program. The numbers who stay in recovery over the long term have been small. We have often seen family members focus intently on their own recoveries until they complete the written work on the 12 steps. Then they soon stop working their programs.

Part of the responsibility for this phenomenon lies with the U.S. healthcare system and its lack of recognition of co-addiction as a treatable condition with as many complications as sex addiction. While many treatment programs spend a relatively small proportion of their therapeutic focus on the family aspects of the disease and on the family members' treatment, the 12-step fellowships for family members have discovered an equal need for recovery between the sex addict and co-addict alike.

As therapists become more educated about the family aspects of the disease of addiction, they can more responsibly inform and offer treatment and 12-step program referrals to family members. Truly successful members soon learn to recognize the steps and the use of a 12-step support system as ongoing tools for a new way of life, not something to complete like homework for school.

Twelve-step fellowships are full of sex addicts in recovery. Most people who enter recovery programs are able to establish abstinence within the first several months, and while both slips and full-blown relapses occur, they then begin to establish true recovery over time. Many therapists have also had the joyous experience of knowing many sex addicts and co-addicts in long-term recovery.

For many partners, the thought of reaching out to a 12-step community can be daunting. Understanding more about the 12-step fellowships may make the process of reaching out easier. Contact information for all of the fellowships may be found in the Resource Guide. One of the promises of the 12 steps is that you will experience a "new freedom." Embracing recovery and allowing yourself to reach out for support may be the first step to experiencing a new freedom in your life.

Chapter 8
What Are the Best Ways
to Take Care of Myself?

Sonja Rudie, M.A., LMHC, C-EMDR, C-EAGALA I, CSAT

Discovering your partner is a sex addict can be a traumatic and stressful event, and can compound the grief of previous unhealed emotional wounds. During times of great difficulty, it's common for people to neglect their own self-care, especially if they are not in the habit of getting their wants and needs met. This chapter underscores some of the fundamental ways partners of sex addicts can take care of themselves after their world is turned upside down.

You're Not Crazy Even Though You May Feel Like It
Many partners report they knew something strange was happening in their relationships, but they had no idea that their spouses or partners were sex addicts. You may have asked: *What's wrong with me? Why am I so mistrustful? Am I crazy? Why am I feeling this way today when some days are just fine?* These are common thoughts for partners attempting to absorb information that feels too overwhelming for them.

As you move from disbelief into reality, you're likely to have many questions. How did I miss this? My gut told me something was wrong, but how reliable was this information?
Feelings of shame or embarrassment often prevent a partner from turning to resources that could normally be a source of comfort. Partners will also blame themselves for the sexual acting out of their spouses/partners because they don't understand that the sex addiction has nothing to do with them. This is especially true if they have not previously colluded with the addict in sexually acting-out behaviors.

Deception may have gone on for a long time, so when the truth comes out a partner's denial may return with a full force. Many times the partner will have knowledge of a few "infractions" against the fidelity of the coupleship, but she or he will dismiss her or his instincts to keep the peace. Sometimes there's only an intuitive sense that there's something wrong.

Often this sense is quickly minimized, then dismissed as paranoid or mistrustful of the addict, especially if the addict has provided convincing evidence of how "insecure" the partner is behaving. This use of an emotional or psychological "smokescreen" can fool partners. Feelings of revulsion are normal when faced with deliberate lies and covert behavior.[1]

In recovery, co-addicts start to listen to their inner voice. Dr. Emeran A. Mayer, a professor of medicine, physiology and psychiatry at UCLA, notes:

The enteric nervous system can be seen as an extension of the emotional center of the brain. Evolution has placed part of our emotion-generating circuits in the gut, an area where you have major mechanical influences such as contractions and a direct interface with the environment.[2]

Mayer hopes to find scientific explanations for "gut-thinking," and that our visceral information is what we have come to understand as our "felt-sense." While this does not give all the facts to a partner who is questioning his or her reality, it certainly gives more understanding of how important it is for a co-addict not to dismiss the body's ability to discern important unconscious recognitions that something is amiss in a relationship.

In his book, *Blink: The Power of Thinking Without Thinking,* Malcolm Gladwell describes the work of Dr. John Gottman, a marital therapist and researcher from the University of Washington.[3] He reports how Gottman was able to determine successful or unsuccessful marital outcomes with remarkable accuracy by the use of mathematics and video observations of couples interacting with one another.

Gladwell uses the term "thin-slicing," defining it as "the ability of our unconscious to find patterns and behaviors based on very narrow slices of experience." He believes when our unconscious engages in thin-slicing, what we are doing is an automated, accelerated, unconscious version of what Gottman does with his videotapes: instinctive processes of rapid cognition.

Often partners of sex addicts may experience truth in their unconscious through this "thin-slicing" process. One some level, they recognize the addict's deceptive behavior.

Taking care of yourself means letting yourself know the truth. Even a private investigator cannot tell you whether your gut is giving you information that's accurate. However, if you're contacting a private investigator, there's normally a good reason for your mistrust. Acknowledging that you're uncomfortable, fearful, uncertain, angry, hurt or feeling betrayed are healthy steps to caring for yourself.

Committing to the reality that you deserve to honor your body wisdom and "thin-slicing" may not mean you have all the details, but it does mean you're absorbing the shock and can begin to take the next steps toward safely making good decisions for yourself. You have the right to your own reality.

What are some ways I can take care of myself?

First, you must recognize your unmet needs. Abraham Maslow provided us with a hierarchy of needs that helps us understand the basics of self-care and why it's important.[4] For instance, by reviewing the pyramid below, you'll see the fundamentals of human needs defined by Maslow:

Fig. 8.1

Are you meeting the basic needs from the bottom rung of the list? Are you safe physically, emotionally and spiritually? If not, how fast can you get yourself there? If the need for sex has been shifted to mean something other than a safe expression of yourself in a healthy, committed, monogamous relationship, how is it possible for you to create that safety with your partner or spouse? Does this mean you need professional assistance?

The hierarchy of needs reflects how we must first get the basic needs on the bottom met before we can proceed toward the top. If we were to take the idea of getting needs met one step further, we could also feasibly add the basics like proper dental care, clothing, friendship, consistently stocked food in the home, a safe neighborhood in which to reside, sufficient rest, mobility, recreation, exercise, or leisure time with family and friends.

This would also include time to create, tinker, build, draw, sketch, write poetry, music, dance, hike, sail, or spend time with animals or nature. Although solitude is not listed on Maslow's hierarchy of needs, some people may argue it's also a fundamental need for self-replenishment because it fosters a connection with one's self and a Higher Power.

What are my blind spots?

Blind spots are untreated illnesses such as eating disorders (ED), PTSD, depression and anxiety. Untreated sex addiction and co-sex addiction can also be considered blind spots. Maybe you're just now considering the possibility that your partner may be a sex addict, or perhaps you made a discovery and are in a significant amount of pain and suffering. If you're attempting to recover from the shock of infidelity, seek a community of people in recovery and a competent professional who can assist you in finding your equilibrium again.

Undiagnosed illnesses, such as depression, can wreak havoc on a person's life. Depression is a treatable illness, and it's important to understand unnecessary suffering can be eliminated. If you believe you may have an illness and are not taking care of getting it treated, you are operating from either a place of poverty or denial. If you are in a place of denial, or have a blind spot, take this opportunity to invest in yourself. You're wiser than you think, you deserve to give and receive love and self care. Make a decision to act on your own behalf!

Discover Your Worth

Cultivating positive regard for yourself and challenging perfectionism are ways to promote self-care. Glenn Schiraldi writes about "Howard's Laws of Human Worth" in *The Self Esteem Workbook*.[5] Schiraldi's book addresses the need for understanding one's core worth. He believes that worth is never determined by externals, such as what kind of car you drive, clothes you wear, your occupation, or how many meetings or therapy sessions you attend. Worth is never in jeopardy, is infinite, unchanging and intrinsic for all human beings as we are created equal from birth. He describes these concepts as vital frameworks for health and healing.

How does your thinking compare with these concepts of unconditional positive regard? Have you been giving yourself the message that you are worth the effort of living a healthy and sane life? Are you continuing to challenge any chaos in your life and take responsibility for creating a healthier way of being? The absence of self-esteem for one's core worth is considered by many to be an invisible handicap.[6] Creating healthier self-esteem is possible by practicing new ways of thinking and behaving toward yourself.

If you have ever traveled by plane, you know that passengers are always instructed on how to use an oxygen mask. Passengers are told, "Put your own oxygen mask on first, then attend to the people around you." Saving yourself first is an act of courage and self-preservation. If you can save yourself with the help of your Higher Power, you're better prepared to consider the needs of others. Children need their parents to be "fully oxygenated." With proper and swift action, children and loved ones can be positively influenced by the resiliency and determination of a stabilized parent. What ways are you "oxygenating" your body and self today?

Learn Your Behavior Cycles

Behaviors have specific patterns. Become a student of learning your own cycle. Find ways to create healthy activities and behaviors in your life. These steps will help bring structure to chaos, sanity to a crazy situation. For more information on how to understand your cycle, examine the recommended list of readings at the back of this book. Educating yourself will give you the empowerment you need to make a difference in your own life circumstances. Taking positive steps toward making changes in the way you live your life is vital for your mental health and, if you have children, for theirs as well.

Learning your own cycle doesn't diminish the appropriateness of feeling angry or devastated about betrayals you may have experienced. If you've been harmed by your partner going outside the covenant of your coupleship, it's possible that your behaviors and emotions have impacted the people around you. You are responsible for your feelings and actions – even when you find out about betrayal. How can you behave in ways that are consistant with your value system and also stay firm within your need for emotional and physical safety?

Self-Care Versus Selfishness

Love is a condition that exists where the other's well-being is AS important AS one's own   -Harry Stack Sullivan

What does self-care mean? There are a variety of ideas about what self-care means or looks like. Self-care refers to a commitment to one's own good health. Pauline Boss, Ph.D., describes health as "relational ... the ability to enjoy a positive connection with another person and with a community of others; preventive health is the presence of resilience in the face of stress and trauma."[7]

Former President Jimmy Carter describes health as "relational, able-bodied, involves self-regard, and includes control over our own affairs, strong ties with other people, and a purpose in life."[8] Carter says some of the best advice he ever received was that it was "better to use recreation to preserve health than to use medicine and treatment to regain health" once it was gone. He goes on to say a few dollars or days spent pursuing a hobby or pastime is a sound investment, paying off both in enjoyment and in avoiding medical expenses.

In the recovery community, people use the acronym HALT, which helps serve as a reminder of self-care concepts. If you're hungry you need to eat; if you're angry, find a way to express anger safely; if you're lonely, reach out and connect with trusted friends, family, or family of choice; if you're tired, then rest. Many times people are taught to believe that taking care of one's needs is being selfish. Sometimes your needs may conflict with the needs of others and that's OK. Selfishness usually is accompanied by a lack of mindfulness, humility or compassion, which isn't the same as self-care. Unless someone is a dependent child, adults can take the responsibility necessary to take care of their own needs and be mindful of their loved ones. Mindfulness doesn't mean behaving in a controlling way; rather it reflects a care deeply felt and observed for the self while considering others.

Sarina was married to a man who was the deacon at their local church. She discovered he had been regularly viewing online pornography of teen girls. She was devastated. She and her husband sought counseling after he was caught by his church and reported to the authorities.

As they began working their program, Sarina began focusing on herself and her unmet needs. She began to make a list for different categories: health, spiritual, friends, social, creative, family and relational. Then she broke these categories down into two or three things that represented her own personal self-care plan. For example, under "Family" she wrote: "Take time to do fun things with the kids, write my siblings, and go to a family reunion." In the category of

"Health" she wrote: "Take time to find my core self, make time to play, and get at least seven hours of sleep each night." Sarina was amazed at how little self-care she had actually done in recent years because she had been so focused on her husband and children. As she began making her own health a priority and her husband continued his own therapy, the couple began making strides toward greater intimacy and healing their marriage.

In the book, *Beyond Codependency,* Melody Beattie writes:

When will we become loveable? When will we feel safe? When will we get all the protection, nurturing, and love we so richly deserve? We will get it when we begin giving to ourselves...[9]

How Do I Relax When There's So Much Going On?

A nap is an adult's version of a child's fort.
-Sark

The Relaxation Response
You may know what you need to do to take care of yourself, but actually taking action is more difficult. Those that are deliberate and create an opportunity for relaxation will reap the many benefits. Stress that builds up cumulatively will wear down our bodies. Our ability to cope with situations becomes quickly compromised when we become exhausted. We are more vulnerable to illness, injuries, accidents and disease when this condition becomes chronic.

It's especially noteworthy to consider how one stressor will be compounded when another stressor is added before the first one is resolved. Illness such as heart disease, high blood pressure, headaches, obesity, ulcers, anxiety, insomnia, depression, arthritis, asthma, colitis, diarrhea, sexual dysfunction and headaches have been linked with prolonged excessive stress.[10]

What are my treatment options?
Psychiatric Care
Making a decision to enter treatment is one of the most important decisions you'll make in your lifetime. First, you must be willing to truthfully explain to a mental healthcare professional what you believe is the primary cause of your distress. Treatment professionals will usually do a thorough assessment of your life events and medical background. Providing this information is essential so they can begin creating a treatment plan. Sometimes this will also include an action plan that recommends a medical evaluation from a physician. This is nothing to be fearful of, rather it means you're receiving careful attention and support.

Full medical evaluations from psychiatrists are often used as a baseline in assessing medical history before a full treatment plan can be effectively completed. The purpose of the evaluation is not intended to corroborate or justify someone "is crazy." It's advisable, therefore, to avoid buying into any societal stigmas associated with medical evaluations. It may help you to know that this is what mental health care providers commonly view as excellence of care. Not everyone will need to see a psychiatrist, nor will everyone who sees a psychiatrist necessarily need medication.

Individual Therapy

There are many treatment options available to you when seeking therapy. If you're seeing a psychiatrist, they will have a specific way of doing therapy that's based on a medical model. Some will manage medications after the initial medical evaluation and others will prefer to do both the therapy and the medication management.

Psychologists, or persons with Ph.D.s, will also have their choice of models of therapy they prefer to use. The same is true for Licensed Clinical Social Workers, Licensed Mental Health Care Professionals, Licensed Professional Counselors, and Licensed Marriage and Family Therapists. There seems to be as many choices of therapy and counseling as there are choices in automobiles to drive!

Obtaining a referral from a trusted family physician, local hospital, crisis line, The Society for the Advancement of Sexual Health (SASH), International Institute of Trauma and Addiction Professionals (IITAP), or member of the 12-step community is often an excellent way to discover names of clinicians who have experience working with co-sex addiction and sex addiction issues.

There are a host of treatment model options and tools available to treat partners, spouses, companions, children and family. Some of these include: art therapy, psychotherapy, psychopharmacology (medication), EMDR (Eye Movement Desensitization Reprocessing), cognitive behavioral therapy (CBT), trauma-focused cognitive behavioral therapy (TFCBT), equine-assisted therapy (EAT), gestalt, somatic experiencing, mindfulness-based cognitive therapy for depression, cognitive therapy, interpersonal therapy, psycho-dynamic psychotherapy, dialectical behavioral therapy (DBT), existential therapy, humanistic therapy and dance therapy.

Many therapists are trained in more than one kind of therapeutic model and may possess skills in several of these areas. They also may have specialized training in the use of psychological tools such as hypnosis, Neurolinguistic Programming (NLP), or Thought Field Therapy (TFT). A comprehensive review of the different types of therapeutic approaches is beyond the scope of this book. However, some of the aforementioned are possible treatments with good results.

If you decide to attend therapy, be sure to pay special attention to the therapeutic relationship. Is this someone you believe you can work with? Does it feel generally like a good fit for you? It's important that you experience a feeling of safety with your therapist to help you gain some sense of control in your life again, especially if you're being treated for PTSD or PTSD-like symptoms.[11]

Effects of traumatic experiences spread throughout the family, so it's important that it not go untreated.[12] If you have experienced trauma, your ability to function with your children, spouse or partner, may be impacted. Other areas of you life, such as work, school, church, social life and finances can also be impacted negatively without appropriate intervention and treatment.

Groups

Counseling and support groups are advisable to help reduce the pain and anguish experienced by infidelity, divorce, or other kinds of traumatic events.[13] The combination of individual therapy with group therapy gives the added benefit of stabilization and comfort for people who are suffering.

Many people struggling with co-sex addiction can find a tremendous amount of support by meeting with other partners and spouses struggling with the same issue. This helps to normalize the situation and reduce shame. Practitioners all over the country have begun to offer groups for partners of sexual addicts.

Inpatient

Sometimes the pain of a situation goes beyond what feels bearable. If you are suicidal or are unable to function, inpatient or residential treatment may be an option. Centers that focus on stabilization will have a shorter length of stay and often focus on medication management. There are also residential programs that focus on the area of codependency or co-sex addiction. Talk with your primary therapist about what level of care is right for you.

Marital and Family Therapy

Your primary individual therapist will be your best resource to determine when couples or family therapy is called for. It is common for couples who decide to stay together and work on recovery from sexual addiction to need the assistance of a marital therapist. If both of you are also in individual therapy, it is advised that your marital therapist is not the same therapist that treats either of you on an individual basis, if possible. However, your marital therapist should work with both of your individual therapists. Ask your therapist about the recommended treatment plan for your situation.

What will the costs of treatment be?

Financial stress is often a key issue in marriages where sex addiction and co-sex addiction exists. Affording proper treatment for self-care can be difficult for many families. This becomes a particular challenge when a specialist is needed.

If you have medical insurance, many plans will not cover marital therapy, but sometimes they will cover individual sessions when there is a clinical diagnosis of depression or some other kinds of legitimate mental-health diagnoses. Insurance coverage is more likely if you see a psychiatrist, psychologist, or a professional who is licensed or certified in the field of mental health. Seeking out qualified professionals either "in network" or "out of network" as provided for in your insurance contract may save you a lot of money.

Therapists who are CSATs (Certified Sex Addiction Therapists), who are also licensed professionals or doctors may help you avoid possible increased financial stressors simply because their more experienced care can save you time in therapy. You may also find there are associates within a company, community mental health facility or hospital under supervision for certification offering a lesser fee for service. You may be able to avoid out of pocket payments for therapy completely if you do your research ahead of time.

What are my needs?
According to Maslow, our progression up the hierarchy of human needs is essential to foster a secure sense of love and belonging. Wants and needs are separated here into different categories because people usually aren't aware that they are so fundamentally different from one another. For example, a person may want to be sexual, but what they may need is the intimacy afforded by a real emotional connection to express feelings of hurt, worry, or frustrations. Maybe they are simply lonely and their unmet need for companionship has been replaced with food. Overeating or poor nutrition can become a substitute for knuckling down and making a real effort to reach out into a healthy community or truly working a recovery plan.

In her book, *Breaking Free: A Recovery Workbook for Facing Codependence,* author Pia Mellody describes the overwhelming sense of loss and devastation that is a hallmark trait of co-dependency. Doing what is best for you may feel strange, wrong or upsetting at first.[14] For example, spending money to get your teeth fixed when family members are clamoring for the latest video game may feel counterintuitive, but it is a terrific exercise in self-care. Picking up the phone and calling a trusted friend or family member instead of eating a quart of ice cream perhaps doesn't seem as easy as simply indulging in overeating.

Communicating the need for safe expression of your pent up hurt or anger is one way to be congruent with yourself by fostering true intimacy and continuing in healthy self-preservation. Your need for a safe intimate connection is valuable and honorable. Being harmonious with yourself is a healthy response and avoids the act of abandoning your core self for the sake of the other.

Professionals have long understood the correlation between repeated abandonment of the self and the shame-bind that perpetuates further cycles of harm and despair. Those who were neglected or abused in childhood will often experience high levels of toxic shame and feelings of unworthiness as an adult. Due to the fact that they may feel "worthless," they may treat themselves as worthless and even reenact unsafe situations in their adulthood.

When faced with repeated exposures to emotional or physical harm, we may further our own destruction through the use of substances or aggressive acts of physical self-harm such as obesity or self-mutilation. We may develop illnesses like eating disorders, chronic pain disorders, or dissociative disorders that impair our ability to properly function in the world.

114

These issues are generally treatable, so if you or a loved one has symptoms similar to those described above, seeking a qualified therapist to sort them out is a step toward relief.

Meeting Your Wants Can Bring You Joy
As mentioned previously, wants are different from needs. Wants are "the essence of a heart decision that evokes pure joy."[16] For example, if you have dreamed of learning to fly, obtaining a degree in higher education, owning a dog, visiting Alaska, parachuting or traveling to a foreign country, these are all examples of wants that can delight the soul.

Some people find it useful to create a list of 50 things they want to experience before they die. Writing down a list of dreams has several purposes. This list can help you define what activities that will enhance your health and well-being or help you move forward in a life that you uniquely aspire to.

Learning to decipher your wants and needs can take you a long way in creating a better life for yourself. Martin Seligman, Ph.D., author of the book *Authentic Happiness,* discusses the million dollar question most of us would like the answer to:

What is it that makes people happy? Is it money? Fame? Marriage? Status? Does happiness depend on what country you live in or your ethnic background? Does happiness depend on what church you belong to, how many children you have, or don't have?[15]

If you have a need for security and safety like Maslow suggests, and a want for personal fulfillment, how do these ideas figure into the equation?

According to Seligman, the secret to happiness is to find your own "flow" or "calling" by utilizing what he calls your "Signature Strengths." He describes these strengths as qualities that each of us possess naturally: the intrinsic strengths that make us unique from others. The feelings of joy, zest and enthusiasm that people experience when operating from their signature strengths are a reflection of what Seligman is talking about when they say such statements as, "This is the real me."

What makes your life worth living? What is it that lights fire in your soul, gives you a chuckle, or brings passion into your existence? Are you using your signature strengths in your day-to-day experiences? How can you begin shifting your focus to create a life filled with abundance, gratitude, and authentic happiness even if you're faced with uncertainty? Start by beginning. Begin by being determined to change the way you think.

How can I rise above this situation and feel stronger?
Resiliency is the ability to rise above difficult circumstances. It can be mastered by diligently focusing on self-care one day at a time. A recognized expert in resiliency, Dr. Albert Sebiert identifies steps to build resiliency in his book, *The*

Resiliency Advantage. These steps are:

- optimize your health and well-being
- develop good problem-solving skills, learning to integrate both positive and negative thinking
- develop strong inner gatekeeper, including self-confidence, self-esteem and self-concept
- develop resiliency skills. Become a student of resiliency and learn how to build these skills
- discover your talent for serendipity. Using a surprising accident or event to lead you into your own wisdom of discovering the hidden unexpected gift or blessing[16]

Sebiert goes on to say,

...resilient people don't wait for others to rescue them, they work through their feelings, set goals, work to reach their goals, and often emerge from it with a better life than before...[17]

It's not enough to "talk the talk" without "walking the walk." This may be one of the most difficult times of your life. You would likely encourage anyone else in your situation to follow through on taking care of themselves. Why not take this advice for yourself? You can begin today by making the choice to discover yourself and find your heart's sincere desire.

Looking at the world from an upside down place may actually give you the impetus to see your circumstances from a new perspective. New perspectives have the potential for propelling you forward into positive change. You can choose to create new dreams or revisit old ones you have not yet fulfilled. You can learn to trust again with the experience of trustworthy loved ones around you. There is a whole world of other people out there who are willing to walk beside you. Are you ready to begin?

PART TWO:
For
Special
Populations

Chapter 9
What Should I Tell the Kids?

Stefanie Carnes, Ph.D., CSAT

Cindy was mortified when she learned about her husband's sexual impropriates at work. She had long suspected Gary might be having an affair with his secretary, but she always believed his explanations: their relationship was plutonic and his long work hours would result in a promotion from dean to provost at the state university. Cindy was shocked when Gary told her he was being investigated for sexual misconduct and harassment – and the allegations had been made by five different women. Moreover, he would probably lose his job. Nothing, however, prepared her for what she learned next: the investigation would be publicized by the news media because of Gary's position at the university.

Cindy and Gary had always been respected members of the community, and she took pride in that. She imagined the way people would gossip about them at church and the country club. She was wrestling with all of these concerns when it dawned on her that they would have to share this information with their twin daughters, Emma and Rachel, age 11.

Emma was a sensitive girl who was very close to her father. Rachel, while always closer to Cindy, was having a difficult time at school. Cindy felt like she was having a nervous breakdown. She couldn't imagine the impact her husband's conduct was going to have on her daughters.

Should the children be told, or should we try to "protect" them?
For many parents, determining how much information to reveal to children represents the biggest dilemma from sex addiction. In the best circumstances, the decision is made after careful discussion and planning with a clinician who has specialized training in treating sexual addiction, and possible additional experience in child development and child counseling.

Determining whether to disclose – and deciding how much to reveal – can be an agonizing decision. Parents must consider many variables, including the age and developmental maturity of the child, content of information to be shared, the child's current level of stability, and the dynamics in the family. And while it's common for clinicians to make recommendations, it's equally important for parents to remember that ultimately how much information is shared is based on the parents' knowledge of their children's personalities.

Disclosure to children is a touchy issue, and even the most seasoned clinicians may struggle when making recommendations to families. There are many types of disclosure scenarios.

Forced Disclosure: This disclosure occurs because the children will soon learn the information through a non-nurturing disclosure process.

Delayed Disclosure: This disclosure occurs when the parents jointly choose to wait to share information until the child is old enough to process the information.

Softened Disclosure: This disclosure usually involves developmentally appropriate sharing that doesn't include detailed information about the sexual behavior. Sometimes a softened disclosure is followed by a delayed disclosure. When the child is older, he or she receives more information.

Unbalanced Disclosure: This disclosure to the children comes from the partner instead of the addict, and often doesn't include the addict. It can be done in anger or with poor boundaries, and usually results in triangulation of the child.

Discovery: This disclosure happens when the child discovers the sexual acting out on his or her own. For example, the child learns of an affair or finds the pornography stash. In some cases, the child may learn this information before the co-sex addict, and in others, the parents may believe the child doesn't know when in fact she or he does.

Some paths of disclosure are healthier than others. It's essential when planning a disclosure process that the best interests of the child always remain the focus. Good reasons for disclosing to children include:

- We want to teach direct, open and honest communication in our family.
- We don't want to perpetuate family secrets.
- We want our children to know us and understand our path to recovery and health. We want to share this part of ourselves with them.
- We want to stop the transmission of addiction from generation to generation in our family by educating our children.

As with most situations that involve children, the child's needs supersede the parent's needs. During trying times it can be difficult for parents to have strong boundaries and protect their children, but this is usually what is in the children's best interest.

I think my child knows something is going on. What should I do?

My best friend saw my dad in a park with man. My parents are now separated and I have to pretend that I have no idea what the problem was. I feel so uncom-

fortable around him now! I put on a happy face when I see my dad, but private-
ly I'm grossed out!
- Jeremy, 11

If your gut is telling you that your child knows what's going on, chances are you
are probably correct. In a survey conducted by Black, Dillon and S. Carnes,
researchers found that in 67 percent of cases, the children already knew about the
sexual acting out prior to the disclosure.[1] If the parents continue to deny or hide
the problem it sends some powerful messages to the children such as:

- This is such a shameful secret I could never talk about it.
- We do not openly discuss difficult issues in this family.
- Sexual acting out is OK as long as it is kept secret in the family.

If you find yourself in this predicament, it's often helpful to uncover more information about what the child does or doesn't know. It may be useful at this point
to involve the child in therapy. The child's therapist can be instrumental in finding out what the child already knows and can work with the parent's therapist in
facilitating a family session that involves a disclosure and open communication
about the addiction.

If the parents only suspect the child knows information about the sexual acting out, they may find themselves in a difficult quandary. On the one hand, they
don't want to perpetuate shame and dishonesty through secrecy and cover-ups,
yet they don't want to disclose information to the child that he or she may not be
ready for. Parents in this situation should work with a qualified therapist in determining the best choice for them given their circumstances.

What is an appropriate age to disclose this type of information?
It's important to keep in mind that no matter the child's age, some open and honest communication can occur. The key to remember is that sharing should be
developmentally appropriate.

Alice's Story
When Alice was just out of her teens, she discovered online pornography. She
soon found herself addicted to the readily available images. She was attracted to
websites that included some romantic and sexualized chat. Her participation
would often lead to hookups with men for casual sexual encounters. She also
dated, looking for Mr. Right. When she met Dan, a corporate attorney, she
instantly fell in love with his romantic and witty personality. But even after she
married Dan, she continued to secretly surf for pornography online. After the couple had two children, Alice attempted to quit looking at porn and tried to put that
lifestyle behind her.

As a stay-at-home mom, Alice's life was full, until her children began attending school. She suddenly found herself with a lot of unstructured time during the day. She soon returned to those old websites that once offered her so much excitement. Alice began feeling increasing isolated from Dan and was stressed about her continued unemployment. Her time online escalated, and it wasn't long before she was hooking up with men she met online for casual sex.

As Alice spent more time online, she began to neglect her role as a mother and wife. She continued to grow distant from her family, and began feeling close to her online buddies. Dan became suspicious when he came across some suggestive pictures on their home computer. When confronted, Alice was initially defensive. There were fights and arguments. Ben, 7, and Tiffany, 5, were puzzled by their parents' sudden moods. Why was Daddy so angry? Why was Mommy so tense? Dan continued to pressure Alice for answers. She reluctantly admitted what she had been doing online. Alice decided to seek treatment for her sexual addiction. Once there, Alice told Dan about her sexual encounters.

Once the couple engaged in the recovery process, there was a renewed commitment to the marriage. They were both concerned about Ben and Tiffany, and they knew the children had experienced the tension between them. They wanted to openly address this tension with the children and be able to speak about their recovery and renewed commitment.

With the help of a therapist, they planned a family session with the children. Alice told the children she had lied to Daddy and caused tension in the relationship. Dan and Alice assured the children that the conflict had nothing to do with them. They also emphasized that they were committed to the marriage and the family, and were working on honesty and recovery with one another. Ben and Tiffany were relieved and could see that their parents were starting to get back to normal.

As you can see in the above example, the disclosure was "softened" because the children were at fragile ages. According to child development expert Jean Piaget, who developed stages of cognitive development for children, children have a limited capacity to understand abstract thinking around concepts such as "addiction" prior to age 12.[2] Additionally, most children have a limited understanding of sexuality prior to mid-adolescence. So the concept of "sexual addiction" is confusing to most children. Not to mention that children are typically uncomfortable discussing sexuality, especially when it refers to their parents.

Parents of older children may consider a full disclosure. A "full disclosure" would include that the parent is in recovery from sex addiction and general information about the acting out. For example, Dad is in recovery from pornography addiction or prostitution use. Ideally, children should be a minimum age of mid-adolescence before considering a full disclosure.

It's also imperative to consider many contextual variables when making this decision: maturity of the child, stress level of the child, family relationships, and other factors specific to one's family. Talking over all the extenuating variables with a good therapist can be helpful. Of course, if the child is likely to learn the information through a non-nurturing disclosure process or already knows, then full disclosure at a younger age should be considered.

Examples of Language Used in Disclosures
Softened disclosure and acknowledgement of reality:

Daddy hurt Mommy, so he's going to sleep in another room for a while.

Mommy and Daddy have been fighting because Daddy lied to Mommy. This is between Daddy and me. We love you and it has nothing to do with you.

Full disclosure if situation warrants:

I am a sex addict. I was dishonest and broke my marriage vows by hiring prostitutes. This has impacted my relationship with you in the following ways. I am in recovery and this is how I'm planning on taking care of myself.

I am a sex addict. My cybersex use has gotten out of control and has impacted my ability to work and stay involved with you and the family. I have received treatment and have a plan around this. I would like to be open with you if you have any questions about this.

My child is struggling in many areas of his life. I'm worried that learning about his father's sex addiction will put him over the edge. Should I go through with this disclosure?
Children also go through difficult times in life. It's wise for parents to assess the proper timing of the disclosure whenever possible. At-risk children should be considered a vulnerable population. The following is a list of indicators that your child may be at risk:

- drug abuse and addiction
- eating disorder
- major mental illness
- suicidal or homicidal ideation
- running away
- school truancy or other school difficulties
- behavioral or conduct problems, such as stealing or vandalism
- problems with social or peer-group functioning (although some is normal).

If your child is exhibiting these issues, you may want to delay or soften the disclosure process. Remember that many children already know about the acting out.

Sometimes if a child is struggling, they may be struggling with information about the acting out and the parents may be unaware that the child already has information. In these circumstances, discussion with a therapist to determine your course of action is warranted.

My children are young adults. I don't think they would ever find out unless I told them. Should I bother sharing this information with them?

While it may be a bit unsettling for an adult child to learn his parent is a sex addict, typically the benefits far outweigh the consequences. Famous psychologist Carl Jung once said,

The most important gift a parent can give their child is to tell them about their dark side. Telling children about your struggles helps them developmentally to have a realistic picture of what it means to be human.[3]

When a parent shares their darkest struggles, sorrows and pain with a child, it normalizes the child's darkness. The child realizes that they, too, will have dark times that they can share with others and overcome them. It also deeply enriches the intimacy between parent and child, and the child will be more likely to share his pain and struggles with the parent.

Of course, when sharing the information with an adult child, reassure him or her that you are working on your recovery, so the child doesn't worry about having to care for the parent. Many addicts in recovery want to avoid talking to their adult children, due to their shame, but the exercise in disclosure can be shame-reducing for the parent as most adult children can handle the information and still demonstrate love for the addict.

Can I share with my oldest child, but not his younger sibling?

It's important to be realistic that when siblings are close they will share information with one another. Most siblings, especially those that are close in age, have a high degree of openness and sharing, especially when it comes to information about their parents. In these circumstances, it's important to use the age of your youngest child when considering disclosure, keeping in mind that they will likely share the information. In the ideal situation, parents will determine what's appropriate to share and keep information consistent for all children. It can be distressing to children when they receive different information from different parents.

For example, if the older child is closer to the addict and the younger one is closer to the spouse and they are given different information, when the children talk it will be confusing for them. They will be hurt that they weren't told everything, or be distrustful of some of the information. If there's a large age gap between your children, you might consider disclosing to the older child.

If your older child is 16 and your younger one is eight, it's likely the 16-year-old is mature enough to not to tell the younger sibling. However, keep in mind that even young children pick up on the subtleties of communication and can be confused by non-verbal communication between an older sibling and parents in a situation such as this.

My partner and I have decided to share this information with the children. How should we do it? How can I make this process easier for them?
Keep in mind that, ultimately, it's the addict's responsibility to disclose to the children. It's a key part of the addict's recovery to take responsibility for his or her behavior and be accountable. This is the foundation of their 12-step work. Family members also need to see the addict as remorseful and accountable. This can provide the necessary healing so the family can move past the shame and pain caused by the addiction.

In an ideal world, the addict and co-addict will plan exactly what will be shared with the children. Corley and Schneider recommend the disclosure focuses on the values that were violated and the direct impact on the child.[4] For example, "I was dishonest, and as a result Mommy was upset," or "I was unavailable because of my addiction, and as a result I wasn't able to attend your baseball games." It's often helpful to spend some time and anticipate questions the children may have and how you'll respond. Below is a chart developed by Corley and Schneider that can assist you in anticipating questions children might bring up.[5]

What Kids Want to Know by Age
It's not necessary or appropriate to disclose to very young children.

> **Preschool (ages 3 to 5):** These children have often been witness to fighting or have heard that you're an addict and don't know what is happening. They may ask:
>
> - *Are you going to die or leave me?*
> - *Am I in trouble?*
> - *Do you love me?*

They need guidelines about genital touching. Too often sex addicted families get hyper-vigilant and worry about a child's normal sexual exploration and genital stimulation.

> **Early Elementary (ages 5 to 6)**
>
> - *Is this my fault?*
> - *Will something bad happen?*
> - *Who are you now?*

Upper Elementary (ages 9 to 13)

- Am I normal?
- Will I get this addiction because I have sexual feelings?
- Am I going to end up a drug addict because you are?
- What will happen to me if you get divorced?

Teen/Adult Years

- How could you do this to Mom? To the family?
- How does this specifically relate to me?
- You've ruined my life.

You can also plan disclosure in a therapeutic context with a family therapist you trust. The addict shares general information, about his or her addiction and the consequences. It's important not to share any detailed information about the sexual acting out with the child if possible. Also, it's beneficial for the addict to share his or her current plan for recovery with the children on an age-appropriate basis. This will provide hope for the children and reduce their anxieties and fears.

The spouse should take a supportive role and be genuine in terms of his or her feelings. Children will pick up on it if the spouse is not genuine. If there are feelings of anger or sadness, the spouse can share with the kids that he/she is hurt, angry or sad. Similarly, the co-addict may need to take accountability for any inappropriate anger he or she may have had in front of the child.

During the disclosure, it's crucial that the spouse doesn't berate or shame the addict in front of the children because they will have so many feelings of their own. This will be a difficult moment for the child, whether they show it or not. You need to make their feelings and ability to process the information a top priority.

Disclosure is a process, not a one-time event, and this applies even with children. Children may have additional questions over time, or as they mature you may feel it's appropriate to share more information. Keep in mind that the strength of your relationship with your child will influence his or her ability to handle this information. Consequently, continue to do fun things together and keep working on the positive aspects of your relationship.

My child is upset because he knows. What can I do to help?
There are times when upsetting information has to be shared with a child. A good example is the "forced" disclosure situation, or circumstances when the child "discovers" the acting-out behavior. The vast majority of children are going to react negatively to the disclosure experience. In the study by Black, Dillon and Carnes, 29 children were asked if they were glad they were told.[6] Of these, 20 said yes. However, the majority of respondents didn't like the process of disclosure and didn't want the information to be true.

Naturally, the more deviant the behavior, the more detailed the information shared with the child, and the more public exposure in the incident, the more distressed the child will be. For example, if the father is the principal at the child's school, was caught with child pornography, and it was in the media, this would be a complex and difficult situation for the child to handle.

Sometimes it can be helpful for children to receive some education about sexual addiction to assist them in normalizing the problem. Data demonstrates sex addiction is a common problem that is typically not discussed, and education can be helpful in reducing shame. If the spouse is involved with the 12-step community, she or he may determine if there are particular events associated with COSA or S-Anon the children may be able to attend. Consider attending a recovery-oriented lecture or meeting, or hearing someone share his or her story, depending on the child's age and the content of the lecture or meeting, can be beneficial. You should also consider therapy for the child. Children do an amazing job of covering up their concerns and pain. If they have a good therapist that they see as an ally, who can also do some occasional family work with the parents, it can do wonders.

One of the most important things parents can do is maintain a sense of stability in the family. Having the addict move in and out of the home, or switching schools will only cause more pain and disruption for the child. Giving your daughter or son permission to still spend time with and love both parents is essential. Some of the most painful situations involve the addict moving out of the home and rarely spending time with the child. For example, if Ben learns his father is a sex addict and his father moves out of the house, then Ben's mother will not let Ben's dad see him, this will only further alienate Ben from both parents. Ben will be hurt and confused by this type of behavior. Of course, if the child is at risk for sexual perpetration that may be an exception.

Giving the child reassurance and hope can make this distressing situation easier. If you feel able to genuinely and confidently reassure the child that nothing is going to change, that can be helpful. Sharing elements of recovery, special things that you and your spouse have learned in the recovery process, can also reassure the child. Introducing the child to safe, strong recovering people can also be positive.

My child was exposed directly to my partners acting out, what can I do to help her?

I don't think I would have ever become a sex addict had it not been for the discovery of my father's pornography stash when I was 8. I was so intrigued with what I saw. Whenever I was in pain, I would reach for that stash. This was the beginning of my addiction.

- Scott, 29, a recovering addict

There are many ways children can be exposed to sexual acting-out behaviors in a parent. For example, they might accidentally discover a parent's pornography collection, or they may find out about an affair. Keep in mind that children are absorbing information about sexuality at all the times during their youth. They learn from their parents, other family members, friends' families and even the media.

When they see a parent's sexual acting out it has the potential to influence the child's developing sexuality. For example, it's not uncommon for affairs to be a repeated pattern of behavior from generation to generation. The child learns affairs are acceptable in relationships after that behavior was modeled for him or her. Similarly, pornography use can also be passed down from generation to generation. Many pornography addicts report being exposed to it at a young age.

If your child has been exposed to sexual acting out, some damage control should take place. It's best to keep from shaming the child or giving negative or puritanical messages. Rather, simply validate that it's normal to be sexually curious at their age and that sexuality is a healthy part of life. An open discussion about intimacy and healthy sexuality is helpful in these circumstances. If the sexual acting out had overtones of objectifying or degrading one partner, then a discussion of healthy sexuality as mutual and respectful should take place.

Occasionally, children will worry if they, too, are going to become a sex addict. This is especially true for boys experiencing raging hormones. An open dialogue normalizing these feelings can reduce anxiety.

In the worst situations, the child may have been molested or experienced incest as part of the sexual acting out. Clearly treatment would be critical for these children. Keep in mind that some children who have been sexually abused do not develop long-term problems, so it's important not to pathologize the child under these circumstances, while still trying to listen, validate and understand the child's experience.

My partner and I cannot agree on whether to disclose. What should I do?
Nothing could describe the pain Mary experienced when she discovered Roger's sex addiction. Not only had he been involved with prostitutes, but he had engaged in several affairs, the last one was with one of her closest friends. She was devastated. She could not bear to talk with him, sit across the table from him, or even look at him. Plus, they had two children together, Jonathon, 9, and Rebecca, 11.

Mary believed the kids needed to know the truth about their father's sexual acting out. Roger, on the other hand, thought it was none of their business. Jonathon and Rebecca had always been close to their dad, so when Mary shared everything with them about Roger's sexual acing out it was quite a shock.

When Roger denied Mary's accusations, Jonathon and Rebecca were hurt and confused. They felt sorry for their mom and they felt like they had to choose sides. Extended family was also dragged into the conflict. Everyone in the family suffered, especially Jonathon and Rebecca.

As seen in this case example, when parents can't agree on a course of action, it's usually the children who suffer the most. Unfortunately, couples struggling with sex addiction are often in so much intense pain, it's hard for the needs of the child to be placed above the needs of the parents. If the couple is heading for a divorce, sometimes separation counseling can be helpful. This type of therapy is not geared toward reconciliation or emotional processing of feelings. Rather, it focuses on issues relating to ongoing contact such as negotiating co-parenting issues and boundaries. This may be a helpful venue for discussing how to share information about the children. Again, remember that the child's needs supersede your needs and in these situations, and it's usually in the child's best interest to work toward an agreement on this issue.

In summary, there are many factors to consider that can make this an easier process for your children. The list below highlights some of the key characteristics that can make this process healthier.

Characteristics of Healthy Disclosure[7]

- Disclosure is facilitated by a therapist.
- Both parents are present and participatory.
- Both parents are in agreement to disclose to the children.
- Both parents articulate why this is important and of value to the child.
- Both parents have strategized and agreed upon what is and is not disclosed.
- Parents speak for themselves. The addict and co-addict each speak about their own behavior.
- The addict speaks in generalities about addictive behavior, not specific details.
- Parents display signs of recovery.
- Neither parent takes the role of victim.
- The child is not used as a confidant.
- Parents are clear that it is not the child's responsibility to fix or take care of them. It's easy for the child to become caught in a triangle, choosing sides, then reacting on behalf of the person or one who is perceived to be the victim parent.
- Open dialogue and discussion with a clinician is demonstrated.
- Set the tone for the child to know he or she can discuss it with you as they need to or as you believe it is appropriate. To say or imply, "We'll talk about this today and never again" reinforces the shame of disclosure and the behavior. Disclosure is not a one-time process.

Educating your children about sex addiction can be one of the most important lessons you can teach. Empowering them with information so they don't repeat the mistakes you've made can save them a lot of pain. Conversely, if they do wander down the same path in the future, your recovery can serve as a source of hope for them and give them the power to stop the cycle of sex addiction in their family.

Chapter 10
Is My Partner a Pedophile?

Barbara Levinson, Ph.D., CSAT

Nearly every day you hear or read something about pedophiles, predators, child molesters or the abduction of children. We are so aware of the issue that we have become a society that sees the boogeyman around every corner. It is important to be knowledgeable about these issues and be sensitive to the needs of our children and keep them safe. However, for people with partners who are sex addicts with behaviors that have included an interest in children, the trauma can be almost too much to bear. Finding out your partner has secret sexual behaviors is enough of a shock and trauma. Add to that the realization that their conduct also includes thoughts, behaviors or fantasies about minors is frightening, abhorrent, mind-boggling, confusing and disgusting. Hopefully this chapter will help clarify some of your questions.

Susie's Story
Susie was angry and frantic. A recent pap test came back positive for the Human Papillomavirus (genital warts), an increasingly common STD, and carcinoma cells. She was confused and had no idea how this could have happened. Although her gynecologist explained she may have contracted the STD long ago and it didn't manifest until recently, Susie was mortified. Her doctor also told her she would need to tell her husband Stan, who had likely also contracted the disease.

Susie had sexual partners before marrying, but had always used protection. Stan had told her he had not been very sexually active while single, and she believed him because he had inhibited attitudes and behaviors about sex.

The couple had been married seven years and had no children together. Susie, however, had a 10-year-old daughter from a previous marriage. Although their sexual relationship was good in the beginning, over the years the couple struggled to keep up an active sex life due to Stan's work obligations. When Susie did suggest sex, Stan would often be uninterested. Susie began to wonder if her desire was abnormal.

Five years into their marriage, Susie's daughter went to live with her father who resided in another state. Once she and Stan were living alone, Susie believed their sex life would become more spontaneous. Instead, the couple had even less sex. Prior to her visit to the gynecologist, the couple had only had sex once in two months. Susie was petrified that Stan would think she contracted the STD through an affair. But she also secretly wondered about Stan's lack of interest in sex. And she had a "gut feeling" that something was odd about the way Stan stared at younger women and made sexual comments such as, "They shouldn't dress like that. They're just asking for it."

He spent hours on the computer, and there were times she couldn't reach him at work, which she also thought was suspicious. She had mentioned these behaviors over the years, and when he got angry, she dropped the subject. Her suspicions only increased after she discovered an open web page that contained pictures of partially dressed teenage models. When she confronted Stan about it, he became angry. She called him a pervert and told him she no longer trusted him.

Despite his denials, Susie couldn't let it go. She became a detective, looking for evidence that Stan was cheating on her. She was soon convinced that not only had Stan had sex with prostitutes, but that he was also interested in viewing images of underage girls. She wondered, *Is my husband a pedophile?*

What is pedophilia?

Pedophilia is defined as a persistent sexual interest in prepubescent children.[1] Clinicians rely on several different sources when considering the diagnosis of pedophilia, including self-report, a history of sexual behavior involving children and psycho-physiological assessments. All of these sources have limitations, and individuals will tend to deny pedophilic interests for fear of being reported and getting caught up in the legal system.

Having interests, thoughts or fantasies is different than acting them out. An individual's history of past sexual offenses in terms of the number, age, gender and relatedness of child victims is informative, but only approximate the person's interest because it is limited to known victims.[2] For a clinical diagnosis of pedophilia, a person will have had:

A) recurrent, intense, sexually arousing fantasies, sexual urges or behaviors involving sexual activity with a prepubescent child or children for a period of at least 6 months. Moreover, the person has acted out on these sexual urges; or

B) The sexual urges or fantasies cause marked distress or interpersonal difficulty. The person is at least 16 years old and at least 5 years older than the child or children.[3]

This diagnosis suggests that the person must suffer internal conflict or social consequences. Only a small percentage of sex offenders meet these criteria for pedophilia.

A pedophile often starts offending at an early age and can have a large number of victims that are not family related. The pedophile is usually driven to offend and has actual sexual contact with victims. All too often, the term pedophile is used incorrectly and is misunderstood. Most of the time, the interest of the sex addict's focus is on much older children who are past puberty and have sexual characteristics that are more developed.

Pedophiles are usually obsessed with children and they can behave in addictive ways. They usually have a belief system that could support a predatory lifestyle. There are also subtypes of pedophilia of the diagnosis to further complicate the issue. These are:

- fixated pedophiles who identify with children and seek sexual relationships with them
- regressed pedophiles who are passively aroused by children

Pedophiles can have a rigid set of double standards and also can be very religious.[4] Some studies report there are a high number of pedophiles that have also been victims of childhood sexual abuse. However, this is not always the case. True pedophiles are simply fascinated with children. They can describe children in very idealistic terms. They're often interested in childlike activities, rather than adult activities, and frequently continue to have the hobbies they had in childhood. That doesn't mean anyone who collects toys or comic books is a pedophile. Collecting behavior can be perfectly normal and appropriate.

Pedophiles will frequently make friends with single parents, or work or volunteer in youth-related activities or professional positions that have contact with children. Again, that doesn't mean every teacher, youth minister or pediatrician is a pedophile. A pedophile usually prefers children who are close to puberty, but others may target younger children. It should be noted if the pedophile was abused as a child, he or she will often target children who are the age that the pedophile was at the time of the abuse.

For the most part, sex addicts are distinguishable from sex offenders, who are also distinguishable from the true pedophile, although there may be some overlap in these groups. Sex offender is a legal term and should only be used for persons who have been adjudicated and involved in the legal system.

If your partner looks or objectifies teenagers, comments on how "hot" they are, or you find some images on a computer, don't panic. It doesn't mean he or she is a pedophile. Sex addicts often explore sexual avenues they may never have thought of before the Internet. Because all kinds of information, images and videos are readily available, the addict can get easily aroused or interested in behaviors that he or she may never thought of before.

There is, however, a difference between curiosity and preferential interest. Finding information about particular websites your partner has visited or downloaded images, although concerning and possibly illegal, again doesn't mean your partner is a pedophile. A careful assessment must be done to understand the behaviors. A pedophile will typically have a large collection of pornography, if they use the computer to gather information and view pictures, and will categorize the images in separate folders. Often the collection will contain particular images or a series of images of particular children.

There are other red flags that can distinguish a true pedophile. For example, the type of movies or videos they buy or rent, souvenirs or the home's décor.

Binoculars by a window facing a school, playground or park can also be indicators. Fixated pedophiles can generate their own "erotic" materials from relatively innocuous sources, such as TV advertisements, clothing catalogues featuring children modeling underwear, and other available sources.[5]

Can pedophiles be cured?

There's much talk in the media about how all pedophiles are dangerous predators with a poor prognosis. In reality, most pedophiles can be treated and managed. Treatment of pedophilia is difficult, but not impossible. But more than likely, your partner is not a pedophile. However, that doesn't mean he or she doesn't have an interest or fantasies about teenagers or "adult-looking children" or "child-like adults."

If you believe your partner is a pedophile, it's essential to start with a comprehensive evaluation or assessment. There are many variables that would direct the course of treatment. Are they regressed or fixated? Are they a pedophile, an incest perpetrator, a child molester, or someone who has had fantasies but never acted on them? The diagnosis may be further complicated if he or she has a personality disorder, developmental problems, or a significant mental illness. Many partners in your situation find tremendous relief when they seek the council of a qualified professional that can assist them in understanding the details of their situations.

Sex Offender or Sex Addict

Sex offender is a legal term that refers to someone who has already committed a crime and has been adjudicated in the legal system. Sex offenders are usually referred to clinicians through the legal system or by attorneys, probation or parole officers. Providers of treatment for sex offenders must have specialized training. In some states, practitioners must be licensed to treat sex offenders in addition to their other licenses. Other states have only certification or registration requirements for treatment providers. Some states have no special training requirements, although this is becoming rare.

The treatment of sex offenders requires a very structured program geared toward group therapy. It's usually a cognitive behavioral and psycho-educational approach, and most often the offender uses a workbook designed specifically for the treatment of sex offenders. In most states there are strict requirements about treatment guidelines and strategies. Homework assignments are almost always given, and the offender must adhere to a strict "treatment contract" that outlines what they can and cannot do. The guidelines are usually prohibitive, and the treatment provider almost always works in conjunction with probation or parole.

The laws governing sex offenders are often prohibitive and outline where they can live and work. There are restrictions regarding contact with children, both theirs and others, and what activities in which they can be involved. The main goals of a sex offender treatment program are:

- no more victims
- community safety
- for the offender to have a successful and happy life

There are, however, some similarities and differences between sex offenders and sex addicts. Not all sex offenders are sex addicts and not all sex addicts are sex offenders. Just because your partner is an addict, it doesn't mean he or she has overtly committed a sexual offense, such as rape or child abuse. Similarities:

- Both sexual compulsives and sex offenders report a loss of control and life consequences.
- They both often come from rigid and disengaged families.
- There is usually a history of addiction in the family and trauma in their childhood, with a high percentage of emotional abuse.
- They may have multiple addictions.
- They typically have high stress levels.
- Use of pornography is present.
- There is also a high use of thinking errors (cognitive distortions), such as rationalization, excuses, blaming, "poor me," victim stance, denial, justification, lying, anger, keeping score and sense of entitlement.
- There is also a history of sexual difficulties.

Sexual offenders are more likely to have the following:

- criminal lifestyle history
- criminogenic thinking
- distrust of authority
- history of violence
- past sexual aggression
- escalation of violence
- overall pattern of assaults

Sex offenders have victims, not only the people they offend against, but their victims' families, friends and loved ones. The offender also abuses people who care for them since they are affected by the crimes they commit. Sex addicts often don't believe they have victimized anyone, which perpetuates their behaviors. The person who looks at child pornography may believe it doesn't hurt anyone; however, the children in those images are living humans who have been victimized.

The partner who finds out that attraction or overt sexual behaviors have been happening without his or her knowledge is deeply hurt. Both sex addicts and sex offenders have victims. A major difference is the sex offender has been accused of or did something that was illegal or criminal.

Will my partner go to jail?
If a crime has been committed, the possibility exists that your partner will be caught up in the legal system. This may be how you became aware of your partner's secret life. Here are some examples:

- A man caught with 20,000 images of child pornography on his computer was sentenced to five years in prison.
- A man who engaged in an online sexual chat with minors was charged with enticement of a minor for sexual purposes and sentenced to three to five years in a federal prison.
- A man caught masturbating in his car was charged with indecent exposure and received a year of probation.
- A man charged with two counts of indecency with a child received six years probation.
- A woman who had sex with her 16-year-old son's friend was sentenced to a lengthy jail term.

All of these people were sex addicts who became sex offenders but were not pedophiles.

I think I found child pornography on my husband's computer! How can I be sure? What should I do?

The legal definition of child porn is:
Any person who knowingly mails, transports, ships, receives, distributes, reproduces, sells, or possesses any book, magazine, periodical, film, videotape, computer disc, or any other material that contains an image of child pornography that has been mailed, shipped, or transported by any means, including the computer....Shall be fined ...or imprisoned not more than 10 years, or both, but if such person has a prior conviction...such person shall be fined under this title and imprisoned for not less than 10 years or more than 20 years.[6]

If your partner has had sexual contact with a minor, consenting or not, he or she can and most probably will go to jail or be given probation, depending on the state, risk level and the circumstances of the crime.

The legal definition of child pornography may not capture all the material that an adult with a sexual interest in children may consider arousing. There are several categories of pictures that may be sexualized by an adult with an interest in children. For example, non-erotic and non-sexualized pictures of children in their underwear or swimming suits from commercial or private sources in which the context and organization by the collector indicates inappropriateness.[7] There may be pictures of children naked or semi-naked in nudist settings. Another form is pictures of children in play areas or other environments showing their underwear or varied degrees of nakedness. These may not fall under the legal definition of child pornography but may be indicative of an interest in children. The legal definition of child pornography has some different phrases in it that often lead to confusion and have been subject to some scrutiny.

As it stands, "child pornography" means any visual depiction, including any photograph, film, video, picture, or computer or computer-generated image or picture, whether made or produced by electronic, mechanical, or other means of sexually explicit conduct where:

A) the production of such visual depiction involves the use of a minor engaging in sexually explicit conduct;

B) such visual depiction is a digital image, computer image, or computer-generated image that is, or is indistinguishable from, that of a minor engaging in sexually explicit conduct; or

C) such visual depiction has been created, adapted, or modified to appear that an identifiable minor is engaging sexually explicit conduct.

"Sexually Explicit Conduct" in the context of child pornography means:

A) graphic sexual intercourse, including genital-genital, oral-genital, anal-genital, or oral-anal, whether between persons of the same or opposite sex or lascivious simulated sexual intercourse where the genitals, breast or pubic area of any person is exhibited;

B) graphic or lascivious bestiality, masturbation, or sadistic or masochistic abuse; or

C) graphic or simulated lascivious exhibition of the genitals or pubic area of any person.[8]

More investigation on the sexual interest of children should be done. The current research doesn't take into account all the new technologies that have developed.[9] The lack of research into this important area can hamper our ability to help individuals and their families, and to distinguish between levels of risk.

The Internet Trap

A high percentage of partners first find hard evidence of questionable sexual behavior on their partners' computers. You may have also stumbled across other information, such as sexual chats involving young children, instant messaging, newsgroups, bulletin boards or websites aimed at children. Taylor and Quale suggest the following four markers for serious online behavior.[10]

- possessing new or recent images or images associated with text
- participating in an online community of offenders
- trading of images
- cataloguing of images

There are also other types of "images" you may become aware of, such as the so-called model sites that have original photographs of scantily clad children. Or perhaps you have evidence of your partner looking at clothing catalogues or family nudist sites. Some of the images in online advertisements show toddlers wearing tight underwear or slightly older children wearing makeup and posing with feather boas.[11]

More than 200 of these sites have been found by the *New York Times* through online advertising aimed at pedophiles. Most legitimate modeling sites are password-protected with access only granted to companies and casting agencies after a background check. The *New York Times* article exposed another site that claimed to be a company that helped children start modeling careers. There is, however, no identifying information on this company, and it was linked to as many as six other sites featuring little girls.

If you have discovered child pornography on your computer, it's possible that your partner may have opened up a site without knowledge of what was there. There are tricks that pornographers play in the recruitment of new customers. Aggressive pornographers are implementing new strategies in marketing and technology in order to push pornography to users. Below is a list of methods and a brief description of each

Porn Napping: The purchase of experienced domain names. They then redirect the user to their own sites.

Cyber Squatting: Purchase legal domain names and put explicit pornography on the site.

Doorway Scams: Pornographers have figured out how to use search engines to get their names high on the search engine list when someone could be searching for perfectly legitimate information.

Misspelling: Pornographers may take domain names of legitimate sites and use the most common misspellings to get the user to their websites.

Advertising: Creative fake system-error messages you believe you have to click, but in reality are clicking on a link to the pornographer's front door.

Entrapment: If you have fallen prey to any of the above scams depending on what was done at the porn site, whether an unintentional or intentional visit, a whole host of problems can be incurred.[12]

What if there is no indication of any computer usage or pornography, but there is a suspicion of interest in children, verbal comments, objectifications like staring or looking at children, a history of sexual abuse of a child, exposure of genitals, past involvement in the criminal justice system, or admission of incest as a young child? Once again, this doesn't necessarily indicate pedophilia. These behaviors can be indicative of other problems and should be evaluated by a trained therapist.

If you suspect any inappropriate behavior with children living in the house, get immediate help and do everything you can to keep the children safe. Contact the local authorities or a 24-hour child abuse hotline to report suspected child abuse. If you're not sure what to do, get in touch with a professional who can immediately assist you.

Other common scenarios include interest in younger children and teenagers, sexualization of teenage girls and boys, and grooming activities that are often used to entice these vulnerable adolescents into consenting to sexual behavior because they "are in love," or see it as an escape for them. Usually a power differential is a significant part of that relationship.

I'm so embarrassed. How do I get help?

Most partners are embarrassed, feel shame, and will not tell anyone. They may even want to protect their partners. There are stories in the media about people being caught in sting operations, going to jail, being beaten up, being ostracized and unable to live in certain areas, losing their jobs or worse. Of course, you want to protect your family, your loved ones, your status, and there doesn't seem to be anywhere to turn or anyone to turn to.

You sometimes wish you could just make it all go away. Maybe you've done that before only to have the problem resurface. You're scared, feel guilty, think the worst, and wonder if you will be held culpable for not reporting this behavior or seeking help. You can't tell your neighbors, the police, your family or even your best friend. You don't know who to trust.

After the initial shock, confrontation, the guilt and shame, you might feel angry, furious, enraged, revengeful, depressed, hopeless, worthless and traumatized. People may tell you that you seem different or suspicious, and you may go into rages or withdrawal, or simply act crazy. You're not crazy, but you do need help. This cannot be dealt with on your own.

No matter how much your partner begs, pleads, threatens or promises to change, you must tell a professional. It's important to know that if you tell a therapist your partner is viewing child pornography, the therapist is not a mandated reporter in that situation. The therapist is still required by law to maintain your confidentiality. This is not the case, however, if you partner is manufacturing child pornography. Creating child pornography is reportable and your therapist will be required to contact the appropriate authorities.

If you feel that by telling someone you will be in danger, make sure you are safe before you take action. There are organizations that can help you find safety for you and your children. There's a list of resources in this book that can guide you in the right direction.

The Decision to Stay or Leave

Diane's Story

When Diane met her future husband, she instantly fell in love. Jack had been looking for the "love of his life." But after being married for only six months, the couple was asked to leave their apartment complex because someone reported that Jack had been exposing himself to young children. Diane couldn't believe it.

This could not possibly be the quiet, gentle man she knew and loved. Jack was arrested, given probation and admitted into a treatment program for sex offenders.

Over the next year, Diane tried to understand and come to terms with Jack's behavior. What unfolded was devastating for her. While in treatment, she discovered Jack had been molested as a child and had been exposing himself to children since he was a young teenager. Jack's past revealed a significant interest in young children, and as a teenager he had been predatory in nature. His compulsivity extended itself to other forms of sexual behaviors, such as pornography, erotica and collecting children's movies.

As time went on, the couple faced many hard choices. Although Diane remained married to Jack, she struggled with the decision. She felt like there was little support for her in group therapy since she felt different than most of the other women whose husbands had not committed a sexual offense. Jack wanted to develop a healthy sexuality and realized that his interests may always be there, but he could manage his behaviors. After soul-searching therapy, Diane was able to set boundaries for herself and was clear about her expectations in the marriage. The couple decided they would never have children, and Jack continued treatment and group therapy. Diane also continued psychotherapy. They both knew what the possibilities for the future may hold if Jack did not maintain his sobriety.

As part of his probation, Jack submitted to polygraph tests. During a test, it showed deception. Jack had violated his probation by looking at child pornography. He was sent to prison for five years for violating his probation. When he left prison, he returned to treatment and Diane took him back.

But shortly after his release, Jack began visiting massage parlors and prostitutes, and viewing catalogues and pornography online at work. Although he had no hands-on contact with children, he was deceitful and violated the treatment contract established in group therapy. He had engaged in high-risk sexual behaviors and put himself and his wife in dangerous situations. Diane asked Jack to move out and is now deciding whether to stay in the marriage or divorce. Jack continues to work on his deviant arousal patterns and his sexually compulsive behaviors.

Each person must make their own decision about what to do about their partners' addiction. There is no right or wrong. You will hear others say, "I could never stay if my partner did....." No one actually knows what they will do in any particular situation. Sometimes you find the courage you never thought you had.

Hopefully, what you are reading in this chapter will help guide you in making whatever decisions you need to make. The best advice is don't make any impulsive decisions and always ask for help. Immediate steps should be taken, however, if someone is in danger.

The Arousal Template

As a child matures, the arousal template is formed.[13] Early childhood experiences, family messages, influence from peers, the media, religious teachings, sexual experiences, and exposure to sexual stimuli, as well as a variety of other factors go into an internal process called sexual arousal. Traumatic experiences, such as early abuse, can also have a tremendous impact on someone's arousal template. Arousal is a physical phenomenon, however, it's influenced by our thoughts, feelings and beliefs we have about ourselves and the world around us.[14] Here are some examples of how an arousal template takes shape in childhood or early adolescence.

Nancy, 43, came into therapy because she was only able to have an orgasm while masturbating with the recurrent fantasy involving a teenage girl seducing an older man. It was apparent that this fantasy had been developed to give her some sense of control over a situation from her childhood where she had felt powerless.

John had grown up in a sexually repressive environment and didn't receive the affection and nurturing a child requires. He can recall soothing himself through genital touching while still in diapers. As John grew, when he was unable to deal with the stresses of life, he experimented with wearing diapers in order to access those old feelings of self-soothing. His use of diapers during masturbation quickly evolved into compulsive use, and he was unable to engage in sex with a partner.

Charlie came into therapy because he realized that his interest in teenage girls was inappropriate, and he was in a position where he had access to them. He realized that if he couldn't get his urges under control, he would have to leave his job. When exploring Charles's background, it became evident that he had been sexualized by a female babysitter, and his attraction to teenage girls didn't change as he grew older. There were other factors that also related to his fixation, such as feeling inadequate as a teenage boy, low self-esteem, growing up in a house with an alcoholic father and a mother who was codependent.

He became fixated on young girls who he could manipulate and would encourage their "admiration" of him. He was married with his own children. Over the years, Charlie explored his arousal template, but had not acted out with any teenagers. Charlie admitted there could have been acting out, but his use of his recovery tools and open and honest communication with his wife helped to avert any damaging behavior.

An arousal template can already be discerned between the ages of five and eight years; hence, events early in life can have a profound impact on the emergent sexual self.[14] Originally, most therapists believed the template was formed in early childhood. But now many acknowledge that the Internet has had a profound ability to expand arousal templates. Old arousal templates can be changed or supplemented. In areas that are illegal or unhealthy, the Internet makes it possible for people to reinforce that undesirable behavior and strengthen an unhealthy arousal template. [15]

The hypnotic affect of the Internet, along with the vast array of sexual information available can become a powerful tool for getting us involved in a world we never knew existed. Many people report feeling as though they are in a trance until somehow by chance or accident, they are abruptly pulled back to reality. Once cognitive awareness returns, they are dismayed by the fantasies, thoughts or behaviors they engaged in, things they never imagined they would participate in. Anything can become part of an arousal template. Sometimes the unlikely paring of two things can form an arousal template. For example:

Cheryl's sleep was often interrupted by her parent's fighting. They would scream and curse at each other. In order to soothe herself, she would masturbate. As an adult, she realized it was only when her partner would use profanity that she was able to reach orgasm. Arousal and profanity had become linked together.

Objects, situations and scenarios can become sexualized. Even anger can become sexualized. Our sexuality is comprised of many things and, hopefully, can grow in a healthy way. When we are affected by our environment and experiences, our sexuality can be influenced and be shameful for us. A healthy understanding of ourselves, values and beliefs will open up a whole world where we can enjoy our bodies, our sexual uniqueness, our fantasies and have sexual and love experiences that will become part of our arousal template.

What do I tell my children, neighbors, family and friends?

This is probably the hardest of all: *Who can you really tell and who will understand?* First, it's not your job to tell anyone. It's the addict's responsibility to tell the people in his life about what has happened. In a perfect world, your partner will not be in denial, will go for help, and understand how this addiction has affected others. However, we don't live in a perfect world and there are many occasions when that doesn't happen. You have to decide where to get support.

The people you tell today may be the very people who will judge you if you decide to stay or even leave the addict. The addict may even ask you to not tell anyone. Sometimes the anger is so overwhelming, you'll want to tell anyone who will listen. But once recovery begins, you may regret sharing such explicit information with others. Keeping all this in and handling it by yourself is also not the answer. If your partner does get into treatment, then the two of you can deal with these questions within the framework of the therapeutic process. If you're struggling with the questions raised in this chapter, be assured that you're not alone. Unfortunately for many people, the pain and confusion you're experiencing now is becoming more common.

Remember, you need a lot of support during this time. *Reach* out for resources in your community. *Seek out* others who have been through what you're going through. *Explore* local support groups. *Find* a qualified therapist. Addiction happens in secrecy, recovery happens in community. Shame is reduced by sharing your stories. Be thoughtful and kind to yourself. Get help and support. You do not have to do this alone.

Chapter 11
Is Sexual Addiction and Spousal Betrayal Different in Gay Men?

Robert Weiss, LCSW, CSAT

It was like he took a knife and slashed my soul. Everything I believed about love, relationships and our future together got twisted up into a frazzled mess that I am still trying to untangle.

> *- Seth, a 34-year-old gay man, after learning that his partner of eight years had been visiting male prostitutes throughout their relationship.*

The inevitable hurt, anger and disorientation that occurs when relationship trust is betrayed transcends sexual orientation. Spousal duplicity unleashes a cascade of powerful emotions. These emotions are equally intense for people who are heterosexual, bi-sexual, homosexual or something in between.

When a committed partner's faith in his or her spouse turns out to have been misplaced and that trust is broken, we all end up in the same place. Fear, remorse, rage, numbness, longing and despair are basic elements of grief that are simply human, no matter the gender of our partner. And while it's useful to be aware of how the significant cultural differences between heterosexuals and homosexuals affect sex and relationships, it's more important to acknowledge feelings are feelings, loss is loss, and broken hearts aren't exclusive to a particular race, gender or sexual orientation.

While this chapter will help illuminate the differing ways spousal betrayal through sexual addiction can be viewed from a gay-male context, it's not intended to provide the sex addict with new ways to justify his sexual acting out under the guise of a gay identity. For clarity, this chapter will first discuss accepted sexual and relational practices within the gay subculture.

How is sex addiction different in gay men?

Approximately 8 to 10 percent of all gay men today have a sexual addiction problem, though this figure may seem low in relationship to the amount of sexual activity readily witnessed in most gay-urban environments and in the gay media.[1] Even those who isolate themselves or rigidly compartmentalize their personal and sex lives still see a densely populated sex culture when entering the larger gay arena of gay online life, bars, street festivals and the gay ghetto. And though many urban gay men today have a greater array of social and recreational options than ever before, such as volunteer and recreational groups, dating and social clubs, professional networking and spiritual organizations, many continue to tie their social lives to environments that either reinforce the use of alcohol and drugs, or the search for sex and romance.

The most well-known and profitable private local businesses in Western gay culture are bars, gyms, bathhouses, online porn sites and sex clubs. Gay publications and Internet venues prosper with dollars earned through advertising focused on working out and diet, sexual massage, prostitution, porn, casual hookups and personals. Thus, the gay man's attention is yanked toward self-pleasuring and distraction. At the same time, he's told that he will find love only through achieving physical perfection in gyms, tanning and cosmetic surgery. The circuit party, Internet chat, sex club, bar, gym and dance club scenes, which can be vital, meaningful reflections of the gay experience for some, also have a dark side, presenting those with restricted emotional resources and limited intimacy skills with a lifestyle which they may be ill equipped to handle.

Gay male sex addicts are not compulsively sexual because they are gay; the impulsive and compulsive sexuality stems from each individual's psychological issues and biological predisposition to addiction. These are exactly the same set of symptoms presented by heterosexual sex addicts. Unfortunately for gay sex addicts and even more so for their partners, the addict's destructive sexual behavior takes place against the cultural background of dramatically greater sexual freedoms than his heterosexual counterpart. The urban gay man is in some ways a prisoner of his freedom. He has fewer opportunities for self-examination and little support for behavior change should his sexual behaviors become obsessive.

Likewise, his partner will find little support or validation in the gay world for the hurt and confusion of being betrayed. Ever vigilant to avoid reinforcing the larger society's image that being gay means being troubled, the public face of gay culture is cautious about pathologizing gay sexuality in any form. Consequently, some gay men and gay media will tolerate and even celebrate sexual practices that are clearly harmful (barebacking being one clear example).

All Gay Men Are Not Equal

There exists vast generational differences among gay men in their concepts and values surrounding intimacy and monogamy. Pre-Baby Boomer men, who grew up in an era when homosexuality was considered a disease and homosexual behavior a prosecutable legal offense, learned to live their personal lives behind closed doors. Men in this period placed a high value on discretion and secrecy, giving these men few chances for healthy partnering. Baby Boomers, who achieved manhood during the wide-open sexual mores of the late 1960s through early 1980s, came to embrace their sexual freedoms as a banner of pride to be openly celebrated.

Yet what followed, the Sex = Death period of HIV/AIDS of the early 1980s through the end of the Twentieth Century, had a profound dampening affect on sexual and relational enthusiasm. Many thousands who might have matured into gay relationship mentors and role models died before age 35. Younger Gen-X and Gen-Y gay men came into their sexual prime during a period of much greater public acceptance and legitimacy of being gay. They have also been surrounded by a culture of "post AIDS" sexual conservatism and have demonstrated less of a need to "be different." They have more interest in long-term committed relationships and raising a family than previous gay generations of men.

Once devalued by gay culture as an attempt to "mimic" heterosexual relationships, gays are increasingly engaging in monogamous coupling, often including the ceremonial acknowledgements of marriage, adopting children, and living a more traditional lifestyle. At the same time, these men, along with the larger heterosexual culture, are faced with the evolving sexual and relational challenges presented by the Internet. Overall, as gay men have moved from being rejected by the larger culture, to grudging cultural acceptance, to helping to define it (in media, business, fashion, design, music), they have embraced more traditional heterosexual relationship models, yet they have retained openness to sexual role and relationship experimentation.

Although the feelings generated by a betrayal of relationship fidelity are similar for all who expect a spouse to be faithful, an unspoken expectation of fidelity is for many gay men a less closely held value than that of their heterosexual counterparts. Lesbian women, who typically have higher expectations of fidelity, rarely if ever present in sexual addiction treatment, even though there are likely many lesbians having problems with compulsive sexuality. These women are more likely to overtly experience the kinds of consequences that would lead them to seek help due to their relationship problems.

Broadly speaking, gay-male culture places less emphasis on monogamy and fidelity than straight culture does, and offers more extensive and accepted opportunities for men to have casual anonymous sex. Many gay men comfortably view sex as a form of play or recreation – with sexuality or even romance not always assumed to be the defining factor or "glue" that holds a couple together. It's against this sometimes confusing background that gay sex addicts and their partners attempt to resolve the turmoil of their broken promises and turbulent emotions and attempt to get help.

Sexual norms in gay culture tend to be different and generally more permissive, tolerant of diversity, and open. As a partner you can't characterize or recognize sex addiction or compulsivity in your spouse based solely on the behaviors he engages or exhibits. While it may be easier to detect sexual addiction in a married, heterosexual man with three kids who secretly sneaks off to the strip club or adult bookstore, it's more difficult to assess addiction or compulsivity in a gay man based on the nature of his behavior. For example, having an Internet profile for hookups, wanting to experiment with a three-way, or going to a bathhouse doesn't necessarily mean your partner is a sex addict – even if you don't agree with or approve of those activities. Here is a list of indicators that your partner may have a problem.

These following factors can be more indicative of a sexual addiction problem than where, how or when he chooses to be sexual:

- If he lies to you about sex or keeps secrets about his sexual activities from you.
- He breaks promises or agreements made between the two of you about his sexual behavior.
- One or both of you have experienced specific consequences due to his sexual behavior, like arrest, disease, job loss, public embarrassment.
- Sex – in whatever form it takes for him – is or has become his primary recreational activity, superseding time with friends, time with you, hobbies or other social activities.
- His sexual behavior is escalating, either in the amount of time he spends doing it or the intensity of the behavior he is involved with or both.
- He has made repeated attempts to stop or reduce his involvement in some sexual behavior, only to return to it later despite those problems.

If the themes described above of lying, secrecy, escalation, consequences and loss of control are the primary concerns you have about your partner, then it is very likely he has a sexual addiction problem, whether or not he acknowledges it.

How is my struggle different as a gay partner?
While the recovering sex addict has much healing work to do to become sexually sober, including cleaning up the consequences of his sexual acting out and negotiating his newly experienced emotional life, his committed spouse has even more challenging tasks ahead. Whereas the sex addict has known about his sexual behaviors all along, partners are often blindsided by the revelation of previously hidden sexual activity or the degree of activities that were occurring. Partners suffer from the fallout of the consequences of the addicts' sexual and romantic exploits and, in a broader sense, from this new, unwelcome problem in their lives, one not of their own making.

Often faced with a history of lies and betrayal by the person in whom they had placed the most trust, spouses can find themselves mentally reviewing and questioning the entire experience of their relationships, looking back to figure out what they missed, what went wrong. For those who had believed they had a monogamous relationship, the revelation of betrayal on a large scale causes questioning of what, if anything, is true about their coupleship. Spouses can have a lot of confusion about how to proceed without trust.

Mark's Story
Mark, who had been fighting to maintain his own self-respect and dignity after discovering hundreds of sexual chats, e-mails and sex-date plans on his significant other's computer, didn't expect support from his gay friends or family. He didn't talk to anyone except a therapist about what he was going through.

I didn't think people would understand how I felt so I didn't bother reaching out. My friends are always talking about everyone they have sex with and how gay guys have sex with everybody they know anyway, so how can I expect them to support me? My lover cheated – "So what?" Honestly, it has been hard enough not to keep blaming myself for thinking that my relationship would somehow be different. And since my family has never supported my being gay, I knew they wouldn't be there for me in a situation like this. I felt like it was better to just deal with it alone. Whose shoulder was I supposed to cry on? I grew up Catholic. It's not like I was going to get help from my local priest.

A heterosexual wife feels confused and inadequate when her husband says, "Looking at a lot of porn and going to strip clubs, it's a guy thing. You couldn't understand so leave me alone." Gay spouses face the same issue when told by a partner, "Hey, you know what it's like to be gay. We just do this, just look at all the gay porn online. Stop bugging me." It can be confusing to a gay partner to define exactly what he has the right to ask of his mate in terms of being faithful. And gay partners experiencing betrayal are also less likely to receive empathic support from peers and family.

Seth, whose quote begins this chapter, speaks further about his experience,

Having my partner lie to me for so many years was by far my greatest hurt. But when it all came out, I was nearly as shocked by how little support I got from gay and straight friends alike. It was almost as if everyone expected that a gay guy is going to cheat, lie and keep secrets. Even people who knew us and loved us were only minimally supportive. Unlike my sister, who had family, church and the law on her side when her husband left her for another woman, the reactions I received after expressing my hurt, fear and sadness seemed to run the gamut from being called "reactive" to being told, "It won't be that hard to find another guy if this doesn't work out." And that was from people who love me and know us well as a couple.
I spent EIGHT YEARS WITH HIM, yet because we are two men together the violation I experienced didn't garner nearly the same consideration or sympathy from those around me as my sister's loss did. And though it was painful and sad for her, she was married for only three years. If that's not a rejection of who I am, I don't know what is!

A lack of affirmation for gay male intimacy flows from the larger culture. Consider the gay man's inability to marry, lack of acceptance into most mainstream religious communities, and unequal legal status for male-male relationships. All of this contributes to the reality that gay-male culture tends to value relationship monogamy differently than heterosexual culture does.

With no established cultural acceptance or significant role models for gay relationships and intimacy, same-sex partnerships often have more room and permission to explore differing models of relating emotionally and sexually, but less support for those attempting a monogamous commitment.

Mark talks about betrayal:

At first I couldn't believe what I saw on that computer screen. How could I have missed it before? I hated him and wanted him to leave. I raged at him and told him I thought I had been better off before we met. How he could say he loved me and be doing this at the same time? I doubted everything he ever said. What's worse, his sexual craziness played into my already low self-esteem. I knew I could never compete with the endless array of hot-bodied guys he had been viewing online and hooking up with. Sometimes I got angry with myself and doubted my worth as a partner. What was wrong with me that I wasn't enough for him? And how could I not have known what was going on, how stupid could I be? Why didn't I ask more questions, voice my doubts and concerns sooner?

Mark's painfully honest account of his experience points out some commonalties among all spouses finding themselves in this situation, straight and gay. His feelings of disillusionment, uncertainty, and self-recrimination are all too familiar to any wife of a sex addict. Much as someone who suffers the death of a friend or parent, he questions whether he could have said or done more.

This is his remorse. As in heterosexual partnerships, shame and embarrassment over the betrayal and the sexual nature of the problem often prevent spouses from reaching out and getting the support they themselves need. This isolation only adds to their difficulties.

Frank, a 43-year-old gay man who contracted HIV from his unfaithful partner, offers this:

Where are you supposed to go when your lover has betrayed and violated you? There's nothing in the 'gay manual' about that. And it wasn't something I was going to talk to my brothers about or my co-workers. Especially since I had spent the better part of four years telling everyone how well things were going in my relationship and that, yes, gay men could be happy together over the long term. I didn't know who to talk to about this or where to turn. I felt like maybe it was my fault, maybe I hadn't been a good enough lover, and it embarrassed me that others might think that as well. Instead I got hungry for information. So I went out and read every book I could on the subject of betrayal and sexual addiction. I wanted to understand the problem so that somehow I could fix it on my own, make it right for both of us.[2]

Gay Men and Monogamy

While most committed or married heterosexual couples would consider any sexual or romantic interactions taking place outside of their relationships to be in violation of their commitment, this is not the case among all gay men. As stated, gay men tend to have greater acceptance of the alternative relational choices, monogamy being only one of them. "Open relationships," where casual sexual involvement with multiple partners is integrated into an existing committed partnership, is a lifestyle choice more readily integrated into homosexual relationships than heterosexual ones. For some, an open relationship offers a negotiated way to "have your cake and eat it too." Agreements for non-monogamy can occur at any point in a relationship or not at all.

Some male couples never seek monogamy, some evolve into monogamy as their intimacy deepens, and still others who have spent many years together may later choose to "open up" their relationship to sex with others in one form or another. They might also choose to be open to romance and sex with others, but this choice leaves both more vulnerable to "falling in love" with someone else, thus having a greater potential for harm.

Some gay men may choose differing forms of non-monogamy, some not based solely on sexual choices. For example, one couple might agree to have emotional monogamy, meaning no affairs, no romances with others, but be open to sex outside of the relationship, while others may chose to be open to both.

Most counselors working in the field of intimacy and healthy sexuality agree that non-monogamous relationships work best when both partners are comfortable with their relationship being "open" and when both agree to well defined rules establishing clear boundaries of the sexual arrangement.

Once this agreement is decided, one or both are free to engage in whatever sexual situations they have settled on as long as the rules are respected.

Some styles of non-monogamous relationships include:

- either partner may have sex and/or romance with whomever they want outside of the relationship and agree not to discuss it
- either partner may engage in sex and/or romance with whomever they want outside of the relationship and are committed to discussing their experiences
- a partner may only engage in sex with other people when both agreed in advance on that specific person or situation
- the couple only has sex outside the relationship when both are present, in other words threesomes
- partners can only have sex with people already known to them
- partners agree to only have sex with anonymous strangers
- partners only have sex with someone else one time, no ongoing romances allowed
- partners who live separate from each other are monogamous when together, free to do as they wish when apart

Gay couples may experiment with differing forms of non-monogamy, but problems are likely to develop if:

- each partner has a different understanding of the rules
- one or the other lies or covers up his sexual activities
- one partner becomes emotionally dependant on someone else
- one or the other isn't fully in agreement with the plan or is just going along with it to "make a partner happy" or "keep the relationship." This frequently occurs with partner's of sex addicts

Misunderstandings of this type breed resentment, hurt, jealousy, and the kind of bad feeling that can severely damage an otherwise functional relationship. Couples that attempt non-monogamy, may later discover that it has created more issues than it resolved, and if there were pre-existing relationship troubles prior to ending monogamy, there are likely to be even more problems on the horizon.

Unfortunately it can be difficult to go back to monogamy once this particular door has been opened. Some sex addicts have tried the open relationship route in an attempt to manage their sexual addiction problem, but even when offered non-monogamous relationship choices they still found themselves embroiled in lies and broken commitments. This defines addiction.

Unlike non-addicted men who can define a sexual boundary and stick to it, sex addicts are "powerless over their sexual behavior." Once they start down a road of sexual adventuring they are unlikely to be able to control where they will end up. In cases where a couple has attempted non-monogamy, only to end up with broken promises, disregarded agreements, sexual secrets or betrayal it may be that:

- non-monogamy isn't really emotionally manageable for them regardless of how appealing it was in theory
- sex with outsiders has taken the place of having sex with each other
- one or both has a sexual-addiction problem
- one partner has a hidden agenda; for example, the desire to pursue an outside relationship
- non-monogamy was introduced as a last-ditch effort to revive a troubled or failing relationship, and this solution is most often doomed to failure

If the couple's problem is sexual addiction, non-monogamy will not likely be an option for them. The absolute key to a successful open relationship is mutual trust. If one partner has been found to be lying, keeping secrets, and otherwise violating the boundaries of a committed relationship, open or monogamous, then that essential trust is broken and not easily regained. Without mutual trust and complete honesty, open relationships are likely to end up disintegrating into bitterness.

My partner entered recovery and now he wants me to get treatment for co-sex addiction. Why would I need treatment?

Many partners of sex addicts vigorously resent being labeled as having a problem themselves. And why wouldn't they? After all, the person who made the broken promises, withheld painful secrets, and sexually acted out is clearly the source of the problem, not the partner who ended up victimized by the situation.

And while it's true that the gay sex addict has a great deal of work to do in addressing his compulsive need for validation and self-soothing through sex and he alone is fully responsible for the consequences of his behavior, many partners also have emotional issues that need to be addressed, concerns often more subtle than the obvious behaviors of the sex addict.

Men who partner with people with addictive personalities can have underlying emotional deficits that are to the addicts they chose, despite the fact that their emotional challenges play out differently. Partners of addicts can at times appear selfless and kindhearted to all, while beneath the surface they struggle with powerful fears of being abandoned. Unconscious though these concerns may be, they do affect who is chosen as an intimate partner and how the relationship is carried out.

Partners of sex addicts often feel most comfortable when being depended upon and can go to great lengths to become indispensable to those around them. Typically unaware of their own deep lack of self-esteem, these men seek out circumstance that encourage them to be givers, a child-like role learned in chaotic, problematic or emotionally neglectful families. They learned early in life that the ability to give, be a peacemaker and consistently attend to the happiness of others above themselves were essential survival tools. And while being a giving person is a positive attribute, these men often give without enough regard for their own self-care or end up giving much to those who have little to offer in return.

Characteristically these men will give and do more for others than is actually healthy. They may be overburdened and over committed. Their greater focus is to ensure the comfort of those around them at all costs, avoiding conflict or dissatisfaction from those they value. Divested of their own emotional and sometimes physical needs, they invest and pride themselves on "being there" for others, often without any awareness of the deep anger and resentment they hold, which can surface when they feel unappreciated or overwhelmed. The dark side of the spouse appears in his expressions of his resentments and feelings of victimization. Using blame, nagging, sarcasm, criticism and devaluing to express anger and disappointment, he leaves those around him feeling guilty, hurt or shameful with no clear path to restore harmony.

Ultimately these partners become angry and disappointed with themselves as well, not liking how negative they have become, but with little understanding of how they got there. Some become dependant on overeating, compulsive exercise, overspending, or other potentially self-destructive behaviors that help soothe their unmet needs and frustrations. These patterns can set up lifelong struggles with body image, weight or finances.

Frank, speaking again about his experience, relates,

I was angry and started calling him every few hours to check up on him, and I also did a lot of detective work. I constantly was going through his things: his wallet, receipts and cell phone charges. I thought that if I could just know everything, then somehow I would know if it was all was going to be OK or not. Eventually, I got tired of the whole thing being focused on him: his acting out, his emotional problems, his shame and embarrassment. What about my loss, my pain, my fear about the future? I got tired of asking him about his meetings, how his sobriety was going, and if we were going to be OK. I found myself becoming more critical and unpredictable, expressing my anger sideways through sarcasm, nagging, and emotionally withholding from him. I started to dislike myself. That's when I finally decided to get some help for me.

More Than Anger

It's not unusual for couples experiencing an addiction problem in their relationship to have to face other dysfunctions as well. Along with sex and drug addiction, domestic violence is one of the most prevalent and destructive problems among lesbians and gays. In sharp contrast to the popular cultural misconceptions of gay men as being effeminate or non-aggressive, gay men can have difficulty expressing their anger and frustration and may resort to physical expressions of their feelings. You have every right to feel extremely violated and angry, but hitting your lover or being hit by him is never acceptable. The law is quite clear about these issues, and those who do lash out physically – gay or straight – can be arrested if reported.

The potential for violence in these circumstances is not exclusive to gay men. Some heterosexual female partners, who may have had no tendency toward violence in the past, have become physically or otherwise abusive when presented with the trauma of sexual betrayal. When confronted with truths they don't wish to hear and the strong feelings that go along with them, some sex addicts can also become abusive. A traumatized partner, particularly one without help and support, can become abusive in ways that were previously uncharacteristic of him. This only highlights the importance of getting support and seeking professional help for you. Beyond physical violence, there are many ways to shame and frighten a spouse that are equally unacceptable. Throwing and breaking things, pinning someone to a bed or wall, refusing to let someone leave by blocking a doorway, or stalking and following someone are all forms of intimidation that indicate a serious problem that needs immediate attention.

Verbally threatening to kill or hurt yourself or your spouse when upset also warrants immediate help. Relationship violence and threats of self-harm should not be ignored. If this is happening, you should find a professional to speak with immediately. Most urban mental health centers, gay and lesbian community centers, and private therapists can help.

What is my next step?
If your trust has been betrayed, you're right to feel mistrustful, distant, hurt and confused. For couples that choose to remain together, it can take up to a year or more before relationship trust will begin to be restored. In the meantime, you're stuck with an unwelcome mess of emotional fallout and consequences. And unfortunately, if you chose as most do, to work though this period and remain in the relationship, there are no guarantees that your addict partner is telling the whole truth, even if he's in therapy, treatment or a 12-step group.

Left with uncertainty about your relationship's past, present and future, you must take healthful actions toward your own emotional self-care. Some of these might reasonably include: asking the addict to sleep in a separate room, move out for a while, or even take a time out from the relationship.

During this stressful and painful time, you must take concrete steps to focus on your own emotional and physical needs and let the sex addict get the much needed help through 12-step support and therapy. Below are some trusted do's and don'ts guaranteed to put a healthy focus on your own healing.

Partner Do's:
Do get tested for STDs, and not just HIV. Most active sex addicts are careless with their own sexual health and the sexual health of their partners. Later, seeking to hide their behaviors, they deny, sometimes even to themselves, the health risks they've taken in their sexual insanity. And HIV is not the only concern. Sex addicts are frequently exposed to a variety of diseases including Hepatitis, Venereal Warts (HPV), Syphilis, Gonorrhea and Herpes.

Once a sex addict has disclosed his sexual acting out, even if he says that he was "always safe," it's best for you to be tested to ensure your physical health. Bear in mind that STDs like HIV and other viruses have an incubation period before tests can detect them, so if you get a first-test clean bill of health, you should be reevaluated in four to six months.

Do investigate your legal rights even if you are planning to stay together. You need to know your rights in the areas of potential separation, financial concerns, and parenting if you have children. Gay spousal rights to property, alimony, etc., vary widely these days depending on the status and length of your relationship and where you live. You need to know where you stand. Those in legal domestic partnerships or with shared property have specific legal concerns to be addressed, which differ from those who have not set up these arrangements.

Finding an informed gay-sensitive family attorney and gathering this information is vital – whether you plan to leave or stay. Much of the needed information is also available online. A simple online search, for example entering the terms same-sex, domestic-partnership law, Texas (or whatever state you live in), will likely take you where you need to go.

Do learn everything you can about addiction, codependency and sex addiction. Read, go to workshops and look online. Like the partner of an alcoholic, you need to learn the facts about sexual addiction and the recovery process, not merely to educate yourself or to understand your spouse, but to help make informed decisions about your own future. Treat sex addiction as if it were a physical illness and get informed.

Do reach out for help. Sometimes sexual issues feel too personal to share with family or friends. Many gay men much prefer to talk about their sexual and relationship successes, than their problems. Nevertheless, getting support both from loved ones and professionals trained in sexual addiction treatment is invaluable.

Whether or not you feel like you have your own issues to address, you need help simply because you are involved with an addict. This journey requires a level of support that goes beyond the life experience of most people. Find out about and attend S-Anon, COSA, CODA, Al-Anon, or a private therapist's support group. Don't worry if they're gay or straight, male or female. As long as you're welcome in the door − go! Remember, others have been through this and survived. Find out what they have to say.

Do explore your own sexual and relationship history. Sex addicts can come in pairs and there may be life issues here for you to address as well. Spouses can also uncover times that they themselves acted out sexually, typically in an attempt to please a sexually addicted spouse, to keep him from going out with other men, or to keep him from leaving.

By considering your own history it's easier to understand how you might have ignored or mistrusted your own feelings in the past, an activity you don't want to repeat going forward. This is the time to get your own therapist if you don't already have one. Let him guide you and act as your support when looking at your own past.

Do let him know about your anger and hurt. It is never your job to protect him from your feelings. Be assured that by expressing your feelings, you're not punishing him or pushing him back into acting out. In fact, the more fully the sex addict comes to understand how his sexual behavior has affected you and others he cares for, the better it is for his own long-term healing and recovery.

Do get help expressing your feelings. You're hurt and angry and this must be let out for you to eventually move on. But an endless barrage of criticism, withholding, giving the silent treatment, or looking down on your partner ultimately won't help anyone heal. Either the sex addict is going to embrace honesty and sexual behavior change or he isn't. A constant vigil to prod him into health by reinforcing fear, shame and guilt is likely to backfire.

Do take an active role in your own healing. The sex addict is either going to work on this or he isn't. Regardless of his choices, you need care, love, and support. You need to talk about what has happened with compassionate friends and family, and you need a stable support network. Exercise, rest, take time off, see family and friends, and make sure to take care of you.

Do trust your feelings and observations. If the sex addict isn't getting help for his sexual behavior problems, isn't attending therapy, or isn't going to support groups, it would be unhealthy to believe things are getting better. His promises to change or stop mean very little, but his concrete actions taken toward change mean a lot.

Do request and expect a full disclosure of his sexual acting out. You have a right to know what you have been kept in the dark about during the course of your relationship. You should expect a disclosure fairly early in the process that will put all past secrets on the table. This is a process that should be done with an involved professional therapist who can organize and manage this difficult but necessary process.

Partner Don'ts:
Don't have sex with him without protection for at least a year – no matter what he says about his past activity or recent tests. It doesn't matter. Even if neither of you are HIV-positive, there are a host of other problems, like Herpes and Hepatitis C.

Don't use sex or romance to make him or you feel better. Some couples seeking to restore the previous intimacy in their relationships will seek instant sexual intensity or romantic honeymoons following the disclosure of a sex addict's problem. It's not unusual for couples that have been having relatively little sex to suddenly start having a lot of it following some disclosure of betrayal and sexual acting out.

While sexual intensity may feel good for the moment, providing each of you with some feeling of reassurance, using sex and intimacy in this way actually moves you further away from healing the deeper, more troubling issues. Sexual intensity to fix the relationship is a form of mutual denial that is bound to fail. It's healthier, though less comfortable, to engage in a relationship cooling-off period, agreeing not to cycle into any sexual or romantic intensity, while in the early stages of recovery.

Avoid making long-term decisions in the beginning. This could include life-changing decisions such as whether to break up or permanently change residences. Wait until you have more clarity about where things are headed. The rule of thumb: *No major changes for the first six months of the recovery/healing process.*

Don't hold yourself responsible if the sex addict acts out. If he wants to act out sexually, he will. Nothing you do makes him act out; he always has choices. No amount of hurt or frustration expressed by a wounded spouse makes him do anything. The addict is always responsible for how he chooses to handle his feelings.

Avoid the temptation to go on your own sexual binge to get even or prove yourself. This is likely to cause more hurt, betrayal, or secrecy and will only make things worse. Getting even never works or feels good over time and usually brings disaster in the end.

Don't randomly talk about the sex addict's behavior or problems to humiliate him. It's one thing to get the help and support you need by telling your story to others. But telling his mother, boss or best friend about his sexual behavior to embarrass or humiliate him is likely to cause regret and unnecessary heartache.

Don't make threats you don't intend to carry out. Threatening to leave him when you're angry, but then taking it back when you feel better, only serves to reduce your credibility. Freely express your hurt, anger and despair, but it's best to not make threats at all – unless you are well prepared to carry them out.

Where do I go for help?
Despite the embarrassment a wife may feel when seeking guidance in working through marital betrayal, if she reaches out, she'll find more abundant emotional, therapeutic, and social support available to her than most gay men will. Unfortunately, many gay spouses have fewer available resources and are less likely to turn to the same sources for help, as might a woman in a committed heterosexual partnership.

Some heterosexuals may turn to their faith for help with family problems, but despite the increase of religious or spiritual organizations that are inclusive of gays and lesbians, a legacy of ongoing prejudice makes it less likely that a gay partner would turn to a faith-based guide for help with male-male spousal betrayal.

Similarly, most gay men are unlikely to turn to an older parent or even a sibling for direction in these circumstances. Especially if – as in Mark's case in the beginning of this chapter – they have previously experienced rejection and a lack of support from those uncomfortable with having a gay son or brother.

Psychotherapists of both sexes who are trained to provide a safe, healing environment to those in emotional pain, may not be as willing or able to provide the same empathic emotional support to a partner suffering from broken trust in a male-male relationship as they might for a heterosexual one.

Many well-meaning professional therapists, gay and straight, may offer less helpful responses for a variety of reasons, such as:

- The therapist, consciously or unconsciously, has difficulty acknowledging a male-male committed relationship as having the same emotional depth or meaning as a heterosexual marriage, thereby underestimating the intensity of a spouse's loss.
- The therapist, mirroring a culture that doesn't support gay marriage or equal rights for gay male couples, may not engage the couple to stay together or encourage the partner to work in therapy with the same intensity and involvement as he or she would if the couple were heterosexual or legally married.
- The therapist with unresolved, uncomfortable feelings when discussing the romantic and sexual details of gay men may avoid or miss important details. And frank, honest sexual discussion is especially important when working with sex addicts and their partners.
- A well-meaning, but under-informed therapist can be misled by the sexually addicted patient who frames his sexual acting out as being "what gay men do" or "how gay men are."
- The therapist who holds an underlying belief that by being a gay man you will inherently have sex and relationship problems will cause harm by dismissing the spouse's expectations of fidelity or by discounting the reality of a sexual-addiction problem.
- Gay therapists unfamiliar with sexual-addiction assessment, diagnosis, and treatment methods may naively attempt to normalize the sexual acting out, thereby missing the problem altogether.

Ideally, the best setting for a sex addict's partner to get help is in the same place where the addict receives it, with a counselor or psychotherapist trained in the treatment of addictive disorders and sexual addiction. While you are well served by being in your own individual therapy, you should expect to have some involvement in your partner's treatment as well. His treatment and recovery process should not be a mystery or a secret.

You need to understand what his problem is about, along with how it affects your relationship. You need a place where his secrets will be honestly disclosed to you, along with a clear-cut plan for recovery. Perhaps most important, you need to hear what other spouses just like you are going through. Thorough and thoughtful treatment for couples with sexual addiction problems will:

- help educate you about sexual addiction
- provide couples therapy
- offer a disclosure process
- provide a partners group where you and others can express your feelings and provide mutual support

Though it can be difficult to find all this in one treatment setting, well-developed outpatient sexual addiction programs are increasingly available in most large cities. Resources can be found at the end of this book. The good news is that you don't have to limit yourself to groups focused solely on gay partners. In fact, sexual addiction treatment ideally mixes both gay and straight addicts together in the same therapy group, and it's equally helpful to give gay and straight partners a chance to learn from each other.

This kind of setting brings you together with women who share the same pain, loss and confusion about their husbands as you do about your partner. Groups like this can offer you validation, because they offer you the chance to hear how similar your emotional experience is to that of these women, despite the fact that they were legally "married" and likely have the support of church and family.

Interestingly, it also gives the women in the group a chance to hear a man's perspective of sex, something they very much need to understand. One woman in a mixed spouses group put it this way:

It wasn't until the gay guys joined our group that the women realized that men really do feel differently about sex than we do. Up until then I kept looking at my husband thinking, "How could you so casually separate sex and love? How can you tell me that your sexual encounters didn't mean anything to you when, for me, having sex always means being connected?" I was floored when some gay partners explained that they really did understand how sex could be casual in that way because they, too, at times had had sex like that.

Yet seeing the gay spouses sense of betrayal and violation, so similar to mine, surrounding the lies and secrecy of their sexually addicted partners, helped me realize that my husband's sexual behavior really wasn't about me or in reaction to me at all. It helped me see that men in general are more able to separate sex and love than women are, and that my husband's betrayal of me has more to do with his own willfulness, dishonesty and double life than it had to do with any other woman in particular or with our sex life.

It's common for many spouses to shun the notion of treatment and therapy for themselves, seeing the sexual issues as being "his problem." Some say things like, "He made this mess for us, why should I have to help clean it up when he was the one who created all this pain?"

While it's true the sex addict is responsible for the actions that have harmed your relationship, the simple fact is couples that heal the fastest and have the best chance of growing beyond hurt, betrayal and recrimination, involve both partners healing and working at the same time.

If therapy is just not for you, there are many partners who found the answers they sought by thoroughly reading about the addictive process and involving themselves in 12-step partners groups like Al-Anon, CODA, COSA and S-Anon.

These support programs offer partners the same safe haven, fellowship and direction as the 12-step sexual addiction programs SAA, SCA, SLAA and SA offer to the sex addict. And though it is a challenging step to get yourself to that first group or meeting, partners who stick with this process report that despite the crisis that initiated their attending, over time they themselves grew in unanticipated ways, becoming more like the men and women they had always wanted to be.

Chapter 12
Straight Guise: Is My Partner Gay?

Joe Kort, M.A., M.S.W., CSAT

Ten years ago, tapping a key to bring the family computer to life, Diane, a 42-year-old Detroit bank teller, found herself staring at an image she came to wish she'd never seen. It was a photo of two men having sex. Checking the computer's history, she discovered this wasn't the only gay porn site someone in her family had visited, and someone had been cruising these sites for some time.

It had to be one of her sons – either Jason, 13, or Ryan, 15. She spent an anxious day waiting for her husband Mark, a 44-year-old real estate agent, to come home. Married for 19 years, Diane and Mark were very close. They lived in a conservative Detroit suburb, were heavily involved with their sons' schools, and went to church each Sunday as a family. "It's probably Ryan, don't you think?" she asked Mark when they finally had a moment alone.

"Yes, you're right. It must be Ryan," Mark said.

Diane was devastated. "We have to see a therapist," she said. "I have no idea how to deal with this. I'm going to call someone tomorrow."

"Slow down," Mark said. "Let's not act too quickly."

But Diane couldn't wait. "I'm going to talk to Ryan about it."

"Not yet. That's not the best way to handle it," Mark replied. They went back and forth like this for days, talking about it every evening, usually ending up in a fight. Finally, when Diane could no longer take it, she told Mark that she was going to confront Ryan with what she knew. "You shouldn't do that," Mark said.

"You're always trying to stop me," Diane cried. "But not this time. I should have done this a week ago."

Only then, when he realized that his wife was a few moments away of confronting their older son, did Mark admit the truth: the photos were his.

Diane was too shocked to speak. In tears, Mark admitted he had been visiting gay chat rooms and porn sites for more than a year. Not only that – he'd met men through the Internet and had multiple sexual encounters with other men. "But I'm not gay," he told her, insisting that these were only sexual encounters, that he had no emotional feelings or ties to any of the men he'd had sex with.

Diane was mortified. She wanted to know when all this began. Though confused, Mark confessed that he'd always had fantasies of men orally pleasing him but never felt the need to act on it until last year when he began visiting gay chat rooms.

"Why then?" she asked. Mark said he didn't know.

By the end of their talk, Mark promised to get help – and he did. He began seeing a therapist and taking anti-depressants. Together, they agreed that Mark had been depressed. They also agreed that Mark's difficult relationship with his father had left him seeking male affection through homosexual sex. But that did not mean he was gay. Mark also promised Diane that he would stop surfing the Internet and meeting men for sex. Mark kept his word – for a year. Then he found his way back to his favorite sites. Only this time, he used his work laptop, which Diane didn't have access to. In an online chat room, Mark met Steven. The two fell in romantic love, something Mark had never counted on. He became preoccupied with Steven, wanting to be with him all the time, thinking about him obsessively when they were apart.

Like many other closeted gay men, it's when they fall in romantic love with another man that they realize they might be gay. This realization ignites the coming-out process, as Mark was discovering.

But he wasn't quite ready to embrace that process just yet. Mark invited Steven to his home to meet Diane and introduced him as a friend. In doing this, Mark hoped that Diane wouldn't be suspicious about his whereabouts and activities.

But Diane knew something was going on, mostly because Steven didn't like her. When she mentioned this to Mark, he dismissed it. "You're imagining things," he said. This made her even more suspicious. She began checking Mark's cell phone, and saw that he made many calls each night to Steven's number. Feeling tormented, she eventually called Steven and asked him what was happening. Steven told her everything.

This revelation drew Diane and Mark to therapy. And only then did Diane find out the truth – that her husband had been cheating on her again.

"So you lied to me?" Diane exclaimed. She was in tears.

"You never asked," Mark responded. He was crying too, despondent over the thought of losing Diane.

"I didn't think I had to ask! You told me that it was a fluke thing and that it was over!" she cried.

"I thought I could manage the urges," Mark said quietly. He thought that if he kept it quiet enough, he'd never have to tell Diane about his true feelings. He didn't want to hurt her; he loved her. And he didn't believe he was gay, only that he had homosexual urges. To Mark, "gay" was an affirmative identity, something that made you want to be in gay pride parades and tell the world who you are. That was never his experience. He was a happily married man with two kids and a successful career who simply felt compelled to have sexual relations with men. Mark was also very much in love with Diane, which complicated his identity issues. How could he be gay if he loved his wife? Maybe he was bisexual. Or maybe he just liked having sex with men.

That rationalization had served him in the past, but no longer. He couldn't deny his love for Steven. Yet he'd never thought what it would mean to live the gay lifestyle, or come out to his family and friends. Inside, he was mortified that he'd hurt his wife so deeply. He knew that he wanted the marriage to work. As he sat weeping, begging Diane's forgiveness, pleading with her to take him back, promising that he wouldn't act out homosexually again, something else very profound was happening: Mark was in the early stages of coming out as a gay man. Falling in love with Steven had only accelerated the process.

Over the months, it became clear that Mark was gay. He came to accept that he'd spent most of his life repressing his homosexuality. Now he felt enormous guilt for all he had done to his wife and to himself – not to mention his children. Mark insisted he didn't want to change his life. He loved Diane, their children and their life together. They'd always had good sex. In fact, since Mark had decided not to pursue acting on his gay identity, sex had become even better, which confused them both even more.

Yet things were complicated. Diane was adamant that she didn't want to be married to a gay man who was sexually active in any way. Mark wanted to assure her that he could be sexually exclusive to her but he could not make that promise. He began negotiating with her about using porn or going into chat rooms, but Diane said that was unacceptable. She was concerned that he'd start seeing men again. "I'm not going through this again," she protested.

Eventually Mark and Steven broke up, but Mark and Diane also separated so that Mark could live as an "out" gay man. This was extremely difficult for both of them. Neither wanted to see their marriage end and both were very much in love with the other. But they couldn't find a way to make it work.

This case illustration is an example of a phenomenon that is increasingly common in our society. The shock and pain of discovering your husband is having sex with other men can be overwhelming. This relationship dynamic has become surprisingly common in recent years. Consider the following statistics:

- According to the Centers for Disease Control and Prevention, more than 3 million women are involved with men who secretly have sex with other men.[1]
- The Straight Spouse Network, a national organization with support groups for mixed-orientation couples, estimates that at least 2 million gay/bisexual people are married to straight partners. This figure also includes men married to lesbians.[2]
- According to the Family Pride Coalition, 20 percent of all gay men in America are in heterosexual marriages.[3]
- Additionally, a recent New York City survey found nearly one in 10 men say they're straight and have sex only with other men. They also found that 70 percent of these straight-identified men having sex with men are married. In fact, 10 percent of all married men in this survey reported same-sex behavior during the past year.[4]

Some of the findings include:
- Straight-identified men who have sex with men reported fewer sex partners than gay men.

- Straight-identified men who have sex with men reported fewer STDs in the past year than gay men.
- Straight-identified men who have sex with men are less likely than gay men to report using a condom during their last sexual encounter.
- Straight-identified men who have sex with men are more likely to be married than a straight man who has sex with women.

Only 54 percent of the men who say they're straight and have sex with women are married, compared with the 70 percent marriage rate among the men who say they're straight but have sex with men.[5] This is different than gay-identified men who are heterosexually married in what I call the "New Mixed Marriage" – when one partner is straight and the other is gay.

This chapter will help the partners of these men, first by separating the two types of men: men who are gay and bisexual; and men who are heterosexual who seek sex with other men. The difference is one of sexual orientation versus sexual preference. It will also help women develop a deeper understanding of their partners' behaviors and recognize that it can have many meanings, and that it may not mean the relationship has to end.

What does it mean when men seek sex with other men?
Not all of men who have sex with men are gay – in fact many are not. There are many reasons men have sex with other men, only some of which have anything to do with homosexuality or bisexuality. These men will be called SMSM (Straight Men Who Have Sex with Men). Just because a man is sexual with the same gender, doesn't necessarily reflect sexual/romantic orientation. He can be heterosexual and enjoy the act of sex with another man. There is a difference between sexual identity, orientation, fantasies and behavior.

It's not up to a therapist or a spouse to make the judgment whether an individual is gay or bisexual – it is up to each man to identify this for himself. Personal judgments and feelings too often enter into the marriage in a rush of reactivity and complicate the situation. What follows is men lying to and cheating on their wives rather than being able to talk it through. The shame of homosexuality causes these men to not even tell their therapists, so they work on it alone. Honoring the fact that this is an individual decision process is difficult for the spouse but is really the only course of action.

What are the differences?
There is a difference between sexual behavior, sexual fantasy, sexual orientation and sexual preferences. How does one know ultimately whether he is heterosexual, gay, bisexual, SMSM or something else? Sexual preference takes into account the desired actions and fantasies with a partner. Sexual orientation encompasses a sexual identity – with all the feelings, fantasies and emotions that excite us sexually. Thus, there is a distinct difference between a gay man and a "male seeking male."

A gay man's sexual orientation is characterized by lasting aesthetic attraction to, romantic love of, and sexual attraction exclusively for his same gender. His sexual thoughts, fantasies and behaviors are aligned exclusively or largely toward men. While some gay men can enjoy women as part of their sexual fantasies, even behaviors (for instance, being sexual with a woman while with her husband), they are mostly, if not totally, attracted to men. If a gay man were walking on the beach, he would notice only the half-naked men; he would not notice women in the same way.

On the other hand, an SMSM might consider sex with a man for sexual gratification. But at the seashore, he would be ogling women. He's a heterosexual who engages in sex with other men for a number of reasons. His same-gender sex acts arise to achieve physical release, not from attraction to or desire for other men. Most SMSMs are left cold, even turned off by images of naked men, but get sexually aroused by women.

These men typically want to bond with – and get affection from – other men. Their behavior may also reflect a desire to experiment, or to express conflicts with their sexual feelings and desires, which have nothing to do with being gay. For SMSMs, same-sex encounters are not about romance or desire, but about sexual and physiological arousal with another who happens to be male. A discussion follows on the differences – and similarities.

- A homosexual is a male who understands he is sexually attracted to other males and may or may not have some romantic interest in males as well, but is not interested or has not yet come out of the closet toward gay-identity development. This man may never come out of the closet or may never act on his impulses. This man is not affirmative about his homosexuality, and if he does move in that direction, may not build a life around it.

- A gay man is a male who is sexually and romantically attracted to other men. He wants to and does develop his life to support his gay identity. He starts his identity development as self-identified as "homosexual" but moves toward a positive and affirmative identity as "gay." A gay man's sexual orientation is characterized by lasting aesthetic attraction to, romantic love of, and sexual attraction exclusively for others of the same gender. A gay man's sexual thoughts, fantasies and behavior are aligned. It's an identity based on affection, emotional, spiritual, psychological and sexual feelings exclusively or mostly toward men.

- A SMSM is a heterosexual male who has homo-erotic and same-sex attractions to sexual behaviors with other men and who may or may not act on them. Again, he is not attracted to the man himself sexually or romantically, but only seeks sexual release. He doesn't have romantic interests in other men whatsoever. These men do not notice other men erotically; rather, they are sexually and romantically interested in women only.

• A bisexual male is one who is sexually, emotionally and romantically interested in other men and women. He may have a stronger desire toward one gender or the other, but understands his identity could go either way and feels affirmative about it.

One's sexual preference takes into account the desired sexual actions and fantasies with a partner. Sexual orientation encompasses a sexual identity with all the thoughts, feelings, fantasies and emotions that cause us to become sexually excited. Thus, there is a distinct difference between a gay man and a SMSM.

What are some reasons men have sex with other men?
Assessing all the possibilities such as homo- or bisexuality, sexual addiction, bi-curiosity, homo-eroticism, sexual abuse and more will help you understand your situation. It's important to note that these categories are not mutually exclusive, in that some individuals may fall into more than one category.

Hetero-Emotional, but Homo-Sexual
These men are romantically attracted to women. Usually heterosexually married, they can be sexual with the women they love, but are predominately aroused and driven by desire for sex with other men – not romance. They see themselves as heterosexuals with only sexual interests in men.

Sex Workers/Male Escorts
These heterosexual men engage in sexual behavior mainly for financial reward. They lack desire for the other men and are aroused by the behavior, not the client.

Shame Seekers
These heterosexual men feel strongly compelled to seek intensely arousing but shameful experiences – dildo sex, bondage, and various sexual experiences and preferences that would typically be labeled as homosexual. To avoid having females identify them in this way, they seek out men whom they perceive as non-judgmental.

Sexual Experimenters
Heterosexual boys often experiment with other males, usually during adolescence and up to age 25, out of sheer curiosity. A heterosexual male might be interested – particularly while intoxicated – to experiment sexually with another man. However, it is simply experimentation and may not happen again. When women experiment with other women, they may see the behavior as only experimentation – often for the arousal of heterosexual men. They are usually not labeled lesbians.

Sexual Addicts
"Gay" behavior can also result from sexual addiction. Sometimes the escalation

of sexual behaviors can compel a man to be sexual with another man for another level of his "sexual high," or provide him with a sexual opportunity because he is so driven to act on his urges.

Opportunists

These straight men have high sex drives and are aroused easily. They connect with men for quick and easy release, avoiding emotional engagement. Heterosexual patients tell me they have done this to avoid having to "wine and dine" a female partner who they perceive won't provide sex without a relational experience, whereas most gay men will. This is not a comment on homosexuality as much as it is about males, as this kind of "quickie, anonymous" sex does not occur with lesbians like it does with gay men.

Father-Hunters

These heterosexual men lacked affection and attention from their fathers, and now seek sex with men as a way of finding that nurturance and male acceptance. These clients will often admit the sex was not enjoyable – and certainly not as enjoyable as with women. They wished they could have sat, talked and just be held by the man they hooked up with. It's an attempt to satisfy their "father hunger."

Narcissists

These self-absorbed straight men have a constant need for attention and acceptance; they use sex as a lure to be worshiped and adored. Here it is not about the other man, it's about an experience for himself using the other man for his own sexual gratification.

Dominants/Submissives

Sometimes during the practice of bondage and sadomasochism there is erotic play between two men. Occasionally it is with women present, other times it is not. Sometimes it's about availability where a man wants to act out his fantasies and women are not interested or around.

Cuckolds

These are men who enjoy fantasies of – or the reality of – their wives and girlfriends having sex with other men in front of them. The proximity of the sexual experiences can be close up or far away as long as they have the knowledge of where and when it's occurring. They're often sexually aroused by feeling humiliated that their wives are being pleased by another male whom they see as more potent or better endowed. Cuckolds are also men who enjoy being sexual with other men's wives in front of the husband. Both of these scenarios may also include sexual contact with the man but only in the presence of the wife or girlfriend.

Homosexually Imprinted

If a heterosexual boy is molested by a male, he may keep reenacting the sexual abuse to defuse and desensitize his emotional pain. If unresolved, this may occur into adulthood. When his original trauma clears up, he may stop reenacting his molestation. At first glance, these men appear to be in early denial about their homosexuality. As a result, many clinicians reassure clients that once their sexual abuse issues are resolved, their same-sex behaviors may evaporate. But this doesn't always happen, particularly if the client is innately gay, lesbian or bisexual.

Again, homosexual behavior doesn't mean the man is gay or even bisexual. He can simply be left with an imprint to reenact his abuse and find "pleasure" in what was inflicted on him as a child. This really isn't pleasure at all, but trauma turned into orgasm. In their book, *Male Victims of Same-Sex Abuse: Addressing Their Sexual Response,* John M. Preble and A. Nicholas Groth write:

... this may actually reflect an effort at mastery of the traumatic event...when he was being sexually victimized, someone else was in control of him sexually. During masturbation he is literally in control of himself sexually, and this may be a way in which he attempts to reclaim mastery over his own sexuality. Likewise, his participation in consensual sex reflects his choice and decision. [6]

The authors go on to say that "the fantasy thoughts are prompted by fear more than desire, by anxiety more than pleasure." In other words, they become a way of managing fear and anxiety.

SMSMs who suffered childhood sexual abuse that may have caused homosexual-behavioral imprinting may have strong, recurring same-sex fantasies, and behaviors which can indicate a deeper social or sexual need. American culture doesn't give permission for men to touch or have affectionate feelings for one another. Oddly enough, sexual contact can become the only way men can display affection for one another and keep it a secret to avoid being shamed by others.

When men are struggling with their sexuality, they're looking for answers about whether they are gay, bisexual or straight. They're usually hoping a therapist will detect something in them that's worth preserving and encouraging, saving any hope of heterosexuality. Typically, such men are at the questioning stage about their sexuality and are trying to find explanations about what they're thinking, doing and feeling. In fact, there can be many answers that don't involve the client being gay or lesbian at all.

What is erotic intelligence?

"Emotional intelligence" has become an increasingly popular term to help people improve performance in the workplace and in educational settings. Employers and teachers recognize that emotional intelligence plays a role in understanding people. Similarly, erotic intelligence – what men and women do and fantasize about sexually – reveals quite a bit about them. Your sexual fantasies are a result of your psychological makeup. Your libido is not separate from who you are. In fact, much of one's identity is embedded in his or her erotic life. Just as you can tell much about people from the friends they keep, so you can tell a lot about anyone by understanding his or her sexual desires.

SMSM's arousal templates have prompted them to be sexually drawn to encounters with other men. Erotic intelligence is not so much about sex, but it is expressed through sex. One's childhood and past experiences become linked and embedded in one's arousal template through sexual fantasies, desires and behaviors.

An arousal template is what turns us on sexually, whether it's role-playing fantasy or sexual positions. Our love and sexual-preference "map" is determined during childhood. At this stage, we're imprinted with family beliefs and societal norms. Imprinting is the psychological process by which specific types of behavior are locked in at an early stage of development. All of us, gay and straight alike, are conditioned to think, feel and act the way our early childhood caretakers nurtured and taught us. We observe and internalize how others love us, neglect or abuse us.

Here is where it's crucial to differentiate sexual orientation and sexual preferences. Sexual mapping and imprinting shapes sexual preferences, not sexual orientation. There are those who believe that one's sexual orientation – how one self-identifies in terms of gay, straight, bisexual – is learned in childhood. One is born with one's orientation and that preferences are learned.

These arousal templates are about more than just love: They enter our erotic minds as well. But most people – male and female, gay and straight – don't need to examine their sexual behaviors and fantasies that aren't interfering with their lives. As a result, they have healthy sexual behaviors and can relate well with sexual partners.

Why did I marry a gay man?

You may be asking yourself, "How could I not know?" Some women, consciously or unconsciously, gravitate toward gay men or SMSMs. This happens for a variety of reasons – most of which are unconscious and subtle. While there are many women who knowingly marry gays or SMSMs, the majority have no conscious awareness of this. Many women who marry gays or SMSMs are enablers and codependent. That is, you may be allowing your spouse to continue his behavior and feel unworthy and powerless to confront it even after you realize it has happened.

You may be unconsciously drawn to men who might betray you. Perhaps while growing up, you experienced lies and witnessed emotional boundary violations that remained unresolved and left you traumatized. Perhaps there was infidelity in your family of origin. This could turn you into a co-addict who unconsciously seeks a "familiar" man who violates your trust all over again. Still other women marry gays or SMSMs out of unconscious codependency and an interest in controlling or micromanaging a "flawed" partner. Some women are drawn to men who aren't anything like their macho, patriarchal, abusive fathers in the hope that their partners will not sexually or otherwise overpower them.

A very common reason women marry men with sexual interests in other men is the desire for sexual and emotional distance within the relationship. You may have sexual issues yourself that have not been addressed and are attracted to men in similar situations. Women are so engrained to not explore their own sexuality and fend off the predatory nature of most heterosexual men that there's a tendency to lack awareness of their male partners' sexuality as well.

Spouses aren't without some accountability as to why they married someone who has limited emotional or sexual availability. Both the straight and gay spouse often have issues, and to ignore the psychological process that's at work for the straight spouse does both a disservice. While straight spouses might not have consciously known their partners were gay, it's not an accident, for example, that they married people who couldn't completely commit or be intimate and available to them as a straight spouse could have been. No matter what the case, it's normal to feel genuine love for your spouse and vise versa. Despite the initial reasons for their attraction, it's important to stress that most of these marriages are built on actual love.

What does my family history have to do with this?
There may be issues in your family that laid the foundation for you to select a partner who is gay. For example, you may have been wounded and traumatized by your father. Perhaps he was abusive emotionally, sexually or physically, had affairs, or was neglectful. You may have decided, consciously or not, to minimize or block any type of sexism or form of abuse coming your way. Or on the opposite extreme, you married a man whose sexual power is distant or troubled, or he may be a sex addict or have a problem with impotence, or be a gay man struggling to squelch his homosexual impulses. This might be your way of protecting yourself from straight men's sexual aggression. Gay men will make women like this feel safe, especially if sex is kept to a minimum.

Most often the reasons stem from dependency needs and fears of being vulnerable. Women who surround themselves with gay men always say they appreciate not feeling judged as harshly as they are by straight men.

Another reason straight women marry gay men is because, in general, gay men tend to honor women more for who they are. With less sexual tension between them, gay husbands can be more sensitive to their wives' needs and willing to overlook physical distractions, such as weight and appearance, that straight men might not. This may be a welcome relief for a woman shunned or rejected sexually or romantically by straight men.

The question at hand is more why these straight spouses were psychologically drawn to gay/lesbian spouses – and why did they stay in the relationship? When these straight spouses look back, most will say they picked up signs that something was missing from their gay spouses, but they paid little attention. They will admit there were times when they began to wonder about certain things that were happening – or not happening – in their marriages. Often straight spouses make excuses for the red flags they noticed in the past. For example, you may have realized your partner was less gender-conforming than other men or women. Denying these warning signs is how you unconsciously maintained a distant, low-intimacy relationship with your partner throughout the relationship. One straight male client who discovered he had a lesbian wife said,

I had no idea. My friends and I felt as if I had died and gone to heaven to have a wife so interested in sports. She would watch more football than me and could kick my butt at basketball. I loved it!

He never attributed her interests to the possibility that she was a lesbian. Instead he believed he found a woman who shared his passion in sports. He reported that she always had gay and lesbian friends and he considered her open-minded.

Understandably, straight spouses will usually deny their own personal stories, particularly at first. Feeling hurt and betrayed, they blame the gay spouse. The initial revelation only aggravates the feelings of betrayal. This is hardly the time for the straight spouse to examine his or her part in the drama. But over time, these straight men and women are often able to make sense of their actions and understand why they chose to marry gay spouses.

Less is written and known about the men who marry lesbians or bisexual women. Some men might like that their wives occasionally enjoy sex with women and find it erotic and they may not equate it with lesbianism.

Some straight spouses may have been sexually abused themselves, which influences them to marry someone with their own sexual problems. In other words, if you have been sexually abused you may be struggling with your own sexual conflicts about the unresolved abuse. Consequently, you may unconsciously look for someone who is also struggling with sexual conflicts. When working with sex addicts, author Dr. Patrick Carnes' research shows a high incidence of sexual abuse in the history of both partners.[7] Understanding sexual abuse in your past and determining if this abuse influenced you to marry a gay/lesbian partner can help you understand your part in the relationship.

"The Seven-Year Switch:" The Gradually Gay Husband
Why do gay men marry straight women?
While some women find themselves in relationships with SMSMs and can salvage them, others end up in relationships with men who, over time, discover that they truly are gay and want to build a life with another man, as in the case example of Diane and Mark. If your spouse has begun to come out or identify himself as gay, you may be wondering "Why didn't they discover this sooner, before getting married?"

Homosexuality is still, by and large, stigmatized. Young people often don't feel comfortable exploring anything but heterosexuality. Thus, it makes sense that gays and lesbians marry heterosexually, both for conformity's sake and because this type of relationship is all they've ever known. Either they hope their urges will go away or, more often, they're genuinely unaware they're even attracted to their own gender. If these men are aware of their same-sex attractions, they would not label it as gay but "kinky," and not self-identify as gay. Most of them truly love the women they fall in love with and marry. They want children and the American dream.

Some gay men will marry a woman who will take care of them, to bond with a mother figure, as a cover for their gay activities, or hope that straight sex will "cure" their desire for men – or at least keep that desire strictly sexual. However, there are many negative psychological consequences to staying in the closet while married, for both the gay and straight spouse, such as decreased sexual fulfillment and reduced intimacy.

Paradoxically, some husbands act out in addictive ways to avoid dealing with their gay identity. Like drinking too much, sex becomes their way of evading the issue. It also serves the same function as any other time-consuming addiction: a way of burning off extra energy that might otherwise lead to introspection. They may make excuses – which many men may actually believe – including, "I'm just doing research for a novel." "It's an assignment for my art class in anatomy." or "A friend at work is gay, so I was curious." On the other hand, some men become flatly asexual. Still others distract themselves from sex by throwing themselves into sports, work or hobbies to suppress unwanted impulses.

Often, these men have no one to confide in, not even a priest, minister or rabbi. They find it hard to find comfort in organized religion and support groups like AA, as struggling straight people would. Without anyone to help them articulate their innermost feelings, these feelings and fears stay bottled up inside, impeding the coming-out process.

Before they consider being honest with themselves and their wives, gay men typically want to have their cake and eat it too, believing they can keep a wife and a boyfriend while keeping quiet about the latter. They change the definition of what they're doing, from cheating to "not wanting to hurt her." Arrangements like the so-called "closed-loop" clubs, where the boyfriend knows about the wife, but she doesn't know about him, damage both relationships and are nothing but a recipe for disaster.

Changing behavior is possible; changing orientation is not. For some men, the process is gradual and may take many years. As in the case of Mark and Diane, some men don't recognize they might be gay until they fall into romantic love with another man. Given this, it might take years before he knows for sure whether he is gay and wants to come out. Unfortunately, this process is usually done privately, completely unbeknownst to the female partner.

Coming to Terms with Disclosure
Many straight spouses react to the news that their partner is gay by going into the very closet their gay spouse is in the process of leaving. Once they acknowledge they knew or suspected on some level their spouse was gay, they then have to deal

with their own denial or, in some cases, their secret homophobia. Other straight spouses feel embarrassed, cheated, fooled. They worry about being judged by others. They're not sure how to move forward - who to tell, how to tell them, and when to tell. Some straight spouses grow so enraged and bitter that they divorce, never to examine themselves and the situation from any other point of view. Instead, they turn their kids against their gay ex, and refuse to reconcile.

Often the straight spouse struggles with feelings that he or she could have been more "man/woman" for the gay/lesbian spouse in order to keep the marriage together. It's important to know that this isn't the issue, the split has nothing to do with one's performance as a spouse. As a matter of fact, the truth is that your gay partner's sexuality has nothing to do with you in the least. You simply married a partner with sexual conflicts.

On some level, I feel as though this is my fault. How do I keep from blaming myself?

Most sexual acting out, straight or gay, results from one or both partners' inability to achieve and keep intimacy. While these factors affect many heterosexual marriages, the SMSM's predominant motive for "straying" is to find his true identity and reveal it to himself. SMSM's typically cheat or act out because they're repressing part of themselves. Their conflict is about their "identity," not about their ability to love and bond with their partner. It is not the result of marital problems.

Sometimes the woman feels as though she did something to cause her partner to seek out affairs with men. As readily as she claims total responsibility for the state of her relationship, her SMSM partner is willing to blame her as well, often claiming that she wasn't responsive to his needs. Once both partners understand the acting out is probably about issues of identity, not dissatisfaction. Once the man begins treating his female partner as a partner rather than as an adversary, they can begin to resolve their relationship. Both partners need to understand that neither gay partners nor straight partners are 100 percent responsible for the crisis in the marriage.

Now that I know, where do I go from here?

Some straight spouses want to stay married, even if they feel embittered and betrayed. Often, this only perpetuates a bad situation. If you find yourself in this situation, examine your reasons for staying and any possible underlying dependency issues. Sometimes the fear of being alone can be overwhelming. It might be helpful to do this with a nurturing therapist who can help you question some of these very painful issues.

Some straight spouses, however, feel relieved. They may have blamed themselves for the problems in their marriage – especially sexual problems – only to now realize that they were not at fault. Others are happy to feel released from having a sexual relationship with their spouse and grateful to enjoy a continuing emotional relationship.

Society typically supports the "betrayed" ex-wife and blames gay men for marrying in the first place. You may find this is initially comforting when you are hurt and angry. However, it can also perpetuate feelings of victimization. It represents tremendous growth for a spouse in this situation to move from blaming to examining her role in the situation. Healing involves moving from victimization to empowerment.

This chapter will help partners of men who have sex with men understand that infidelity means something different than in "traditional" marriages. In marriages when both partners are straight, an affair can be an expression of a problematic marriage as well as hostility toward the spouse. In couples where the male partner seeks sex with other males, the adultery is often about the man's personal identity and can have little to do with the health of the marriage. The roots of these behaviors are more complex than simply gay-versus-straight, homosexual-versus-heterosexual. A man does not always need to make a choice between the two; it's possible to reconcile a gay arousal template with a heterosexual identity. Determining if the sexual acting out is about orientation, opportunity, sexual abuse, or addiction is critical to understanding these men and these couples.

Mixed orientation marriages – where one spouse is gay and the other is straight – and marriages where men are discovered to be sexual with men frequently end in divorce. These marriages do not have to end. It demands the willingness of both partners to communicate calmly and effectively about the sexual behaviors and understand what it means. Only then can they decide how to proceed with the marriage. Some of these relationships can be salvaged and eventually turn into vital and successful partnerships.

Chapter 13
Can We Really Make It?
A Couple Talks about Long-Term Recovery

Virginia Hartman, MA, LPC, CSAT
Paul Hartman, MS, LMFT, CSAT

There is good news and bad news for couples in recovery from sexual addiction and co-addiction. The good news is recovery for the couple is possible. The bad news is couple's recovery requires hard work, commitment and patience. Still, the effort is worth it.

This chapter reflects the personal experience of a sexual addict and co-addict. We talk about how we achieved recovery and how we sustain recovery. While we focus primarily on long-term couple's recovery, we also refer to our individual recoveries, because our couple's recovery depends on individual recovery. We began our recovery journeys more than 30 years ago. As of this writing, we have been married more than 45 years. We hope to share how a long-term recovering relationship can be fulfilling, satisfying, passionate, romantic and fun.

Is it possible to have a relationship with a person who betrayed me so deeply?
Dr. Patrick Carnes identified six stages in recovery from sex addiction.[1] (See Chapters 3 and 4 for more on the Six Stages.) In our experience, these same stages apply to our coupleship. In the developing stage, we both knew that we were dissatisfied and unhappy in the relationship. We did not know why specifically. The crisis/decision stage began when the co-addict discovered some of the addict's sexual acting-out behaviors. As the co-addict, my thoughts were:

- this is too much
- this is the one thing I can never forgive or accept
- this is the end of the marriage

At this point, many co-addicts seek help from an attorney. I did myself. Many of these cases do result in divorce. Looking back, I feel fortunate and grateful that I sought help from a therapist instead. Back then there were few if any therapists who specialized in just sex addiction. I was already attending Al-Anon meetings. From recommendations there, I found a therapist who did group therapy, had expertise in multiple addictions and could refer me to 12-step meetings as part of the treatment plan.

Even with help from a therapist, I did not believe that I could stay in the marriage. We had three young children, so part of me wanted to keep the family together. However, another part of me felt so betrayed that the thought of staying in the relationship seemed impossible. I needed time apart from the addict.

My therapist agreed. She recommended a clinical separation rather than a legal separation. One of the most important lessons I learned then was that I did not have to make long-term decisions. I did have to learn to live in the present moment. My therapist kept reminding me that over time – in my case about six months – I would get through the pain of betrayal and loss, and that my own inner wisdom would know what to do about the marriage. Instead of obsessing about my partner and whether or not to divorce, I learned to focus on me. My main tasks were to learn and practice self-care, reduce shame, stop blaming myself, build self-esteem and stop obsessing.

While all this was happening, my partner felt tremendous shame, humiliation, remorse, fear and hopelessness. In recovery language, this state is sometimes referred to as "hitting bottom." Even today with all the advances in addiction medicine, hitting bottom still seems to be a necessary part of the recovery process for addicts.

In this condition of hopelessness and surrender, the addict begged for another chance, saying "I will do anything." That turned out to be an exaggeration. The therapist recommended inpatient treatment that would take at least four weeks, maybe longer. The addict refused. The addict used the excuse that inpatient took too long and cost too much. Those are very common excuses. The real reason was my partner was still in some denial about the disease and lacked willingness.

The addict did agree to some things that proved to be essential, including group therapy, attending 12-step meetings and the clinical separation. Many addicts identify with the phrase "recovery is doing the things you do not want to do."

Primarily because we both had the help of a good therapist, we progressed from Carnes' second stage of crisis to the third stage – shock. We both knew that there once had been a time when we truly loved and trusted each other. We could not believe what was happening to us. We both began the recovery process as victims. Without therapy and a 12-step program, we would have continued to recycle through the dysfunctional roles of victim, rescuer and persecutor. Only because we had the willingness to seek and accept help, we learned to move from victim to choice maker. We learned that we were not bad people. We were people with a disease. One was an addict and the other was a codependent. These two separate disorders share a common etiology – childhood trauma.

For a young child, fear equals trauma. We were both traumatized in childhood. Carnes' research shows that 83 percent of sex addicts are also trauma survivors.[2]

Some contend that this disease model enables the addict and co-addict to avoid taking responsibility. On the contrary, our experience demonstrates that each of us had to take responsibility for our own recovery. Understanding addiction and co-addiction as the diseases that they are may be one of the most important steps in our early recovery – individually and as a couple.

With this new paradigm, we each moved from vacillating between blaming the partner and blaming ourselves to a new dynamic of empowerment through self-focus. Neither of us knew yet if we wanted to stay married. We did know that whatever happened, we both had a disease and each of us was responsible for our own recovery.

What does the addict need to share and what does the co-addict have a right to know?
Our therapist assisted us with the disclosure process. This crucial step has the potential to lead to disaster when mishandled. Remember that the addict and co-addict are both trauma survivors. The disclosure process itself can be trauma-inducing. When couples attempt to do disclosure on their own, each of them risks being re-traumatized. The co-addict often demands detailed information about the sexual acting out. Some therapists refer to this as "pain-shopping." If the addict gives in to the demands for too much detail, those details may become imprinted into the brain of the co-addict and make recovery virtually impossible.

The addict often attempts to disclose only what the partner already knows and withhold everything that might successfully be kept secret. This dishonesty during disclosure reinforces the co-addict's belief that the addict can never be trusted.

A skilled therapist will coach the co-addict into waiting for disclosure until the co-addict is strong enough to hear it without the risk of being re-traumatized. The addict needs to become willing to be "rigorously" honest. The addict will sometimes withhold information out of fear that the partner will leave if she or he knows everything. Attempts at information management set up a power imbalance with the addict one-up and the co-addict one-down. Mutuality cannot exist from this dynamic. Thus, couples recovery cannot happen.

Keep in mind that disclosure is not a one-way street. In an attempt to get unmet needs met, the co-addict may have lived a secret life also. No secrets, no information management, no inappropriate detail, no dishonesty, and no unnecessary trauma risks apply equally to the addict and the co-addict.

The addict did the despicable behaviors. Why am I labeled co-addict and why do I have to join in the work?
Details of individual recovery exceed the scope of this chapter. We simply need to emphasize that both addict and co-addict need their own recovery before there is any hope for coupleship recovery. Two wounded people cannot form a functional coupleship. Sex addiction exceeds behavioral problems. Addiction is a brain disease. Recovery means healing the brain, healing core wounds and changing behavior. Co-addiction exceeds healing the wounds of betrayal. Co-addiction is a disease. It has its own symptoms and core issues. We both believe

that we are together today because in the beginning of the recovery process we experienced the miracle of self-focus. Twelve-step recovery is all about self-examination.

Why not just move on?
We learned to view our coupleship as "the third entity." Just as each individual entity has needs, the third entity of coupleship has its own needs. If we did not have children, we don't know if we would have chosen to stay together and work on the coupleship.

Our therapist encouraged us to work on a relationship even before we chose to stay in the marriage. The therapist taught us that we could divorce and become ex-spouses, but that we would never be ex-parents. Our original goal was simply to become friendly co-parents.

We embraced the idea that a successful marriage is not the result of finding the right partner. A successful marriage is the result of learning how to function in relationship. We agreed that if we were going to do the work of learning how to behave in a healthy relationship, we might as well learn with each other and see what happened.

Many couples caught up in the pain of sex addition do choose to move on without doing this difficult healing work. Many of them go on to new relationships only to experience the same problems all over again with the new partner. This is an example of first-order change: "The more things change, the more they stay the same."

Specifically, what do we need to do?
Our "third entity" of coupleship needed many of the same tools for recovery that we needed individually. Visualize a three-legged stool. Two legs represent both partners and the third leg represents the coupleship. The tools needed include marital therapy, couples group therapy, and 12-steps for the coupleship.

When we began this work, Recovering Couples Anonymous (RCA) did not exist. We found a culture of support through other couples in 12-step recovery. Our coupleship suffered some of the same wounds as the individual addict and co-addict, which included leading a secret life, couple shame and couple trauma. Slowly we both came to see that we had problems that could not be fixed by simply changing partners. We began to see why so many people divorce only to perpetuate the dysfunction.

We believe that we did not fix the old relationship. The old relationship was so damaged by sexual betrayal and other traumas that it was beyond repair. Rather we chose to build a new relationship with each other. We sometimes joke that this is our second marriage. Actually we have only been married once, but we are in relationship with a brand new person as the result of recovery.

What do you mean "we create our own reality"?
The following axiom reveals itself most vividly in the process of trust building

and forgiveness: Whether you believe you can or believe that you cannot, you are right. Both the addict and the co-addict often begin the process believing they cannot do it.

The reality is that the behavior of many sex addicts is so despicable that it is understandable for the co-addict to think, *I can never trust or forgive.* And on our own, most could not. This is one of the reasons we must become part of a culture of support. We need the experience of seeing others do that which we think cannot be done. This is difficult, but not impossible. Thousands of recovering couples have done it. If our goal is to have a successful coupleship with our current partner, we must surround ourselves with others who are doing it.

Will I ever be able to trust my partner again?

Trust building for the co-addict falls into the category of "life is not fair." The addict's behavior broke trust, and the co-addict must be willing to do part of the work to rebuild that trust. Believing that trust can be restored is difficult for the addict as well. Often addicts are so shame-filled from the double hit of childhood trauma and current compulsive behavior that they believe no one, including themselves, will ever see them as trustworthy. Trust becomes the foundation of the new relationship that needs to be built. We must both choose to believe that we can build trust with our partner.

Fortunately there is a formula for trust building. Al-Anon has an expression for such a formula: Talk's easy, work's hard. *Consistent* trustworthy behavior over time equals trust. Notice the word consistent is emphasized. *Consistency* is the key to the process. This becomes an even greater challenge because "addiction is a disorder that is characterized by relapse." Left to our own devices, the sex addict will relapse. However, Carnes' research informs us that addicts who work the tasks and live a 12-step recovery can live a life free of slips and relapses. Consistent trustworthy behavior is attainable even for a sex addict. The co-addict's role in all this starts with choosing to believe that it can be done even though all the co-addict's experience screams to the contrary.

The other part of the formula states over time. Even with all the recommended recovery resources in place, this process takes a long time. And it always takes longer than the addict thinks it should! In SAA meetings all over the country, newly recovering sex addicts can be heard whining about how they have been so good for so long and their partner still doesn't trust them. Often such complaints can be heard after only a few weeks of abstinence from the compulsive behaviors that broke trust in the first place. Trust cannot be rebuilt in days or weeks. It takes months and years. The addict needs to bring patience to the process. The addict's core belief needs to be: I can do this and it will take time. Every time the co-addict expresses distrust or fear and the addict reacts with impatience and anger, the coupleship experiences a setback and the trust-building process suffers.

Even now, after all our years of recovery and relapse-free behavior, the co-addict can still experience triggers that provoke doubt, suspicion, fear, wonder or painful memories. When the addict reacts with gentle, loving, reassuring, messages, we move through these experiences with barely a hiccup to our coupleship. Addicts can respond from recovery rather than dysfunction when they remind themselves that the trigger is often the result of the scar tissue from the old wound of sex addiction.

Accountability is another part of the trust-building process. The addict must be willing to give the co-addict access to all the information needed for reassurance. This includes passwords, cell phone records, access to voice mail and e-mail, financial records, and anything else that the co-addict requests. We may need to change jobs in order to discontinue the need to travel on business. The co-addict may need us to stop going certain places or spending time with certain people. Remember this quote from Alcoholics Anonymous: "We must be willing to go to any length to get it."

Obviously, this is not legal advice for couples going through divorce. Protecting yourself in a divorce action is a totally different process than the process of building a relationship. Helpful self-talk at this point is: *This is difficult, but it is worth it.*

We use one other resource for trust building. It comes from Don Miguel Ruiz's The Four Agreements: Be impeccable with your word.[3] Many know this old joke: "How do you know if an addict is lying?" "If their lips are moving." Many of us grew up in dysfunctional family systems where we learned to distort the truth as part of our survival system. In recovery, we must say what we mean and mean what we say. To live in recovery we must become people of integrity. When we live from integrity our actions match our words. We become trustworthy.

Can I ever truly forgive?

Another cornerstone for the foundation we are building is forgiveness. Like choosing to trust, this is another very tall order. The tools we learned for trust building help us in the forgiveness process. It starts with choosing to believe that you can do it. Again this is true for both the addict and co-addict. Sometimes the co-addict learns about betraying behavior and retaliates in ways that are inappropriate, hurtful and vengeful. Sometimes co-addicts act outside their value system in an attempt to get their needs met. The addict and co-addict must both choose to forgive.

The strongest case we can make for forgiveness is to look at the alternative. What happens if we do not forgive? In 12-step recovery we learn that the opposite of forgiveness is resentment. In the 12-step program resentment is sometimes described as taking poison in hopes that the offending person will die. Choosing resentment does not work. It only hurts the person holding the resentment. Does this mean that forgiveness must always be granted? No!

Many of us come out of a faith system that teaches that the betrayed must always forgive. Whatever our religious background, many of us have heard the instruction, "turn the other cheek." Janis Abrahms Spring's *How Can I Forgive You* provides excellent guidance for both the offended and the offender on this topic.[4] She emphasizes that the offender must earn forgiveness in contrast to the offended who must grant forgiveness. We found this to be an excellent model for healing the coupleship from the betrayal of sex addiction.

We learned that unconditional forgiveness and resentment are the opposite extremes on the forgiveness scale. We strive for the healthy middle of acceptance or genuine forgiveness when earned. When resentment remains buried and hidden, Spring calls this *false forgiveness.* The unresolved resentment may surface years later. Resentment blocks healing and coupleship recovery.

Twelve-step recovery provides another resource for earning forgiveness. The ninth step instructs us to make amends to people we harmed. We learn that the main people we harmed were ourselves and our family. Making an amend goes way beyond saying, "I'm sorry."

Many addicts have said sorry so many times that the word becomes meaningless or even annoying. If we really mean it, Dr. Joe Cruse suggested a format that we find effective.[5] There are five parts to the apology:

- I was wrong.
- You didn't deserve that.
- I'm sorry.
- Please forgive me.
- I love you.

When delivered with sincerity, this can be a means for earning forgiveness. Amend means change. The best way to earn forgiveness is to change behavior. The entire recovery process helps us achieve real and lasting change.

Many of us have heard the phrase "forgive and forget." If we embrace this approach to forgiveness we may wrongly conclude that forgiveness is not possible for us because we know that we cannot forget. Our experience teaches us that we can choose to forgive even though we may never forget.

In summary, coupleship recovery requires forgiveness. We cannot fake it. Working the 12 steps and committing to therapy helped us work through and let go of resentments.

Getting to the belief that our partner was trustworthy and that we each could forgive the other, took us significant time. Neither of us remembers exactly how long. We both agree that this part of the healing process took not months, but years.

Will I ever feel safe enough to be vulnerable with my partner?
In the Carnes' model, we were at the grief stage. We both reached this stage earlier in our individual recoveries. With the help of the 12-step program and therapy, we separately acknowledged the losses we experienced over a lifetime. We learned to grieve those losses. John James' book, *Grief-Recovery Handbook,* provided invaluable help with this process.[6]

Remember, we are working in a model that recognizes our coupleship as the third entity. So even though each of us had grieved separately, we needed to grieve our losses as a couple. Couples can only do this when they feel safe enough to be vulnerable with each other. Grieving is an emotionally intense encounter. This cannot be done together until trust and forgiveness have been established.

We will share one example of a loss that was both an individual and couple's loss. After the birth of our second daughter, we experienced our third pregnancy. That pregnancy ended in a late-term miscarriage. That child who died before birth was a son. At the time of the miscarriage, we barely acknowledged the loss. We were both too caught up in the busyness of our lives and the distraction of our addiction and co-addiction to grieve the loss at the time. With help, we learned to face our losses together and grieve together.

We named our unborn son, talked about how our life as a family would have been different if he survived, cried together, and continue to talk to each other about him whenever either of us think of him. Grief is a process of healing. In addition to healing our coupleship, grief also provided us with our early experiences of emotional intimacy.

Can we ever stop blaming, attacking and defending?

We both needed to admit that we didn't know how to talk or how to listen to each other. Like most people, we learned couples' communication by watching it modeled by our parents when we were young children. For both of us, our parents modeled dysfunctional communication. Also, our resentments toward one another made respectful, intimate communication very difficult. Once again, we needed therapy to teach us how to do it differently. RCA gave us opportunities to watch recovering couples model new methods of communication.

Entire books have been written on couples' communication, and a thorough discussion of strategies is beyond the scope of this chapter (see The Resource Guide for books on couples' communication). However, we will share a few highlights that helped us communicate without attacking and defending. Take time to decide who will talk first and who will listen first. We cannot listen and talk at the same time.

Two sayings help us remember this: When the mouth opens, the ears close, and there is a reason we are created with one mouth and two ears. Also, we remind ourselves that we are communicating to know our partner better. That means listening to the other's reality and talking to share our reality. Functional couples' communication is not about blaming, defending, case-building or getting your way. It is about being vulnerable enough to share our reality and being respectful enough to listen without judging or defending.

Can we ever have intimacy in this relationship?

We learned that we had not known emotional intimacy with each other even before sex addiction took over the relationship. We didn't need a new partner to have intimacy. Both of us needed to stop blaming the other and learn how to create intimacy. The following behaviors helped heal the coupleship and helped create emotional intimacy:

- stop blaming
- risk trusting
- earning and give forgiveness
- reduce shame individually and as a couple
- grieve together
- communicate with boundaries – simply to know and be known

Going through this process requires us to risk being vulnerable with one another. We learned to communicate in feelings-related language. One day we recognized that we had created a functional, emotionally intimate coupleship – without the need to change partners. We still had more work to do, but we had the start of a new relationship.

Can we ever experience healthy sexuality together?
We began learning about healthy sexuality early in our healing process. However, we didn't experience true sexual intimacy until we achieved emotional intimacy that resulted from practicing all of the tasks listed above. The sex addict needed to change the core belief that sex was the most important need. The partner needed to stop believing that being sexual to please the addict, or avoiding sex to punish the addict or protect the self would result in power and control over the chaos that resulted from living in sex addiction.

In early recovery, we both needed time out from sex. We achieved that by agreeing to a celibacy contract. Our therapist recommended 90 days of no sexuality together, alone (masturbation), or in any way. Since we were getting back together after a time apart without sex for about six months, we abstained from sex for about nine months total before we were ready to begin this extremely vulnerable and intimate step.

We needed to learn how to nurture ourselves and each other in non-genital ways. Our therapist instructed us to have "skin time" at least twice a week. That was a time of holding each other in bed while nude. We learned to enjoy this form of touch without progressing to intercourse or any form of genital stimulation. This assignment was especially difficult for the sex addict. Over time, even the addict learned to enjoy this form of nurturing and intimacy.

We both needed to admit that we did not know a lot about sex. We needed to learn about the human sexual response cycle. There is so much more to good sex than orgasm. We learned together to enjoy every stage of the cycle. We recommend Carnes' book, *Sexual Anorexia,* as a resource for couples desiring better sexual intimacy.[7] About two thirds of the book is devoted to healthy sexuality. Reading through and discussing each of the chapters together will enhance both emotional and sexual intimacy.

er we attempt to emphasize that we felt powerless ov
owerless to heal our relationship. Working the 12-step
ual recoveries gave us the hope that we could recover if
epted help. We applied that same principle to our coupleship
With help, ...d do what we could not do alone. To paraphrase *Alcoholics Anonymous - Big Book,* we admitted that:

- we were addicted and could not manage our relationship
- no human power could relieve our pain
- we could recover if we were willing to accept help

Neither of us thought of spirituality as a way of experiencing intimacy. We automatically thought of religion. Although we both grow up in similar denominations and raised our children in a faith community, we rarely talked about religion. In our individual recoveries we learned to differentiate religion and spirituality.

In RCA we learned that spirituality for the coupleship was just as important as our individual spiritual progress. We learned that we could have different religious beliefs and still connect with each other spiritually. The key here is connection. Both addict and co-addict learned to live in isolation. Many addicts relate to the expression "feeling alone in a crowd." We experienced any form of connection, not just connection to God, as spiritual progress.

Individually, both of us spent time in prayer and meditation each morning. We began to do that spiritual practice together. We would take turns reading from a meditation book from our recovery program. We would discuss it together. Then we would pray out loud together. We sat facing close enough to hold hands. We prayed with eyes open looking into each others' eyes. We do not know whether this is an effective way to talk to God. We do know that it is a very powerful way to connect with each other.

Both of us love to spend time outside in nature. We learned that this too can be spiritual practice. Everything that results in feeling connected, whether to the universe, the planet, the community, family or to another person, all of this is spiritual. We spend time together in nature on a regular basis. We love beaches, mountains, rivers and deserts. All of these places help us feel connected to the earth, to each other and to the spiritual realm.

For us, finding a place we could both worship a Higher Power together was an important part of our couple's spirituality. We no longer worship out of a sense of obligation but rather as an expression of gratitude, and a way to experience spiritual intimacy together.

We learned that there are two parts to spirituality – spiritual principles and spiritual practice. If it is true that one spiritual principle is love, then everything we do to grow in intimacy together is spiritual practice.

...will all this just come naturally?

...s, the answer is never. We will celebrate our 46 anniversary this year. ...e been recovering together for about 30 years. We still have to work at hav- ...g a great coupleship. The problem is time. In order to have intimacy together ...e need time together. At every life stage, things get in the way. Many recovering sex addicts replace their sex addiction with work addiction.

Just like a precious child, our coupleship requires, time, nurturing and valuing. We still schedule a date night together. When we don't, a whole week can slip by without time for intimacy and fun. It seems like everybody is too busy. We do find time for the things that are really important to us. Here is a model for couple's time to strive for:

- 30 minutes a day
- one day a week
- one weekend per month
- one week every six months

We rarely hit the goal. However, by striving for the goal we have much more quality couples' time than we would without a goal.

When will we stop hurting each other?
Even after many years of individual and couples' recovery, we are still imperfect human beings. We still make mistakes. One of our most useful tools comes from RCA. Once a week (daily in the beginning) we review the week (day) together. The talker shares "one thing I did this week that was hurtful to our coupleship..." and "your gift to me was...." Then we switch roles and the listener shares in the same way. Notice the taking of responsibility and validating of our partner. We have come full circle from blaming and defending.

We close with this reminder: A successful coupleship is not about being lucky enough to find the right partner. It is about learning how to function respectfully in a relationship. Even when the betrayal cuts so deep, as in sex addiction, couples can choose to build something brand new together that is better than what they had in the first place. That is what is possible when both partners bring individual recovery to the coupleship.

The 12 Steps
of Sex Addicts Anonymous

Step One: We admitted we were powerless over addictive sexual behavior - that our lives had become unmanageable.

Step Two: Came to believe that a Power greater than ourselves could restore us to sanity.

Step Three: Made a decision to turn our will and our lives over to the care of God as we understood God.

Step Four: Made a searching and fearless moral inventory of ourselves.

Step Five: Admitted to God, to ourselves, and to another human being the exact nature of our wrongs.

Step Six: Were entirely ready to have God remove all these defects of character.

Step Seven: Humbly asked God to remove our shortcomings.

Step Eight: Made a list of all persons we had harmed and became willing to make amends to them all.

Step Nine: Made direct amends to such people wherever possible, except when to do so would injure them or others.

Step Ten: Continued to take personal inventory and when we were wrong promptly admitted it.

Step Eleven: Sought through prayer and meditation to improve our conscious contact with God as we understood God, praying only for knowledge of God's will for us and the power to carry that through.

Step Twelve: Having had a spiritual awakening as the result of these steps, we tried to carry this message to other sex addicts, and to practice these principles in our lives.

Adapted from the International Service Organization of SAA, Inc., 2005.

Resource Guide

The following is a list of recovery fellowships that will help you on your journey to healing.

Adult Children of Alcoholics
310-534-1815
www.adultchildren.org

Al-Anon
800-344-2666
www.al-anon-alateen.org

Alateen (ages 12-17)
800-356-9996
www.al-anon-alateen.org

Alcoholics Anonymous
212-870-3400
www.aa.org

CoAnon
www.co-anon.org

Cocaine Anonymous
800-347-8998
www.ca.org

Co-Dependents Anonymous
602-277-7991
www.codependents.org

Co-Dependents of Sex Addicts (COSA)
612-537-6904
www.cosa-recovery.org

Debtors Anonymous
781-453-2743
www.debtorsanonymous.org

Emotions Anonymous
651-647-9712
www.emotionsanonymous.org

Families Anonymous
310-815-8010
www.familiesanonymous.org

Gamblers Anonymous
213-386-8789
www.gamblersanonymous.org

International Institute for Trauma and Addiction Professionals (IITAP)
P.O. Box 2112
Carefree, AZ 85377
480.575.6853
www.iitap.com; e-mail info@iitap.com

Marijuana Anonymous
212-459-4423
www.marijuana-anonymous.org

Narcotics Anonymous
818-773-9999
www.na.org

National Council for Couple and Family Recovery
314-997-9808

Nicotine Anonymous
www.nicotine-anonymous.org

Overeaters Anonymous
www.oa.org

Recovering Couples Anonymous
314-997-9808
www.recovering-couples.org

Runaway and Suicide Hotline
800-RUN-AWAY
www.1800runaway.org

S-Anon
615-833-3152
www.sanon.org

Sex and Love Addicts Anonymous
210-828-7900
www.slaafws.org

Sex Addicts Anonymous
713-869-4902
www.sexaa.org

Sexual Addiction Resources/Dr. Patrick Carnes
www.sexhelp.com

Sexual Compulsives Anonymous
310-859-5585
www.sca-recovery.org

Sexaholics Anonymous
866-424-8777
www.sa.org

Society for the Advancement of Sexual Health
770-541-9912
www.sash.net

Survivors of Incest Anonymous
410-282-3400
www.siawso.org

Recommended Reading

ADULT CHILDREN OF ALCOHOLICS

It Will Never Happen to Me
Claudia Black

Adult Children of Alcoholics
Janet G. Woititz

Marriage on the Rocks
Janet G. Woititz

Healthy Parenting: An Empowering Guide For Adult Children
Janet G. Woititz

Grandchildren of Alcoholics: Another Generation Of Codependency
Ann W. Smith

My Dad Loves Me, My Dad has a Disease
Claudia Black

CODEPENDENCY

Codependent No More
Melody Beattie

Boundaries: Where You End and I Begin
Anne Katherine

Choice Making
Sharon Wegscheider-Cruse

Learning to Say No
Carle Wills-Brandon

Living in the Comfort Zone: The Gift of Boundaries in Relationships
Rokelle Lerner

Is It Love or Is It Addiction?
Brenda Schaeffer

Facing Codependence
Pia Melody & Andrea Miller

Codependency, Sexuality and Depression
Author

The Drama of the Gifted Child
Alice Miller

CO-SEX ADDICTION

Open Hearts
Patrick Carnes, Mark Laaser, Deborah Laaser

Women Who Love Sex Addicts
Douglas Weiss & Donna DeBusk

Back from Betrayal
Jennifer Schneider

Healing Together
Wayne Kritsberg

Sex, Lies and Forgiveness
Jennifer Schneider & Burt Schneider

Relationships in Recovery
Emily Marlin

Rebuilding Trust
Jennifer Schneider & Burt Schneider

FAMILY OF ORIGIN
Healing the Shame that Binds You
John Bradshaw

It Will Never Happen to Me
Claudia Black

Changing Course
Claudia Black

Healing the Child Within
Charles Whitfield

MEN'S ISSUES
Fire in the Belly
Sam Keen

If Only He Knew
Gary Smalley & Norma Smalley

The Knight in Rusty Armor
Robert Fisher

Longing for Dad
Beth Erickson

When He's Married to Mom
Ken Adams

MONEY ISSUES
Deadly Odds
Ken Estes & Mike Brubaker

Money Drunk, Money Sober
Mark Bryan &: Julia Cameron

Money and the Meaning of Life
Jacob Needleman

RECOVERY AND 12-STEP BOOKS
Alcoholics Anonymous
Anon

Al-Anon Faces Alcoholism
Anon

Al-Anon's Twelve Steps and Twelve Traditions
Anon

One Day at a Time in Al-Anon
Anon

The Dilemma of the Alcoholic Marriage
Anon

The Courage to Change
Anon

Hope for Today
Anon

Alateen - A Day at a Time
Anon

Alateen - Hope for Children of Alcoholics
Anon

Having Had a Spiritual Awakening
Anon

Twelve Steps for Adult Children
Veronica Ray

A Woman's Way Through the Twelve Steps
Stephanie Covington

Sex and Love Addicts Anonymous
Anon

Twelve Steps for Overeaters
Anon

Twelve-Step Prayer Book
Anon

Trust the Process
Shaun Mcniff

The Addictive Personality
Craig Nakken

Codependents Anonymous
Anon

SEX ADDICTION
Don't Call it Love
Patrick Carnes

Out of the Shadows
Patrick Carnes

Contrary to Love
Patrick Carnes

The Betrayal Bond
Patrick Carnes

Facing the Shadow
Patrick Carnes

A Gentle Path Through the 12 Steps
Patrick Carnes

Sexual Anorexia
Patrick Carnes

Disclosing Secrets
Deborah Corley & Jennifer Schneider

Cybersex Unhooked
David Delmonico & Elizabeth Griffin

In the Shadows of the Net
Patrick Carnes, David Delmonico &
Elizabeth Griffin

Cruise Control
Robert Weiss

Women, Sex and Addiction
Charlotte Kasl

*The Clinical Management of Sex
Addiction*
Patrick Carnes & Kenneth Adams

Untangling the Web
Rob Weiss & Jennifer Schneider

SEXUAL ABUSE
Silently Seduced
Kenneth Adams

Abused Boys
Mic Hunter

Against Our Will
Susan Brownmiller

The Courage to Heal
Laura Bass

Victims No Longer
Mike Lew

Broken Trust
Patrick Fleming, Sue Lauber-Fleming
& Mark T. Matousek

SPIRITUALITY AND MEDITATION
The Spirituality of Imperfection
Ernest Kurtz & Stephanie Ketchum

Each Day a New Beginning
Karen Casey

The Language of Letting Go
Melody Beattie Answers in the Heart
Anon

Addiction and Grace
Gerald G. May

Journey to the Heart
Melody Beattie

The Courage to Change
Anon

Days of Healing, Days of Joy
Anon

Yesterday's Tomorrow: Recovery Meditations For Hard Cases
Barry L.

Food for Thought: Daily Meditations for Dieters And Overeaters
Anon

Spiritual Skill Set - Guided Imagery Meditations CD
Patrick Carnes & the Voices from AFAR

Serenity Through Meditation - CD
Sue Nuefeld-Ellis

Women Who Love Sex Addicts
Douglas Weiss & Diane DeBusk

Women Who Hurt Themselves
Dusty Miller

The Princess Who Believed in Fairy Tales
Marcia Grad

My Mother, Myself
Nancy Friday

Perfect Daughters
Robert Ackerman

Motherless Daughters
Hope Edelman

She Has a Secret
Douglas Weiss

Father Hunger
Margo Maine

TRAUMA
The Betrayal Bond
Patrick Carnes

Waking the Tiger
Peter Levine & Ann Frederick

Heartwounds
Tian Dayton

Trauma and Addiction
Tian Dayton

WOMEN'S ISSUES
Women, Sex and Addiction
Charlotte Kasl

Women, Anger and Depression
Lois Frankel

About the Authors

Stefanie Carnes, Ph.D., CSAT, is the director of family services, research and intensive workshops at Pine Grove. In this capacity she supervises and manages the family therapy services for numerous programs, including the drug and alcohol rehabilitation unit, the sexual addiction program and the eating disorders program. In her role as research director, she oversees all research projects at Pine Grove. Dr. Carnes is a licensed marriage and family therapist and an AAMFT-approved supervisor. Dr. Carnes is also a certified sex addiction therapist, with expertise in therapy for couples and families struggling with sexual addiction. She is the author of numerous publications and presents regularly at conferences at both the state and national levels.

Patrick Carnes, Ph.D., C.A.S., CSAT, is a nationally known speaker on addiction and recovery issues. He is the author of numerous books, including *Out of the Shadows: Understanding Sexual Addiction* (1992), *Contrary to Love: Helping the Sexual Addict* (1989), *The Betrayal Bond: Breaking Free of Exploitive Relationships* (1997), *Facing the Shadow* (2001), *In the Shadows of the Net* (2001), *The Clinical Management of Sex Addiction* (2002) and *The Recovery Start Kit* (2007). Dr. Carnes is currently the Executive Director of the Gentle Path program at Pine Grove Behavioral Center in Hattiesburg, Miss. He is the primary architect of Gentle Path treatment programs for the treatment of sexual and addictive disorders. He also pioneered the founding of the Certified Sex Addiction Therapist program and the International Institute for Trauma and Addiction Professionals.

Paul Hartman, MS, LMFT, CSAT, began a second career in counseling after graduating from Fuller Theological Seminary where he attended both the School of Theology and School of Psychology. Upon earning his license in marriage and family therapy, Mr. Hartman and his wife, Virginia, went into private practice together, opening The Healing Center. The couple specialized in treating addiction, co-addiction, couples and families. Mr. Hartman trained with Dr. Patrick Carnes to become a certified sex addiction therapist and follows Carnes' model of a program practice. He retired from his Michigan practice in 2005 but continues to work with Carnes and the International Institute for Trauma and Addiction Professionals.

Virginia Hartman, MA, LPC, CSAT, began her professional career as an elementary school teacher before earning a MA in counseling psychology from Western Michigan University and becoming a Licensed Professional Counselor. After becoming certified as a substance abuse interventionist by the Johnson

Institute, she gained experience in intervention, after-care, family treatment and primary treatment. She worked with several leaders in the field of addiction, then went into private practice with her husband Paul in Michigan. She trained with Dr. Patrick Carnes, using the task-based approach to treat trauma. She became a certified sex addiction therapist, specializing in treating sexually anorexic women. Although now retired, Ms. Hartman continues to teach, consult and supervise CSATs, and also holds workshops for women and couples.

For more than 20 years, **Mavis Humes Baird, CSAT,** has developed several intervention and treatment programs in various modalities for addicts, family members and whole families. She consults with providers for their own program development. She is a CSAT Supervisor and an original member of Dr. Patrick Carnes' Practice Improvement Program. She worked in central and eastern Pennsylvania first as a drug and alcohol therapist, educator and interventionist, and then as a codependency and trauma therapist, treating eating disorders, sexual abuse and family systems issues. She also developed an effective treatment model for multiply-diagnosed clients. She has been working with sex addicts and co-addicts since 1988. With the help of a national rights organization, she is launching a legislative initiative to help educate society and aid sex addicts who want to find help.

Since 1985, **Joe Kort, MA, MSW, CSAT,** has specialized in Gay Affirmative Psychotherapy, Marital Affairs, Mixed-Orientation Marriages, Sexual Addiction, Sexual Abuse and Imago Relationship Therapy through weekend workshops for singles and couples. He provides trainings to straight clinicians about Gay Affirmative Therapy around the country. Mr. Kort is the author of two books on gay-male identity and relationships as well as journal articles on sexual addiction. His newest book is *Gay Affirmative Therapy for the Straight Clinician: The Essential Guide.* An adjunct professor teaching Gay and Lesbian Studies at Wayne State University's School of Social Work, Mr. Kort maintains a regularly updated website at www.joekort.com.

Barbara S. Levinson, Ph.D, CSAT, is the Director of the Center for Healthy Sexuality in Houston. She offers specialized programs for the treatment of sex addicts and sex offenders and their partners. She also specializes in the treatment of Internet addictions. Dr. Levinson provides individual and couples therapy for persons who have intimacy and relationship problems. As a Certified Sex Therapist Diplomat for the American Association of Sexuality Educators, Counselors and Therapists, she deals with sexual issues of individuals and couples. At the Center for Healthy Sexuality, Dr. Levinson provides group therapy in many specialty areas. She is also a Licensed Marriage & Family Therapist, a Licensed Sex Offender Treatment Provider and a Therapist Supervisor for the International Institute for Trauma and Addiction Professionals Certified Sex Addiction Therapists.

Omar Minwalla, Ph.D., CSAT is a Licensed Psychologist and Clinical Sexologist, and the Clinical Director of the Sexual Recovery Institute in Los Angeles. Dr. Minwalla earned his doctorate in Clinical Psychology from the Illinois School of Professional Psychology in Chicago and completed his post-doctoral fellowship at the University of Minnesota Medical School's Program in Human Sexuality. His specializations include sexual compulsivity/sex addiction, sexual offending, sexual dysfunction, transgender populations, sexual orientation, BDSM and paraphilias. He also has a private practice specializing in marginalized sexuality and gender concerns.

Sonja Rudie, MA, LMHC, C-EMDR, C-EAGALA I, CSAT, specializes in the treatment of trauma healing and recovery. Ms. Rudie is a Licensed Mental Health Counselor, Certified EMDR clinician, Certified Equine Assisted Therapist and a Certified Sex Addiction Therapist. She provides innovative and interesting treatment options for clients suffering from trauma in addition to the standard primary treatment protocol of Cognitive Behavioral Therapy. Ms. Rudie has provided therapy groups in resiliency skill-building, self-esteem, reality testing and creating mastery. She is the president and founder of La Perla Counseling and Trauma Response Services, Inc., which provides counseling for individuals, couples, families, youth and groups.

Jennifer Schneider, M.D., Ph.D., CSAT, is a physician in Tucson, Ariz., specializing in addiction medicine and pain management. For 20 years she has been a researcher, speaker and author in the field of sex addiction, with a particular interest in the effects of sex addiction on the family. Dr. Schneider is the author of *Back From Betrayal: Recovering From his Affairs* (3rd Edition, 2005), *Sex, Lies, and Forgiveness: Couples Speak on Healing From Sex Addiction* (3rd Edition, 2004); *The Wounded Healer: Addiction-sensitive Approach to the Sexually Exploitative Professional* (with Dr. Richard Irons, 1998); *Disclosing Secrets: What, to Whom, and How Much to Reveal* (with Dr. Deborah Corley, 2002); and *Untangling the Web: Breaking Free from Sex, Porn, and Fantasy Addiction in the Internet Age* (with Robert Weiss, 2006).

Cara W. Tripodi, LCSW, MSS, CSAT, is the Executive Director and owner of S.T.A.R.-Sexual Trauma & Recovery, Inc., an outpatient practice in Wynnewood, Penn., devoted to the identification and treatment of sexual addiction, sexual anorexia and sexual codependency. She graduated in 1991 from Bryn Mawr College Graduate School of Social Work & Social Research and has trained with Dr. Patrick Carnes. She is a Level II practitioner in EMDR. Ms. Tripodi is a local and national speaker on sexual addiction and sexual co-addiction, and has published an article, *Long-term treatment of partners of sex addicts: A multiphase approach to healing.*

Robert Weiss, LCSW, CSAT, is founder and Executive Director of The Sexual Recovery Institute in Los Angeles. Mr. Weiss is the author of *Cruise Control: Understanding Sex Addiction in Gay Men* (2005) and co-author of *Untangling the Web: Sex, Porn and Fantasy Addiction in the Internet Age* (with Dr. Jennifer Schneider, 2006), *Cybersex Exposed: Simple Fantasy to Obsession* (with Dr. Jennifer Schneider, 2001), and numerous professional articles on sexual addiction and offending. A UCLA MSW, Mr. Weiss received post-graduate sexual addiction training with Dr. Patrick Carnes. In addition to his clinical work, he is a professional lecturer and trainer, providing clinical education and program development. Mr. Weiss' recent media appearances include *The Oprah Winfrey Show, The Today Show, Dateline NBC* and CNN.

Notes

Chapter 1
1. Melody Beattie, *Codependent No More* (Center City, MN: Hazelden, 1987).

2. Timmen Cermak, D*iagnosing and Treating Co-Dependence* (Minneapolis, MN: Johnson Institute, 1986).

3. Pia Mellody, *Facing Co-Dependence* (New York: Harper Collins Publishers, Inc., 1989).

4. Chart "Characteristics of Co-Addiction" Adapted by P. Carnes, *Don't Call it Love* (Minneapolis: The Gentle Path Press, 1991).

5, 7. P.J. Carnes, *Don't Call It Love: Recovery from Sexual Sddiction* (New York: Bantam Books, 1991).

6. Barbara Steffens & Robyn Rennie, "The Traumatic Nature of Disclosure for Wives of Sexual Addicts." Sexual Addiction & Compulsivity, 13:247-267, (2006).

8. www.sash.net

9. P.J. Carnes, *Facing the Shadow* (Carefree, AZ: Gentle Path Press, 2001).

Chapter 2
1. D. Corley & J. Schneider, *Disclosing Secrets: When, to Whom, and How Much to Reveal* (Scottsdale, AZ: Gentle Path Press, 2002), 118.

2. D. Corley & J. Schneider, *Disclosing Secrets: When, to Whom, and How Much to Reveal* (Scottsdale, AZ: Gentle Path Press, 2002), 119.

3, 4, 5. J.P. Schneider, D. Corley and R. Irons, "Surviving disclosure of infidelity: Results of an international survey of 164 recovering sex addicts and partners." Sexual Addiction & Compulsivity, 5:189-217. (1998).

6. J.P. Schneider & B. Schneider, *Sex, Lies & Forgiveness: Couples speaking out on healing from sex addictions, 3*ʳᵈ *Ed.* (Tucson, AZ: Recovery Resources Press, 2004), 103.

7. P.J. Carnes, *Don't Call It Love: Recovery from Sexual Addiction* (New York: Bantam Books, 1991).

Chapter 3
1. P.J. Carnes, *Don't Call It Love: Recovery from Sexual Addiction* (New York: Bantam Books, 1991).

2. *Alcoholics Anonymous - Big Book* (New York: Alcoholics Anonymous World Services, 3rd Ed., 1939), 83-84.

3. *Alcoholics Anonymous - Big Book* (Alcoholics Anonymous World Services, 4th Ed., 2001).

Chapter 4
1. M. Beattie & P. Carnes, "Interview with Melody Beattie," *Contrary to Love* (Carefree, AZ: Gentle Path Press, 1999).

2. E.D. Payson, *The Wizard of Oz and Other Narcissists: Coping with the One-Way Relationship in Work, Love, and Family* (Royal Oaks, MI: Julian Day Publications, 2002).

3. P.J. Carnes, *Don't Call It Love: Recovery from Sexual Addiction* (New York: Bantam Books, 1991).

4. R. H. Coombs, *Handbook of Addictive Disorders: A Practical Guide to Diagnosis and Treatment* (Hoboken, NJ: Wiley, 2004).
B.J. Sadock & V.A. Sadock, *Comprehensive Textbook of Psychiatry, 8th Ed.* (Philadelphia, PA: Lippincott, Williams & Wilkins, 2005), 1991-2001.

5. L. Cozolino, *The Neuroscience of Psychotherapy: Building and rebuilding the human brain* (New York: W. W. Norton & Company, 2002).

6. Recovering Couples Anonymous World Service Organization. http://www.recovering-couples.org.

7. *Shall We Dance* (Miramax, 2004). http://www.miramax.com/shallwedance

Chapter 5
Ann Katherine, *Boundaries: Where you end and I begin* (New York: Fireside Books, 1993).

Ann Katherine, *Where to Draw the Line: How to Set Healthy Boundaries Every Day* (New York: Fireside Books, 2000).

Lisa M. Najavits, *Seeking Safety: A Treatment Manual for PTSD and Substance Abuse* (New York: The Guilford Press 2002).

Elenor Payson, D M.S.W., *The Wizard of Oz and Other Narcissists* (Royal Oak: Julian Day Publications, 2002).

Douglass Weiss, Ph.D., *Partner's Recovery Guide: 100 Empowering Exercises* (Fort Worth: Douglass Weiss, 1997).

Charles L. Whitfield, M.D., *Boundaries and Relationships: Knowing, Protecting, and Enjoying the Self* (Florida: Health Communications Inc., 1993).

Chapter 6
1, 2. W. Maltz, *The Sexual Healing Journey: A Guide for Survivors of Sexual Abuse* (Harper Collins Publishers, 1991).

Chapter 7
1, 4, 5. *Alcoholics Anonymous* (New York: Alcoholics Anonymous World Services, 3rd Ed., 1976).

2. Sexual Recovery Anonymous (SRA) Literature.
http://www.sexualrecovery.org/SRA%20Literature.htm

3. ISO of COSA literature, www.cosa-recovery.org

6. E. Kurtz & K. Ketcham, *The Spirituality of Imperfection* (New York: Bantam Book, 1993)

7. P.J. Carnes, *Don't Call It Love: Recovery from sexual addiction* (New York: Bantam Books, 1991).

Chapter 8
1. M. Scott Peck, M.D., *People of the Lie: The Hope for Healing Human Evil* (New York: Touchstone, Simon & Schuster, 2nd Ed., 1998), 62-75.

2. Chip Brown, *I've Got A Feeling...;* quoting Dr. Emeran A. Mayer. (*Oprah Magazine*, March 2007), 224-269.

3. Malcolm Gladwell, *Blink: The Power of Thinking Without Thinking* (New York: Little, Brown and Company, Time Warner Book Group, 2005).

4. Maslow & the Hierarchy of Needs from P. Carnes, Ph.D. & John Bradshaw, MA, "The Two Faces of Sexual Shame: Ecstasy & Agony," April 2001, Seattle, Washington.

5, 6. Dr. Glenn R. Schiraldi, *The Self-Esteem Workbook* (Oakland, CA: New Harbinger Publications, Inc., 2001).

7. P. Boss quotes T.H. Rainbolt, LMHC, "Building Resilience," quote on handout, April 2007.

8. J. Carter, *The Virtues of Aging* (New York: Ballantine Books, 1998).

9. Melody Beattie, *The Language of Letting Go; Daily Meditations for Codependents* (San Francisco: Harper & Row; New York: Hazelden Foundation, 1990).

10. Glenn R. Schiraldi, Ph.D., *Facts to Relax By; A Guide to Relaxation and Stress Reduction* (Utah Valley Medical Center, 1982, 1987, 1996).

11. U. Schnyder, "Psychotherapies pour les PTSD-une vue d' ensemble. (Psychotherapies for PTSD-An Overview)." Psychotherapies, 25, (1) :39, (2005).

12. A. Bardin, "EMDR within a family system perspective," Journal of Family Psychotherapy, 15(3), 47-61. (2004).

13. R.J. Taylor, "Therapeutic intervention of trauma and stress brought on by divorce," Journal of Divorce & Remarriage. 41(1-2), 129-135, (2004).

14. Pia Mellody & Andrea Wells Miller, *Breaking Free, A Recovery Workbook for Facing Codependence* (New York: HarperSanFransisco, 1989) vii, ix.

15. Martin E. Seligman, Ph. D., *Authentic Happiness: Using the New Positive Psychology to Realize Your Potential for Lasting Fulfillment* (New York: The Free Press, A Division of Simon & Schuster, Inc., 2002), 160, 168, 266.

16. Dr. Al Siebert, *The Resiliency Advantage: Master Change, Thrive Under Pressure, and Bounce Back From Setbacks* (San Francisco, Berrett-Koehler Publishers, Inc., 2005).

17. Dr. Al Siebert, *The Resiliency Advantage: Master Change, Thrive Under Pressure, and Bounce Back From Setbacks* (San Francisco, Berrett-Koehler Publishers, Inc., 2005), 21.

Also:
American Psychiatric Association, *Diagnostic & Statistical Manual of Mental Disorders, 4ᵗʰ Ed., DSM-IV-TR* (Arlington, VA, 2000).

Sonja Rudie, MA, "Listening to your Body: What is Your Stress Level?" (Seattle: Free Public Lecture Series sponsored by The Meadows Institute, 2000).

Chapter 9
1, 6, 7. C. Black, D. Dillon and S. Carnes, "Disclosure to Children: Hearing the Child's Experience." Sexual Addiction and Compulsivity 10: 67-78.

2. J. Piaget and B. Inhelder, *The Psychology of the Child* (New York: Basic Books, 1969).

3. C. Jung, *The Structure and Dynamics of the Psyche, Collected Works* (Princeton, NJ: Princeton University Press, 1969).

4, 5. D. Corley & J. Schneider, *Disclosing Secrets: When, to Whom & How Much to Reveal* (Wickenburg, AZ: Gentle Path Press, 2002).

Chapter 10
1. American Psychiatric Association, 2000, *Diagnostic and Statistical Manual of Mental Disorders, 4th Ed.* (Washington, DC).

2. M.C. Seto & M.L. Lalumiere, "A brief screening scale to identify pedophilic interests among child molesters." *Sexual Abuse: A Journal of Research and Treatment,* 13, 15-25 (2001).

3. P. Kulbarsh,: http://www.officer.com/article/article.jsp?siteSection=18&id=31904. (2006) "Are child molesters mentally ill? Pedophiles and other predators." www.Officers.com

4. *Diagnostic and Statistical Manual IV-revised* (American Psychiatric Association, 2004).

5. M.C. Seto, J.M. Cantor & R. Blanchard, "Child pornography offenses are a valid diagnostic indicator of pedophilia." Journal of Abnormal Psychology, 115, 610-615 (2006).

6. 18 United States Criminal Code 2252A.

7. Tony Krone, "A typology of online child pornography offending." Trends and issues in crime and criminal justice, No. 279 (2004).

8. 18 United States Criminal Code 2256.

9, 10. M. Taylor & E. Quale "Child pornography and Internet crime." (Howe: Brennan Routledge, 2003.)

11. K. Eichenwald, newyorktimes.com/2006/08/21tecnology/21pedo.html

12. Ropalato, TopTenReviews.com/tricks-pornographers-play.html

13, 14. P.J. Carnes "The arousal template" *Facing the Shadow* (Carefree, AZ: Gentle Path Press, 2005), 227-230.

15. P.J. Carnes, D.L. Delmonico, E. Griffin & J.M. Moriarity, *In the Shadows of the Net: Breaking Free of Compulsive Online Sexual Behavior* (Center City, MN: Hazelden, 2001).

Chapter 11
1, 2. R. Weiss, *Cruise Control: Understanding Sex Addiction in Gay Men* (Los Angeles: Alyson Books, 2005).

Chapter 12
1. Center for Disease Control, Revised June 2007.

2. www.straightspouse.org

3. www.familypride.org

4. Pathela et al. (2006). "Discordance Between Sexual Behavior and Self-Reported Sexual Identity: A Population-Based Survey of New York City Men." Annals of Internal Medicine, v. 145, pp. 416-425.

5. J. Kort "The new mixed marriage: Working with a couple when one partner is gay." (Psychotherapy Networker, September-October 2005), 83-89.

6 . John M. Preble and A. Nicholas Groth, "Male Victims of Same-Sex Abuse: Addressing Their Sexual Response."

7. P.J. Carnes, *Don't Call it Love: Recovery from Sexual Addiction* (New York: Bantam Books, 1991).

Chapter 13
1, 2. P.J. Carnes, *Don't Call it Love: Recovery from Sexual Addiction* (New York: Bantam Books, 1991).

3. D.M. Ruiz, *The Four Agreements: A Toltec Wisdom Book* (San Rafael, CA: Amber-Allen, 2001).

4. J.A. Spring, *How Can I Forgive You? The Courage To Forgive, The Freedom Not To.* (New York: HarperCollins, 2004).

5. Presentation by Dr. Joe Cruse.

6. J. W. James, *The Grief Recovery Handbook* (New York: HarperCollins, 1998).

7. P.J. Carnes, *Sexual Anorexia: Overcoming Sexual Self-Hatred* (Center City, MN: Hazelden, 1997).

Also:
Alcoholics Anonymous - Big Book (New York: Alcoholics Anonymous World Services, 3rd Ed., 1976).

Recovering Couples Anonymous Blue Book (Oakland, CA: Recovering Couples Anonymous, 1996).